Praise for

What's This India Business?

"Very well timed ... and well placed to advise any companies thinking of taking the plunge.
Such advice is invaluable. It is hard to resist a chuckle when Davies points out that any meeting scheduled a week or more in advance is unlikely to take place."
Financial Times

"This nuts and bolts guide will show you how you can surge ahead of market trends, build a sustainable new business model and unleash the power of Indian business people to gain an advantage for both your business and the international economy."
The Weekly Telegraph

"A must read for anyone trying to understand the Indian BPO industry or even the minds of Western managers and their concerns when they do business in India. Gives a fresh perspective and his anecdotes drive home his point and provide for some entertainment too."
The Economic Times

"Paul Davies has performed a timely service in writing this book. Davies writes with a sympathetic understanding of the businessperson's concerns. But he does not flinch from giving very pointed advice. Indeed, the book opens with this challenging statement: "If you can successfully carry out a business process with a colleague who is in the next-door office with the door shut, you can carry it out in India." But this is not to say that doing business in India will be straight-forward. Davies highlights the many, many ways in which the unwitting can come unstuck. There is plenty of useful information here, in particular on what to expect when potential suppliers tender for business."
Book of the Month, Accounting & Business

What's This India Business?

Offshoring, Outsourcing, and the Global Services Revolution

Paul Davies

nb

NICHOLAS BREALEY
INTERNATIONAL

LONDON · BOSTON

First published by
Nicholas Brealey International in 2004
Reprinted in 2004, 2005, 2006

3-5 Spafield Street
Clerkenwell, London
EC1R 4QB, UK
Tel: +44 (0)20 7239 0360

100 City Hall Plaza, Suite 501
Boston
MA 02108, USA
Tel: (888) BREALEY

Fax: +44 (0)20 7239 0370

Fax: (617) 523 3708

http://www.nbrealey-books.com

© Paul Davies 2004
The right of Paul Davies to be identified as the author of this work has been
asserted in accordance with the Copyright, Designs and Patents Act 1988.

ISBN 1-904838-00-6

Library of Congress Cataloging-in-Publication Data

What's this India Business?: offshoring, outsourcing, and the global services revolution /
Paul Davies.
p. cm.
Includes bibliographical references.
ISBN 1-904838-00-6
1. Subcontracting—India. 2. Computer service industry—Subcontracting-India
3. International business enterprises. 4. Business etiquette—India. 5. India—
Economic conditions.

HD2385.15W48 2004
658.4'058'0954—dc22

2004043522

British Library Cataloguing in Publication Data
A catalogue record for this book is available from the British Library.

Printed and bound by Replika Press Pvt. Ltd., India

For
...all those days when I would follow you and you would follow me...
and for
Suresh and Selwyn

Contents

Preface   1

1 India Today and Tomorrow   7
The Indian economy   7
Some recent history   9
Some geography   11
The weather   12
Traveling around   13
Education   14
The offshoring revolution   16

PART I WHAT'S THIS OFFSHORING BUSINESS?   19

2 Business Process Offshoring   21
The initial business drivers   21
Core and non-core   22
Revenue distance   23
Local knowledge   24
The importance of the process   25
The incredible shrinking core   26
IT offshoring   28
Business process offshoring   29
Do it yourself or outsource   31
All or part of the process   35
Dirty or clean   36
Data protection   37

3	**India and the Global Services Revolution**	40
	The Indian IT services industry	41
	The Indian business process outsourcing industry	43
	ITES	45
	Quality	46
	Other countries	49
4	**Where to Start**	51
	Identifying suitable suppliers or partners	52
	Fact finding in India	53
	The tender process	53
	The Indian company's presentation	55
	Seven criteria for choosing a supplier	57
	Management capability	57
	Alignment with western business practice	59
	Competitive threats	59
	Size	61
	Understanding each other's strategic objectives	63
	Shared objectives	64
	Intention	65
	Summary	66
	Language and communication	66
	International Indian companies	67
	PART II WELCOME TO INDIA	71
5	**Your Arrival**	75
	Immigration	75
	Currency exchange	77
	Lakhs and crores	77
	From airport to hotel	78
	Tipping – and begging	82
	Hotels and other experiences	84
	The phone system	85
	Settling down for your first night	87

6	**Preparing for Day One**	**89**
	Dress code	89
	Eating…	91
	…and drinking	93
	An introduction to names	94
	Hierarchy	97
	The family	99
	Sexual equality	100
	Religion and religious observance	101
7	**Getting Around**	**103**
	Taxis, taxi drivers, and private hire	103
	Walking in India	106
	Elevators and personal space	108
	Place names	112
	Off you go	114
8	**IST – Indian S t r e t c h a b l e Time**	**115**
	Indian Stretchable Time – the full story	116
	Arranging times for meetings	119
	Holidays – national and local, official and unofficial	122
9	**Meeting Differences**	**125**
	Traders first and last	127
	Politeness	129
	Yes	129
	Other linguistic traps	131
	Corruption	131
	Management consultancies	133
	Individual insecurity	134
	Understanding each other	135
	Ending the meeting	136
	Making it work in India	137

PART III WHAT'S RIGHT FOR YOU   **139**

10   Making the Right Decision   **141**
       Assumptions   142
       Measurements   143
       Financial projection   145
       Start-up costs   145
       Hidden costs   147
       Social costs and development benefits   151
       Return on investment   152
       Cost avoidance   152
       Contingency, disaster recovery, and business continuity   154
       The pilot   155
       Your final plan   156

11   Due Diligence and Avoiding Risks   **157**
       Recognizing rogues   157
       Indian civil law   159
       The Indian Administrative Service   160
       The contract   161
       The agreement   162
       Exit strategy and risk analysis   163
       Account management   164
       Company accounts   165
       Regulation   166
       Public and employee relations   167
       Your own team   168
       Be prepared   171

12   Negotiations and the Art of Haggling   **172**
       Body language   173
       International negotiation styles   175
       Negotiations in India   177
       Market testing   180
       Recognizing when you have a deal   182
       The agreement   182

13	**The Right Result**	**184**
	Internal expectations	186
	Micro-stepping	187
	Don't manage – monitor	188
	Reporting framework	189
	Account manager	190
	No surprises	191
	Structural difficulties	192
	This isn't working	193
	Staying on track	193
14	**Creating Further Advantage**	**194**
	Reexamining what is core	195
	Changing what you do as well	196
	Staff quality	199
	Sweating the assets	202
	The real output	203
	The Indian value add	203
	New directions	205
15	**Breaking into the Indian Market**	**206**
	IT and telecommunications	207
	Price sensitivity	209
	Being number one	211
	The scale of the opportunities	211
	Reciprocity	213
16	**Corporate Social Responsibility**	**216**
	Your local economy	219
	The wider perspective	221
	The Luddites	223
	References	225
	Bibliography	227
	Useful websites	231

Preface

If you can successfully carry out a business process with a colleague who is in the next-door office with the door shut, you can carry it out in India.

Geography can become history. Distance no longer matters as much. The internet is the new piece of the jigsaw that has enabled the widespread transfer of business processes from the West to offshore locations. In 2005 there will be revenues from business process offshoring in India alone approaching $5 billion.

Outsourcing is said to be the answer, if only we knew what the question was. Outsourcing offshore is probably the answer to even more questions. Though this may sound like clever use of words, there is a serious thrust to these statements.

Outsourcing covers a huge range of possibilities. It is also surrounded by a great deal of jargon, including new words and phrases like rightsourcing, strategic sourcing, and insourcing, not to mention inshoring, offshoring, nearshoring, and rightshoring. This book will help you consider what going offshore can do for your company and whether it is the correct solution for your circumstances. I hope it will also give you the confidence to deal with India's culture and business at first hand.

If the question is what can you outsource to India, the simplest answer is what do you want India to do for you? You will almost certainly find a way of doing virtually anything there. That is a good starting point, although not everything you consider will turn out to be appropriate.

There is going to be a revolution in attitudes and understanding, and we are still at the early stages of the process. We are also at the start of an information war on the importance, threat, opportunity, weakness, or inappropriateness of transferring services jobs offshore. Newspapers throughout the western world, and not only those focused on business, carry articles almost daily about outsourcing offshore. Television programs have been commissioned and elected representatives from most western countries are going on fact-finding trips to

India and other countries to get to grips with what is going on. There is a huge amount of academic research that ranges from vast surveys to really quite punishing analysis. These are all the signs of something that is important and relatively new.

When Citigroup claims to have saved $75 million in one year alone by going offshore, when Prudential Insurance declares cost savings of more than 30 percent, when American Express is reported to have saved more than 50 percent, it is obvious there is a clear imperative for business to establish a serious strategy for sourcing, whether offshore or not. That this applies to businesses of almost any size is no exaggeration. Many companies, ranging from actuaries to education suppliers, from headhunters to health care, from consultancies to lawyers, from architects to civil engineers, have already started the analysis and appraisal. Those companies that have not yet begun to face the challenges, for whatever reason, will need to do so soon.

India is a developing economic powerhouse in the global economy. The World Bank is predicting it will be the fourth largest economy in the world before the year 2050. The domestic economy is still growing at around 5–7 percent in the midst of a global slowdown. There are major parts of that economy that are squarely facing up to deregulation and increased international competition, with investment increasing at over 20 percent per annum. By any standards, India and its one billion people will be *the* country of the twenty-first century.

India has become the natural home of information technology development and support and is fast becoming the global services center for business. How to be part of that economic revolution, which is transforming the business environment in the West, is the main burden of this book. To be able to comprehend the scale of the change and what India can do for your business, it is really necessary to experience India at first hand. In addition to a conventional business approach to the opportunities and challenges that business process offshoring to India involves, the book is a personal introduction to India's culture and how things really work there, particularly if you want to gain the greatest business advantage from what the country has to offer.

Reading this book will start you on a journey that will change your outlook on life and your approach to business. As we move from the challenges and fun of getting to know India to the serious issues of how to work most effectively with India and Indian business, you will gain a different perspective that will unlock the real value that India holds.

How to read this book

My aim is to help you engage with Indian business people on an equal footing. It is likely that your knowledge of India and Indian business will be much less than your Indian counterpart's knowledge of western culture and business. They will have watched western television and films, received an education based largely on western approaches, and be well versed in western business books. That is a huge initial advantage. They may well also have visited or lived in countries in the West. Already 10 percent of the very richest Californians are of Indian extraction, and probably living in Silicon Valley.

I start with four chapters that will help you get the measure of India as a country and the global services revolution as a phenomenon. I discuss what services you can take offshore and how to select an appropriate supplier or business partner, whether you are outsourcing to India or setting up your own services center there.

My next objective is to make you feel comfortable in your own mind about going to India, so you can deal effectively with the many necessary cultural adjustments and be able to concentrate fully on the business in hand. Chapters 5–9 will prepare you for coping with India on a daily basis.

This introduction to India is very personal, of course, and is related directly to how I started to understand India, Indians, and Indian business, and then how I began to deal with it effectively. I want you to share my enjoyment of India and I've tried to draw out some of the fun and excitement, the paradoxes and challenges. These chapters are deliberately light and anecdotal and are probably best read either immediately before you set out for India or on the plane itself, but I hope they amuse you and prepare you for the adventure of getting to know India.

According to industry analysts Gartner, about half of all outsourcing projects fail. Taking that outsourcing work offshore obviously puts additional strains on projects and programs. Chapters 10–13 include important pointers to where the pitfalls are and how to avoid them. This section is more than that, however, as it will show you which routes are most successful. I start with the early days of a project or program, which will become most useful as you begin implementation in earnest.

The inevitable step change that working with Indian business creates sometimes obscures how successful you really are. You will inevitably cut costs and probably produce more effective and productive processes, yet if you only benchmark that change against what you would have been able to achieve in your domestic market, you will have made progress but not necessarily have gained as much benefit as possible. The early wins you will obtain from working in India or with Indian business are a pale reflection of the long-term benefits on offer. It is the added value that will come, perhaps unexpectedly, from the relationship that will provide the real return. These longer-term opportunities are detailed in Chapter 14, and Chapter 15 covers how you can perhaps penetrate the Indian domestic market as well.

Finally, Chapter 16 focuses on how to create responsible developments offshore, fair and advantageous to both India and your domestic economy. You will be introduced to some of the solutions that are becoming viable and that will help build a sustainable corporate social responsibility program.

The need for awareness of these issues is all the sharper because of the scale of the business revolution that is taking place. That scale may be difficult to comprehend. If we change the measure to people's lives, you will understand more. Some estimates suggest that between 32 million and 39 million services jobs will be created in India alone on behalf of western business over the next 15 years. That may mean that 30 million jobs are transferred from the West. If each job affects a further three people directly, that is over 200 million people whose lives will change as a direct effect of this revolution. The indirect effects will be immeasurable.

Pack your suitcase

Someone who goes through life without experiencing India misses a whole range of opportunities, paradoxes, and contradictions. Where else in the world would you see electronic voting machines being transported to far-flung locations on the back of an elephant or the most advanced communications fiber being laid into the ground with only the help of pick and shovel? At the same time, there is a vibrancy about the business environment in India that can restore enthusiasm and make you want to take on the market anew.

Be warned, however. Most foreigners either love India or hate it – it's very hard to be indifferent to the country. As will be obvious, I love India and delight in its flaws, challenges, and amazing qualities. It has the most exciting and different business culture, as well as a sense of the ridiculous that will make you know you are alive. I had been in the country for less than a day when the local managing director of a multinational's Indian subsidiary told me with an absolutely deadpan face: "As you can see, we've got all the chiefs in place. All we need now is a few Indians."

A colleague of mine rolled up in India with two suitcases, one full of business clothes and toiletries, and one packed with chocolate bars – in case he couldn't get hold of any "civilized" food. I was also uncertain and unsure on my first visit, because India does feel daunting in the West. But I was convinced it was going to be so different that it would change the way I saw both life and business.

I got to know life and business life in India over a number of years, some of which I spent as managing director of Unisys India. It was the most challenging and exciting period of my life. Without ever quite being able to anticipate what was going to happen, I had some real successes. I also made all the mistakes there are and learned from them. I hope you can be more wise and learn, not from your own mistakes, but from the mistakes of others – or, more particularly, from mine.

So throw away that second suitcase and let's begin.

1
India Today and Tomorrow

The Indian government says in its official plan for 2020: "Our vision of India in 2020 is of a nation bustling with energy, entrepreneurship and innovation."[1] That word "bustling" in an official document conveys much of the spirit that is being created.

This book covers a mass of significant points that show India as the natural home of business process offshoring, such as the number of graduates, the obsession with quality, the engagement with life, how to use the time zone to advantage, and the new-found flexibility you will have. Underlying all of these qualities is a concept best encapsulated in one word: *attitude*.

It is the best shorthand for the absolute determination to lift India into the forefront of the world's economy that radiates in and from the country. There is a relentless focus on competing with the rest of the world and succeeding. Eliminating poverty is a daunting program, but India is steadfastly single-minded in its goal. If old enmities stand in the way, they are cast aside. Look for example at the alliance between China and India that has been newly forged to ensure that rich countries remove subsidies from agricultural goods. Such an alliance would have been unthinkable only a few years ago. Now the perspective in India is: We are going to succeed in changing the global economy.

Attitude is the word that sums this up. Bear this concept in mind throughout this book, and by the end of it you will have a better insight into what makes India so important and how it will be changing lives all over the world.

The Indian economy

After independence, India had a highly centralized economy with the type of regulations that made you wonder at the attention to detail the civil servants of the Indian Administrative Service brought to bear on very small matters. On occasion manufacturers even had to apply to the government for permission to make their products in the quantities they wanted to sell.

There are food subsidies and rations still, and complex support mechanisms, but the Indian economy is radically different now. Structural problems with the economy remain, particularly in energy supply, and there may be shanty towns just outside your five-star hotel, but the dynamics of that new economy are evident if only in the type of cars on the road. Four years ago a Mercedes was a rare sight even in Mumbai, but now there are enough for them not to be of that much interest.

Since the early 1990s, the economy has been shaken up, deregulated, partly exposed to the full force of the global economy, privatized spasmodically, and generally loosened. With membership of the World Trade Organization, the final barriers are supposed to be disappearing. Customs tariffs, which still seem to average around 40 percent, have indeed been coming down, but there are invisible barriers to trade that defy deregulation. They include, for example, the delay and obfuscation that occur in the import and export processes. Yet there is a willingness to admit the existence of such practices and an evident determination to address them that will convince you that something very special is happening in India.

There are six free trade zones, called Export Processing Zones (EPZs). For example in Mumbai there is SEEPZ, the Santacruz Electronics Export Processing Zone. These are designed to provide internationally competitive infrastructure facilities in a duty-free, low-cost environment, and they work very well.

It is difficult to trust any particular numbers about the Indian economy, partly because you will find it difficult to get just one number for any statistic. The precise numbers are not worth worrying unduly about – and it is just as appropriate to appreciate what the general trend is. Growth in the economy is apparent and substantial, but may not be at the level that the Indian National Government believes it needs to sustain its plan to rid India of poverty by 2020.

The Economist usually ranks India as the third fastest-growing economy in the world. Even it currently puts GDP growth at about 4.9 percent, industrial production growth at 5.7 percent, and consumer price inflation at about 5.8 percent. When you are there, especially if you've been to the other countries that are generally in that sort of frame, these figures feel right, if not an understatement.

The contrast with China, the fastest-growing economy as far as *The Economist* is concerned, is instructive. China has figures of 6.7 percent growth in GDP and 16.5 percent growth in industrial production. The disparity in industrial production growth between the two countries is highly relevant. India has far higher growth in services revenues than China and this is significant for the whole discussion about business process outsourcing offshore.

Some recent history

The British were merely the latest in a long line of imperial rulers or invaders, and that line included the Moguls – who built the Taj Mahal – the Guptas, and even the Aryans. The Portuguese had a colony, Goa, on the west coast up until 1961, and the French finally left India in 1954, seven years after the Brits – though you won't get many Brits to recognize this fact.

British rule started with the East India Company, which was based in Calcutta. It was only after 1757, when Clive of India beat the locals at the Battle of Plessey, that this base was expanded until the whole of India eventually became a colony of the British Crown.

India gained independence from the United Kingdom and the British Empire in August 1947. English is no longer one of the country's 18 official languages: the Official Language Amendment Act of 1967 granted it the status of an additional language. It is the language of administration, nevertheless, and of the judiciary. It is mostly the language of higher education.

Indian law is based on UK law, trains derail just like British ones do, there is a free and exciting press, and the fiscal year starts in April, as in the UK.

There is an elected Parliament, the Lok Sabha, with an upper chamber, the Rajya Sabha, which is a selected Council of States. Regular democratic elections currently produce Union governments based on coalitions of nearly 30 parties. India remains a secular democracy, with occasional tensions between religious and sectarian groups. Despite the creation of Pakistan in 1947, as a separate Muslim state carved out of the Raj with an East and West territory, there are more Muslims in India than in Pakistan or Bangladesh. Bangladesh was originally East Pakistan, but is now a separate state following a bloody civil war in the early 1970s.

The caste system, with its roots in the various conquests of India, divided the population, so that you couldn't cross caste to marry. That concept still exists in people's consciousness. There is, however, a sense of national identity focused on the Union government, often referred to as *The Centre*, as strong a contempt for politicians and civil servants as in any western country, 28 states with their own governments and civil apparatus and as much sense of independence from the Centre as you might wish, seven Union and special territories, and armed forces equipped with a nuclear arsenal.

Paradoxically in view of later history, one might think, India was very Moscow centered all through the Cold War, whereas Pakistan, the specially created Muslim state, was even more paradoxically western oriented and very close to the USA.

There are various hot spots of terrorist and other violent activity, notably in Jammu and Kashmir, which is a legacy of the fixes and compromises the British inflicted on India when they left. The Tamil conflict in Sri Lanka has sometimes threatened to spill over properly into India. In Andhra Pradesh the Naxalite movement is serious enough for the Chief Minister, Chandrababu Naidu, to have at least four identical white cars, all with the same number plate. In the northeast, the tensions with Bangladesh can cause problems. In addition, there has been communal rioting in Gujarat, and even tensions over water usage between states.

The dispute over the razing of a mosque at Ayodhya in 1992 by Hindus, who claimed that it was on the original site of a Hindu temple, has caused endless confrontations and outrages. The anniversary of that attack may have provoked the bombings in Mumbai in 2003 that left around 50 people dead and 150 seriously injured. These bombings are the most serious in a pattern of outrages going back spasmodically over more than ten years.

These outrages were high profile and extreme, but I have been at meetings where the city mayor turned up accompanied by two rather unsavory-looking men with submachine guns at the ready. Nevertheless, such flash points are rare and visitors aren't generally aware of them.

Some geography

Everyone knows that India is that triangular appendage hanging off the bottom of Asia, just below the Himalayas. It's about one third the land mass of the USA, about the size of western Europe, and the seventh largest country in the world.

Down in the south India is lush and green and amazing. There are tropical rainforests falling down to stunning beaches. Elsewhere there are huge deserts and arid yet cultivated land. There are all sorts of crops, including vineyards, and some excellent wines. The sparkling champagne-like ones can be stunning in quality and it is worth experimenting with the other wines too.

In the west facing the Arabian Gulf, the sea is generally gray. To use a British frame of reference, it is like the North Sea at West Hartlepool in February. It is uninviting, but people swim in it. In the east facing the Bay of Bengal, the sea is green. In the south, the Indian Ocean is blue, and a ravishing blue at that.

There are enormous rivers and high mountains and spectacular examples of most geographical concepts in India.

There are six important cities known collectively as the metros. The first is Delhi, really New Delhi now, positioned toward the top, to the left of the middle. Calcutta, officially Kolkata, the original capital of the British Empire's version of India, is in the northeast at the extreme right, about where the triangle of India meets the main land mass of Asia at the bird's foot delta of the Ganges river. Mumbai, previously Bombay, is about a third of the way down on the western or left-hand coast. Hyderabad is a bit further south, in the middle. Bangalore is about a quarter of the way up from the southerly tip, in the middle too, and Chennai, formerly Madras, is to the East of Bangalore, on the right-hand coast.

Delhi is the national capital. Mumbai is the financial center and where the films are also made. As it was called Bombay in imperial times, the movies, by analogy with Hollywood, are often said to be made in Bollywood.

Calcutta is a major port and has been very poor. Mother Teresa based herself and her mission there. The economy is now picking up following some major investments, particularly in information technology businesses.

Bangalore led the high-tech revolution in India, is extremely prosperous, and is a leading force in the business process outsourcing movement. It has become a shorthand reference for much of the outsourcing going to India, but it is by no means the only or necessarily the obvious choice. Many major US companies have based their operations there, from GE to American Express. There are sometimes acute pressures on staff availability and this is one factor why Bangalore may not be the most appropriate metro for your operations.

Hyderabad is coming up fast and is an amazingly dynamic place. Up until independence it was a separate territory, ruled by the Nizam. His grandson is still in Hyderabad and works for the group that owns the Sheraton Hotels. Chennai, also a port, is becoming extraordinarily prosperous, with many foreign companies and major organizations choosing to put their offshore centers there, including the World Bank.

The weather

India can be very hot. Before the invention of air conditioning, at the point in the year when a punkah wallah – a person whose job it was to wave a fan or move a vane with a string and pulley – became inadequate to mitigate the heat, the governing-class Brits used to decamp from Delhi to Shimla in the north, nearer the mountains. Delhi is hotter than it might be because the Himalayas, to the north, act as a natural barrier and ensure that the hot air recirculates right back across the country.

You don't usually need weather forecasts and you normally don't get them, except on the international satellite channels. I did wake up one morning in Hyderabad to a message that it would be a lot cooler today, *down* to around 44° Centigrade, which is very hot in Fahrenheit too.

Delhi gets fog bound in the winter and the temperature goes below freezing even before the air conditioning is turned on. That fog can be a problem and lead to flights being diverted and canceled, especially in January, stranding passengers.

Then there is the monsoon. Regularly every year, from around the beginning of June, the rain belt creeps up the subcontinent. This is a matter of some discussion and analysis for the very good reason that lives depend on a good – that is, heavy – monsoon.

Like most cities, as soon as it rains even a little, Mumbai quickly comes to a halt. When the monsoon deluge starts it is like a massive seizure. If a taxi driver, without a second thought, moves himself out of the driving seat, rests his head against the door pillar, puts his feet up on the dashboard behind the steering wheel, and goes to sleep, that is some indication of how long the ensuing traffic jam will last.

This illustrates two points about India. The first is that the monsoon is seriously wet. The second is that taxi drivers go to sleep at the drop of a hat. You will learn the extenuating circumstances for that in a later chapter.

Once the monsoon starts in early June it will continue right to the end of September, give or take a week or two. It's not continuous rain, but when it is raining, you will know what it means to see wet people.

A raincoat won't be much protection for the quick dash from your car. Use an umbrella – at least it may keep your hair dry.

Traveling around

Americans don't underestimate the distances in India, but Europeans – especially the British – do. There are railways linking most major centers, but they tend to be slow and are probably better suited to tourists. The road network is improving, with dual carriageways planned to link all the metros. Driving, unless for a specific adventure, is not recommended; there are examples of what being driven in India may mean in Part II.

The air network is good and efficient, with three internal airlines competing: Indian Airlines, which is government owned, Jet Airways, and Sahara. The flying time between metros is about two hours. Frequencies between metros are generally good and the reliability isn't much different from Europe or the US, with Jet Air having a particularly good record and superb customer service.

Even before the events in the US on September 11, 2001, security was commendably tight at Indian airports. Now it is a lesson to every civil aviation authority in the world. The thoroughness for internal flights is reassuring: your luggage is scanned before you check in, your hand luggage is screened, and you are frisked as you go airside. As you go through the gate you are frisked again, usually twice, your hand baggage is thoroughly searched, and there is normally a final check just before you board the plane.

Compared with some western airports where the checks often appear insubstantial, the conscientiousness of these security checks is outstanding.

The whole process is anything but cursory, and does require a very Indian sense of resignation to cope with at times.

Education

Universal primary education is available by law to everyone in India and there are about 184 million schoolchildren. In fact, despite that massive number, the dropout rates for government-provided education are alarming, and over the age of 11 fewer than 50 percent of Indian children are in full-time education in most states.

There are massive programs to address this issue, but without significant efforts the malaise will not be cured. Teachers in rural areas are still not paid adequately or regularly. In urban areas they may draw their salaries and not turn up. This causes widespread resentment. In fact, there are signs that the teachers themselves are organizing to change how the system works, as parents, politicians, and bureaucrats alike have started to focus on the ills of the current approach.

The aim is to have universal literacy by 2020. The Ministry of Education claims that, according to the 2001 Census, 65.4 percent of adults are literate, which breaks down to 75.9 percent for males, but only 54.2 percent for females. The overall literacy rate has increased by 13 percent in ten years.

India is one of the three biggest book markets in the world by volume, according to the Federation of Publishers' and Booksellers' Associations in India (FPBAI). The market in 2002 is said to be have been worth around INR70 billion, about $1.4 billion or nearly £1 billion, so each person spent about £1 on books. This is a low spending figure by global standards, but it should be remembered that the vast majority of Indians are very poor. The books purchased are mostly education oriented, about 70 percent, with the rest bought by the educated professional classes. Some 40 percent of all books purchased are in English.

I have had the privilege of working to help create a not-for-profit education services company in India. The focus on education among the poorest people is humbling. Since government schools don't provide a proper education, parents are willing to pay, out of their minuscule wages, to send their children to very poor – that is, not rich – private schools, with English as the medium of instruction. The poorest school I know charges each of its pupils one rupee per day for their schooling, equivalent to 2¢. When the whole family is living on less than $2 a day, that's still a major sacrifice.

From that sometimes heart-breaking and sometimes inspiring end of the spectrum, you will see private schools that put to shame the best in the West. These are the sort of schools where polo is the compulsory sport. And it may be another paradoxical insight into how India is organized to discover how important Christian schools are. Less than 3 percent of the population is Christian, yet one of my friends in India told me that the best schools are the Jesuit ones. He remains a Hindu, but he went to a Jesuit private school and he is adamant that it was the best education one could want.

At the tertiary level, India comes into its own. Perhaps because the caste system gave the highest caste the leisure for study, the country has long had a high reputation for learning. There are about 250 universities, heavily biased toward the hard sciences and business management, but these do little undergraduate teaching. They focus on postgraduate teaching and research.

Undergraduate teaching is carried out at 10,000 or so affiliated colleges, which are expanding fast, and there are about eight million undergraduates at any one time. Lecturers number about a third of a million. Fifty engineering colleges and the same number of business management colleges were opened every year up to 2003.[2] Teaching is mostly in English and undergraduate teaching usually follows the UK approach, whereas postgraduate teaching tends to be more US oriented.

The number of universities in India is growing at around five per year. The investment in them is huge. The universities are first-rate and, from a shaky reputation in the 1960s in most fields other than mathematics and the physical sciences, they have become home to some of the best applied research in the world. Pharmaceutical research especially is becoming more and more effective and India is starting to be a force in the world pharma industry as a major producer of new molecules. There are about 250 medical colleges, 175 dental colleges, and 150 pharmaceutical colleges. The transition of Indian pharma companies from producers of generic drugs coming out of patent protection to innovators is a timely reminder of how India's value proposition and position in the world's value chain can change in this new world.

The Indian Institutes of Technology (IITs) are world leaders – they are the benchmark by which equivalent institutions round the world have to be judged. When you start to interact with the alumni of the IITs, you will be amazed. The quality of their training and education is superb and the quantity of extremely capable graduates will amaze you.

The offshoring revolution

The revenues to Indian companies from offshore IT services are estimated – with the usual health warnings about not trusting a single figure but appreciating the trends – at over $7 billion in 2002, a growth rate below the apparently expected 40 percent, but still a respectable 26 percent.

McKinsey–NASSCOM's original estimate of IT services revenues by the year 2008 was $87 billion. No one thought this was achievable, because it adds up to an astonishing number of people engaged in the business. In fact, McKinsey and NASSCOM have toned down their estimate so that it is now only $78 billion by 2008. Even that figure looks challenging. All that you need to realize, however, is that Indian IT services companies are going to dominate the global IT services industry for some time to come.

Offshore business process outsourcing is confidently predicted to be a larger market, from a base of about $2.35 billion in 2002 rising to $3.6 billion in 2003. McKinsey's current prediction for revenues to Indian services companies from IT enabled services (see Chapter 3) in 2008 is $142 billion. Again, the trend is what's important, not the exact figures.

It is obvious from the numbers of people employed that this is a huge business. It is equally clear, if only from the number of new office developments in the metros to house call centers, that this business is growing at more than 40 percent. Whole new office complexes in places like Gurgaon, outside Delhi, appear on what seems like a daily basis, and because of the speed of construction in India that appearance is close to reality.

Some 40 percent of American Express's back-office processing is already done offshore – not all in India, but a good proportion is there. Amex is planning to take 60 percent of all back-office processing offshore.

GE has over 12,000 employees in India and is planning to expand. GE Capital India provides claims processing, credit evaluation, accounting, and many other functions for 80 GE branches throughout the world. It is the largest IT enabled services provider in India, and last year alone hired 6,000 employees. There are signs around its premises warning "Trespassers Will Be Recruited." Its president, Pramod Bhasin, comments: "I can't tell you how much we depend on India in GE. We're at the stage where we believe all back-office operations should be carried out in low-cost countries."[3]

CitiBank has more than 2,000 direct employees of its local subsidiary in India. Dell has 400; while it was reported to be repatriating some customer support roles to the US at the end of 2003 following complaints from business customers, it was also not reducing its work force in India. Many other companies, such as travel and entertainment website lastminute.com, supermarket retailer Tesco, and telecommunications company BT in the UK, have contracted work offshore, and the number of companies is growing all the time. In 2003 the pace of going offshore really quickened, with HSBC alone announcing more than 4,000 jobs going offshore to India.

It is to precisely what is involved in this offshoring revolution that we turn in Chapter 2.

Part I

What's This Offshoring Business?

2
Business Process Offshoring

Outsourcing your processes *offshore* – now often termed "offshoring" – does not rewrite the rules about outsourcing. To be confident about the most appropriate sourcing of any service, you have to understand the key guidelines for outsourcing in general. In business process outsourcing (BPO) offshore you do have to apply those guidelines more rigorously, but it is a question of degree, not a completely different set of parameters. Even though your supplier is thousands of miles away, its staff will only be a moment away on the telephone or by video conference. If you and your supplier or partner manage this properly and only outsource what is appropriate, the geographical distance will hardly matter, you will gain benefits from the different time zones and not find them an obstacle, and you will scarcely notice that your supplier is not on a different floor in the same office as you.

Get that initial analysis wrong, however, and you will be in trouble.

The initial business drivers

Outsourcing is a common practice in the West. Over half of the UK FTSE 100 companies, for example, now contract some portion of their IT and business processes to outside organizations. One in every five has a single outsourcing contract worth 3 percent or more of its market capitalization.[1] In that context, it is important to appreciate the business drivers behind offshore outsourcing. In a survey reported by Kshema Technologies,[2] which focused on the IT industry but will resonate with what is happening in business process offshoring, the results were not unexpected, but they did give an insight into the wider reasons for going offshore.

The desire to reduce costs was the highest priority or business driver for outsourcing offshore, with 43 percent of companies identifying this as one of the factors. 30 percent also pointed to increasing the ratio of profit to revenue, which may be part of the same story. Focus on core competencies (35 percent), access to special expertise (32 percent), speeded-up delivery (27 percent), relieving resource constraints (25 percent), access to new technologies and eliminating a problem area (24 percent) were all significant. Particular projects came next with 16 percent, followed by some apparently contradictory measures: reduction in IT staff (15 percent) and augmenting existing staff (11 percent).

The difference once we move into business process outsourcing is not that marked yet, partly because experience is not generally shared, but there are signs that increased productivity and better use of physical assets are beginning to be appreciated.

Core and non-core

The conventional wisdom on outsourcing is that you should not outsource anything that is a fundamental part of your value proposition. Anything that doesn't give you competitive advantage not only *can* be outsourced but *should* be outsourced, or at least considered for outsourcing. This may not be quite as logical as it seems, but when making your analysis about what to consider for outsourcing it makes good sense.

Another way of expressing this concept suggests that you should concentrate on what you're best at, and that will almost certainly be your core activity. Anything that isn't core is a candidate for outsourcing, whether offshore or not. Third-party companies that are better focused or equipped and have that particular process as a core competence can take on what is non-core to you. They can do this work for many companies, increasing their capability and skills, and give you the benefit of greater scale.

In following this set of principles, Microsoft, the largest software company in the world, does virtually nothing for itself except IT research and development. It doesn't print anything, package anything, do any internal administration, distribute anything, provide meals, clean its office toilets, or staff its security desks. Research and development is its self-proclaimed area of core competence and that is all it does, if it can help it.

You don't have to be that purist, but it is worth bearing in mind and is a great concept to use as your starting point.

The objective behind outsourcing is usually therefore expressed as a way to achieve competitive advantage. In practice it may only be about achieving competitive parity. Of course, you've got to have the latter at least, but one of the real objectives of this chapter is to identify how to achieve competitive *advantage.*

One further but key benefit that you should achieve from outsourcing is gaining management time to consider running the business more effectively. It is difficult to quantify that, and there will be cynics who regard it as a thoroughly bad development as it will increase senior management interference. Nevertheless, any time taken to reconsider what you are doing and how you are doing it has to be beneficial to your business.

Outsourcing non-core activities should allow you more time to concentrate on real value generation. If it doesn't, there is probably a deeper malaise, whether with what you are outsourcing or with the way you have done it.

In summary, if any particular process is merely a commodity to you, so that you could buy from another supplier without it affecting the quality of your products and services, it is highly unlikely to be worth keeping in house. For example, running your payroll is something you can do and something other companies can do. If running your own payroll does not add any particular value to your business, consider seriously whether to outsource it.

On the other hand, something may be such a small proportion of your costs that outsourcing it is not worth the effort. There will be occasions when this argument is true, but often it is a way of avoiding what appear to be difficult questions.

Revenue distance

Ravi Aron of the Wharton Business School uses a different perspective that also might help you resolve any internal debates about what you should keep in house: the concept of revenue distance. At a simple level, this focuses on two aspects of a process and how close those are to the customer.

The first is what *value* a particular process creates. The nearer to the customer the process is, the less likely it is that it can be effectively outsourced. Secondly, he asks how close this process is to generating *revenue*, with the general view that if it is very close, it is less likely to be amenable to outsourcing.

He adds in more variables, the first of which is the *criticality* of the process, by which he means how much effect making one mistake can have. For example, a mistake in cash-flow analysis for a corporation can be highly critical to the whole business, whereas a mistake in an invoice figure to one customer will usually have much less impact on your strategic planning.

Aron's second variable is process *complexity*. His view is that the more complex the process, the less likely it is to be outsourced successfully. This view is in useful tension with the progress of outsourcing in general, but is something else to bear in mind, particularly when considering whether to outsource a whole process or simply part of it.

A key way of resolving this issue is to have regard not so much to the complexity of the overall process, but to the simplicity of each step. One useful test is whether the process is currently carried out in a separate office, perhaps in the same building, and whether that makes any difference at all. If it doesn't, outsourcing it shouldn't make a difference either.

Local knowledge

Taking a process offshore can add difficulties to those normally involved in outsourcing. There are domain skill issues – that is, knowing what is appropriate for a particular industry or vertical market. These can usually be overcome with training, although you may not initially realize the extra costs involved. If local knowledge is required – of place names, shop names, or abbreviations, for example – training will be even more expensive. In these cases, it may mean that even though the process is non-core, it is not suitable for offshore outsourcing. There have been significant numbers of complaints about the UK's directory inquiries services that are now handled from India, because the operators lack the necessary knowledge of where locations are and how they are spelled.

That notwithstanding, Network Rail in the UK decided to outsource its timetable inquiries to India in 2003. While there is a huge training requirement to ensure familiarity with local area knowledge and how the railways operate, there are undoubted cost savings, and Network Rail has even claimed that the main reason is to avoid the power cuts it has suffered when providing the service in the UK.

Before you outsource offshore, then, it is doubly important to know what can actually be outsourced to the benefit of your business. One shorthand way is examine what is core and what is non-core in your business, and then to ask whether local knowledge or domain skills are significant in the process.

The importance of the process

Outsourcing work offshore to a low-cost country like India does change one aspect of how you look at your business and what is core. While it adds a rider to the rules above, it doesn't really alter their impact.

It should, however, change the way you look at your business. This approach looks at the difference between what is *important* to your business and how that is different from its being core.

You may already, for example, have the firm view that customer service is absolutely core to your business and the aspect that gives you at least some of your competitive edge. As a result, you may not even want to consider outsourcing any element of customer care to India. On the other hand, you should at least consider taking some of the customer care *processes* offshore. Even if in the end you don't make that step for good reasons, you will have been through a productive exercise that will have helped you redefine what you want from your customer care. What outsourcing to India should make you address is whether something being extremely important to you is the same as it being core.

The starting point could be whether you can carry out all of the customer service functions you need cost-effectively compared with India. If you cannot, as is likely, you will be in a dilemma. Can you outsource that function, or at least some of it, and gain competitive edge without undermining your strategic position in the market?

For instance, US airline Delta decided to outsource some of its reservation processes to India, including general sales calls, frequent flyer services, and baggage sales calls. It claims that this has not only reduced costs but also improved service quality and productivity.[3] Hutchison, a mobile phone operator across Europe, Asia, and Australia, has also outsourced most of its customer support operations to India.

You may conclude that you cannot outsource any part of your customer care without losing control of how you address your market and it is therefore not merely important, but core to your business. In that case, you will have to accept that, in order to retain competitive advantage, your customer service has to add significant value in addition to what it is able to do now, because your costs will otherwise be out of line.

The incredible shrinking core

Over time, you will find that no matter how good your initial analysis has been, what you regard as core to your business will be redefined, and will in all like-lihood shrink. Because business process outsourcing to India has only a relatively short history, this isn't quite as visible as it is in the IT software and services market.

The history of IT outsourcing is instructive, and we will consider this fur-ther in the next chapter. A huge proportion of software development has been outsourced to India. However, western software companies, which made a liv-ing out of developing software and applications, were initially extremely reluc-tant to outsource software development, which many saw as their core compe-tence and their competitive advantage. As time moved on, attitudes changed.

Reanalysis of what was core depended on breaking down software develop-ment into its different activities. At a relatively high level, these stages were seen as initial analysis of the business need; creation of a requirements definition; translation of that definition into a software specification; software design and the development of a software architecture; software writing or coding; fol-lowed by implementation and testing.

It was relatively easy to see that coding, the actual writing of the software, is one process among many and, in effect, is a relatively minor activity that is hardly core, whereas design is highly skilled and therefore core. On this basis, coding could readily be outsourced to India. A rather offensive phrase was coined for the Indians to whom this was initially outsourced: "techno-coolies." This phrase has haunted one or two of the earlier analysts.

As Indian software companies became more experienced, and had writ-ten and then begun to support software, the ability to design software was more obviously within their skill set. Testing and implementation became part of their offer. Western IT companies, as a result, moved further away from software, and created another different understanding of what was core to them.

There was one sticking point in this redefinition process. For a long time domain skills were seen as a key differentiator for western IT companies and not something that could be outsourced. Latterly even these domain skills have been viewed as not necessarily core, and Indian services companies have gained remarkable expertise in them. In some western IT software services companies, the core competence is now seen as marketing and selling.

You can have one of two reactions here. The first may be to want nothing to do with anything like this. Outsourcing looks like a Trojan horse that, once it enters your citadel, will destroy you from the inside out. Alternatively, you can look at what happened to western IT companies, short-cut some of the analysis, take a hard look at what is really core in your company processes, and gain a competitive advantage that will be longer lasting.

Being radical with your analysis of what is and isn't core can secure a major leap that will move beyond the survival of your company. You may then flourish in a rapidly developing world where the assumptions all have to be challenged. This may be a step too far and create unforeseen risks, but it is nevertheless advantageous to reassess your business and its component parts.

A key lesson I gained from academic research in an altogether different field has helped me considerably over the years. Rather than strain for new options or ideas, it is often most beneficial to look at what you already apparently know, challenging your assumptions and being prepared to reevaluate what you are thinking and doing, and changing your approach as a result.

As business processing is considered for offshoring, confronting what is core and non-core should become a continuous activity, in just the same way as it did in the IT industry.

There is a great deal of resistance to this concept, nevertheless. Many senior managers will tell you that what is core and non-core in a particular company is understood completely and give that as a reason for not conducting any further analysis. That is a trap. As pricing and cost structures change, the balance between what is core and non-core must change.

What is core to any one business will inevitably shrink over time. This argument can be reduced to absurdity, but it is a perspective that helps you understand the issues. As you reduce what you regard as core, you will inevitably look at what else can go.

An analogy is with what has happened to the value chain in most industries. We have gone from an ideal where everything was vertically integrated to one of smaller and smaller activities being linked together to form the whole. If you look at any value chain over the last ten years, it will most likely have been broken into smaller and smaller segments, and more and more segments will have been taken over by niche or specialist players. In terms of what is core, we are in the same position.

IT offshoring

From the previous discussion you can see that anything related to IT will be a natural to put offshore, whether you are an IT company of any description or a company with an IT department. It's as well to remember that there won't be much, if any, competitive edge in outsourcing any IT, as this will be a me-too business development. Most of your competitors will have already done some, and some will have done a great deal. That means that if you haven't, you should do so as soon as possible simply to achieve competitive parity.

The first question you should ask about IT outsourcing is not whether, but what. If you need a place to start, the answer is quite simple. In the IT world there are two tasks to which most IT professionals are averse: application maintenance and support.

IT professionals like to be at the cutting edge, working on next year's project or code. Maintenance centers on last year's efforts. Outsource it and you will have the nearest thing possible to happy IT professionals in house. The service your users, internal or external, receive will also improve, partly because there are people focused on it who don't resent it, and partly just because there are people focused on it.

There are downsides, such as loss of continuity and knowledge, but these are controllable and relatively insignificant against one extremely important benefit that you will see as a business. IT maintenance will be an aspect of your IT systems for which you will have more or less accurate costs. You will know how many people you have got doing it, or how much of their time it consumes, the cost of the machines, the cost of related telecommunications, and the cost of all ancillary aspects. By getting it for a fixed price from an offshore Indian company, you will probably halve your costs. Most importantly, you will know how much cost you have saved. You will also see how good the service is from India and be able to judge your supplier pretty accurately. This will be an excellent basis and spur for going on to consider all aspects of your IT systems and which parts can and should be outsourced.

Since Indians are not incapable IT professionals, you might raise the objection that they will not favor doing maintenance either. You will be right. However, while it's simply the pits for your department, it's a means to an end for the Indian company. If it does a good job it knows there is much more important work to come. This may start with simple bug fixes or changes, but could become much more rewarding. At the most extreme, it could be taking over your IT department, leaving only a small team in your domestic market. More immediately, and as both sides gain confidence in each other, it could be giving direct support to your customers.

At that point we are almost in a cross-over from the IT world into business process outsourcing. Supplying direct support to your IT users, internal or external, is a big step from outsourcing the maintenance, but after a very short while the only people with real expertise in your current application release will be your Indian software company. Then, of course, why not transfer that email and telephone support to India too?

Business process offshoring

Business process outsourcing offshore is where the real competitive edge is and will be for a few years. In this context BPO covers, for example, internal finance and administration, human resource administration, most back-office systems, procurement, and many forms of customer contact and relationship management.

A call center may be where you start your engagement with BPO offshore. To all intents and purposes, as long as this isn't a core activity, any form of customer response and customer management could be outsourced with significant cost savings.

Apart from those cost savings, there are significant advantages in transferring your call center activity to India. Depending on the service you require, you will find that the agents staffing the phones on your behalf are probably graduates. Call center jobs carry status in India – certainly more than the equivalent job does in Massachusetts or Fife – and you will find that the responsiveness, customer care, and general focus on the work are also much higher. It is certainly not a low-quality alternative.

• If you think about your own experience of call centers – that is, the ones you have to call to get service from – you will no doubt have a long list of the problems they have caused you. You will have been driven mindless by what was originally called automatic voice response (AVR), but which some joker seems to have renamed intelligent voice response (IVR). There is a technological difference, but no real improvement in the customer experience.

Indian call center agents' standard of education may offer you a chance to differentiate your customer service on quality and at the same time give you lower costs. That could provide you with a real competitive edge.

When you start looking at which internal processes to offshore, you can seriously consider all forms of human resource administration, internal accounting, administering expenses, day-to-day audit, procurement, many of the less country-specific legal processes carried out by a company secretary or the office of the general counsel, some marketing communications, and a whole range of ticketing, timetable, and aligned activities. There will be good reasons for not taking some out of your company, let alone out of the country. Yet it is clearly advantageous to start with the question of why not rather than why when the cost savings alone are so significant.

Once you have carried out the analysis of the relatively straightforward processes in your business, there are the more complex and demanding ones.

I was directly involved in the transfer of life insurance claims processing offshore. Claims processing usually relies on a great deal of domain experience, knowledge of products and services, insight into how clients have purchased the products, and what the outcomes might be in any situation. It requires an ability to grapple with complex processes, customer issues of some intricacy, and cultural concerns. It is in the process of being transferred to India and is but one example of much more demanding processes being outsourced offshore. Whether India is the right place to put such work, especially in the short term, is still an open question. It certainly *will* be the right place and, with the careful approach being adopted, this project will be successful, although the initial training costs will be higher than is comfortable.

With the Indian focus on mathematics, it is only a matter of time before actuarial work is moved successfully offshore in quantity. If hard sums like that are taken offshore, many of the professions will be facing challenges about what *can* next go offshore – not whether it *should*.

Don't ignore the research that your company does either. Whether this is applied research, testing, and test analysis for a pharmaceutical company developing a new molecule, or more arcane research into customer satisfaction, it may well be a candidate for outsourcing to India and should certainly be on your list.

The answer to the question of what to place in India is therefore to look at what you do and work out whether it requires a physical presence rather closer than 5,000 miles away. If it doesn't, you need to be thinking about outsourcing it, and taking it offshore, as a significant step to competitive advantage.

I do have reservations about whether some processes are appropriate to take offshore, even if you can define them as non-core, but I have absolute confidence that the process of working out whether you should or should not is a key priority for senior managers in western businesses. If you're not part of this global services revolution, you will lose competitive advantage through missed cost savings, driven by productivity improvements as well as lower wage rates, and, probably more significantly, through poorer quality. You will lose competitive advantage because you will not have the most responsive process management, the most focused approach to your key processes, and access to a flexible and dynamic, highly educated work force.

This is a key advantage behind the success of Indian services companies. Flexibility and agility of response are right at the heart of how Indians conceive of business. You will be able to reconfigure what you do, even though it is remote and at least 5,000 miles away, much more effectively and quickly than if it was in the same building as you in the West.

Do it yourself or outsource

As business process offshoring develops, there are continuing discussions about the approach any company should take to creating its presence offshore, whether in India or elsewhere. There is no universally appropriate right answer, but there are a number of guidelines that should help you come to the best conclusion for your own business.

It is best to see outsourcing as one element in your sourcing strategy. Gartner has coined the term "right sourcing," which encompasses most of the ways to source internal services. The real value of right sourcing is that it places outsourcing within an overall strategy and encourages you to think of the range of your processes within a flexible perspective, what is sometimes called "intelligent resourcing." Outsourcing, offshore or not, then becomes one element in your overall business strategy.

At a much more tactical level, you will also come across terms like "co-sourcing." At first it is easy to dismiss such terms as marketing speak, but there is an underlying value in seeing how potential suppliers or partners view the relationship with you. It may also encourage your business to approach potential suppliers or partners in a different way. It is best to view any investment in India as part of a long-term strategy, and although there will be quick wins, it is the longer term that will give you most benefit.

There are many variations of how to take work offshore even within the broader categories and any number of TLAs (three-letter acronyms) to describe how they are achieved. The following brief overview of the various approaches will introduce you to those acronyms and also start to indicate the various possibilities to consider.

The term business process outsourcing itself encompasses a range of actual outcomes, some of which are not necessarily outsourcing in the conventional sense of a third party taking over a function for another business. Nevertheless, it is widely used in this inexact way. Where there is a huge geographical distance between head office and the subsidiary and there is a locally recruited management, this insourcing, as it is sometimes known, can resemble outsourcing much more than not. In characterizing the various types of BPO offshore, I am accepting it as a generic term and will start by looking at the results.

It may be that you will end up with what is known as a captive, shared service center; that is, a subsidiary of your own company that provides business services for you offshore. At the opposite extreme, you may end up with a service provided for you in a facility that carries out such services for many companies, or one center devoted to your processes but wholly owned by a third party. In between there are many variations: you may establish a joint venture or work in partnership with an Indian company so you have a direct interest in the offshore processing center.

To acquire a captive service center, you may have taken a completely do-it-yourself approach, or an ABO, BTO, or BOT route.

- ❏ The do-it-yourself method is self-explanatory and will involve your in-house team being located in India and subcontracting the various elements involved, including land acquisition, obtaining of permits, building, and recruitment.
- ❏ ABO might more properly be ABTO, and stands for Assisted Build, Transfer and Operate. Instead of your own team entirely working offshore and using subcontractors, you employ consultants to handle the specialized local sub-contracting and the more difficult interfaces with government and other authorities, for example.
- ❏ The second acronym stands for a Build, Transfer, Operate commercial arrangement, where a third party builds the center and then transfers it to you.
- ❏ The final acronym stands for Build, Operate, Transfer, where the third party, as well as building the structure, establishes the initial operation and then transfers it to you as a fully functioning center, not necessarily immediately.

This isn't by any means a full list of the acronyms in this area. DBOT, with the D standing for Design, is one variation, and others are coming by the day.

Where the final service center is not a subsidiary but a proper outsourcing arrangement, you may have a BOO, a Build, Own, Operate contract. The purest form will have little offshore involvement on your side and the center will operate entirely according to service level agreements. In practice, most such arrangements involve more direct intervention than this, especially where there is a partnership or even a formal joint venture. Nevertheless, one company I know adopted this approach because its own internal approval procedures were so difficult that it was easier to obtain one overall agreement to go ahead and then not have to return at each discrete stage for further intervention.

Experience suggests that the pure do-it-yourself model is usually the most expensive, not only because of the costs of an expatriate team, but because delays inevitably get into the system as each stage of selecting subcontractors lengthens. Many companies do not have accounting procedures sophisticated enough to turn these delays into costs, but where a new service center is going to cut your costs by, say, 40 percent, every month's delay is a real cost, however hidden it is. To a lesser extent, the same issues are brought into play with an ABO contract. While there are successful implementations of the do-it-yourself approach, of which the World Bank in Chennai is a prime example, in general this method is fraught with too many difficulties.

There *are* good reasons for taking this approach, if you need this level of control. One is that the second or third exercise you undertake to create a service center in India in this way will be cheaper than contracting with an Indian company to do it. The second reason is more indirect: the Indian government is keen to encourage foreign direct investment, and the do-it-yourself method looks more like that sort of investment. This may not be as convincing to you and your business, however.

You should also be aware that there is a new development in the possibility of taking space inside an existing facility that is used by other companies. Non-Indian companies have started to work out how to provide such services in this way. GE, for example, has declared that it is actively going to market its capability in India to provide services to other western companies.

Finally, you may consider going to any of the international outsourcing companies established in your domestic market and outsourcing your processes to them, leaving that third party to work out where the processes are actually carried out. These outsourcing companies claim that this is the least expensive option. That concept is counterintuitive, but may have some value. There is an issue of scale here. If your processes warrant outsourcing on any reasonable scale that can support you creating your own project, it is probably not the most effective way of achieving your ends. Whatever the cost advantage, if it exists, it is the engagement with India and Indian business that is the real prize.

There is a continuing debate about the right way to approach BPO offshore in India – and there are no right answers that are equally valid across all circumstances. If you are at this point set on doing it yourself, perhaps because you feel that your company's needs are different, my advice is to have a serious debate on an informed basis.

All or part of the process

A second set of issues revolves around whether you can take part of a process and move it offshore, or whether you need to take a complete process each time. This debate becomes theological in its intensity, because many of the proponents will finally have a different definition of what constitutes a complete process. On the other hand, there are a number of serious issues here that you should be aware of as you consider what you have to do, as outlined in the following chapters.

You know yourself that each time a part of a process that is still being carried out in house in your home country is transferred from one individual to another, let alone between departments, the opportunities increase for mistakes and communication issues to bedevil the result. Responsibility is one of the first casualties of too fine a granularity in the division of work, no matter that efficiency is apparently increased if each person is focused on a small part of the process.

Against that logic, however, the tendency in outsourcing offshore will be to consider isolating a particular element of a process and transferring that. Once it has been done successfully, more of the process is allowed to go offshore. If you don't consider this aspect, you may find you end up with a messy compromise. This is not helped by the fact that the subject is usually in shades of gray, not stark black and white.

In one example, it was left to a compromise of sorts, as might be inevitable without sustained analysis. The question centered on how expense claims were dealt with. The initial plan proposed that the process of checking whether the numbers added up could be transferred while the questioning of whether the amounts fell within authorized levels would not be outsourced. The result was an unsatisfactory compromise, where the second stage was duplicated in both sites.

It is not important to concentrate on this example, but to focus on understanding what can be sourced offshore and what should be. Have the debate in the sure knowledge that the people who advocate taking a partial process will in any case lose the argument over time. Of course, that doesn't mean they are wrong to start like that, but in practice it is usually better to err on the side of more rather than less.

Dirty or clean

Another area has bedeviled outsourcing discussions for nearly 40 years. It is whether you take the current process as is, in its rather dirty, distinctly unorthogonal state, and transfer it to someone else to deal with, or whether you should clean it up first. In this debate, unlike the previous two, there is now a right answer, although that doesn't mean that everyone agrees.

A dirty, as opposed to a clean, process is one that does the job reasonably well, but is over-demanding in time and effort, duplicates work, or gets twisted into knots when exceptions occur.

Ensuring that the process is cleaned up and reengineered first before outsourcing it is often advocated by those who feel there is an awful lot of surplus in the system. They want to realize that value for themselves or their company and not let a third party gain unfairly. The argument was originally reasonably soundly based, in that the large outsourcing companies very definitely achieved commercial advantage from squeezing costs out of processes they took over. Such western outsourcing companies very often accepted a loss in the first two years or so of a contract, knowing that good, and perhaps excessive, profits would be made later.

Nowadays this argument is usually majored on by those who don't actually want any outsourcing to take place. Experience has shown that it is falsely based for a number of reasons. Putting any process in the hands of an outsourcer in its rough-and-ready state is by any measure the right thing to do.

If, for example, you've had all this time and you and your company haven't cleaned the process up, is there any realistic chance you will do so now? The answer is obvious, yet managements have accepted somewhat emotional arguments that it will be done this time. In practice, the best that can happen is usually unsatisfactory. The attachment to the old ways and the resistance to change will still be there during the cleaning-up process.

Secondly, you only have to consider what a fresh set of eyes and a new set of analytical skills can do, when there are no false expectations and very little history, to see that whatever the downsides of taking a rather inefficient process offshore as it is, the benefits are likely to outweigh them. If you have a contractual foundation saying that benefits to be gained will be shared on some equitable basis, then both sides should win whatever happens.

There is one caveat, which relates to the seriousness of the issues with the current process. If you have a really difficult process problem that is extremely challenging to resolve, outsourcing that process probably won't do anything more than create an even larger problem. If what you are currently doing is inadequate or failing lamentably, outsourcing is not an answer on its own.

Data protection

One concept that has been invoked as a problem in business process offshoring is data protection. There is no doubt that this is a serious subject and one that has to be taken account of in planning any such project.

At the moment there are many issues and objections being raised on the basis of data protection and country-specific data protection legislation. Some of the objections are valid, and as citizens we have an interest in ensuring that such individual protection exists.

Various data protection laws in the US and across the EU already apply to onshore outsourcing. Offshore outsourcing, however, is certainly viewed with more doubt by national legislatures and a number of arguments about data protection are being used to hinder offshoring.

The dynamics of taking business processes offshore are too strong for these unqualified objections to stand for long, especially where it is only a ruse to stop jobs being lost. Just as quickly as an objection is raised, there will be a riposte that is probably equally poorly researched and unsoundly based.

A few years ago the suggestion was mooted that an image of data is different from data stored as text. Interestingly enough, this approach has achieved a high degree of abstract acceptance, but probably at the level of an urban myth. If the objective is to maintain personal privacy, the way information is stored is really less important than how it could be used.

I have discussed some of the issues with a number of UK lawyers, in-house legal people, external consultants, and Indian lawyers. It is true to say that there is little unanimity in opinion. A cynical view could be that the opinion given at any one time tends to support the vested interest of the person with the opinion. This is harsh and not universally true, but whatever the motivation or content of the objections, you need to be aware that there are issues here and that the whole area is more gray than black and white.

It is necessary to understand that the names of the various pieces of legislation throughout the western world are misleading. It is not the data that is the object of the protection, but the identity of individuals. If particular individuals can be identified by a third-party company to whom work has been outsourced, then there is a justified concern that the objects of the legislation itself, and by extension the individuals, are being threatened. It is not impossible to outsource work where the identity of individuals could be ascertained, but special care has to be taken. If you adopt the view that legislation is there to prevent something happening and lawyers are there to find a way round the legislation, you may find that you are at risk.

In these circumstances, we all have to be careful not to flout the guidelines and even the spirit of the legislation. The usual ideas of obtaining customers' consent, encryption, or assigning reference numbers rather than names may well be deemed adequate, but the real question is whether they are practical. As a spur to taking this seriously, it is worth remembering that there can be no cap, contractual or otherwise, on damages for breaches of confidentiality.

New approaches are being developed all the time. Within the EU there are a number of concepts that may well gain international recognition. The main one is adequacy of protection and ensuring that adequate rights and freedom are maintained. In recognition of its domestic issues, the US is also developing safeguards for individuals and protection for businesses.

As far as the EU is concerned, the concept of adequate protection has been made palpable. A number of countries outside the EU at the time of writing, such as Switzerland, Canada, and Hungary, are deemed to have adequate statutory legal safeguards. Businesses there are seen as knowing exactly what they can and cannot do. India does not yet fall into this category, although legislation to provide statutory adequate protection is promised as imminent. Even now, legal judgments inside EU courts can be enforced in Indian courts.

The EU is also creating standard clauses that can be inserted into contracts to give companies some peace of mind about compliance with the various pieces of legislation. The US is taking similar steps, although from a different perspective. The EU tends to use all-encompassing legislation, whereas the US approach is to build a protective environment through legal injunctions, regulations, directives, and finally laws on the statute book.

To counter the difficulties that having two systems can create, there is a scheme called Safe Harbor.[4] Companies can join the Safe Harbor if they can voluntarily comply in distinct areas that include:

❏ Notice – individuals must be notified about the purposes for which information about them is being used.
❏ Choice – giving individuals the opportunity to opt out of having their personal information disclosed.
❏ Onward transfer – if information is disclosed to a third party, both notice and choice have to be applied.
❏ Access – so that individuals can correct information held about them.
❏ Security – reasonable precautions must be taken to protect any personal information.
❏ Data integrity – the information must be relevant for the process in hand.
❏ Enforcement – there should be a readily available way of ensuring compliance with these principles.

A model contract approach is integral to the Safe Harbor scheme. The European Commission has approved its draft of the model contract provisions, after consultation with the US. It may be that this approach will become more widely adopted, as an interim measure if nothing else.

Changes happen rapidly in this field and you need to have up-to-date information and take professional advice. The areas of legislation that apply are also wide and changing to cater for newer technologies. Data protection legislation and directives are buttressed by telecommunications regulations and, of course, electronic communications directives and regulations, and there is a plethora of rules and guidance notices.

The penalties for failure to comply adequately may be unimaginable, but it is also obvious that the various legislatures involved recognize that outsourcing offshore will happen and that only by creating a proper set of safeguards can the objectives of the legislation be met. Data protection legislation is thus not there to prevent business process offshoring, but to make it acceptable.

3
India and the Global Services Revolution

W hen you visit India today, even if you stay in a five-star hotel, engage with rich and successful Indians, and eat some of the best food in the world, you may find the World Bank's projection that it will become the fourth largest economy in the world an astonishing forecast. You will see people begging by the roadside, erecting shanties on every unoccupied part of the sidewalk or pavement, and obviously suffering from malnutrition. You will become accustomed to buildings in a terrible state of repair. There will be reports of wage rates so low that by any measure the people are in poverty, and stories of drought ravaging whole parts of the country. Faced with that direct experience, it will seem impossible to imagine that such a change could come at all, let alone so swiftly.

India will do it. When the chips are down, Indians will always come through. They will bend the rules, change the approach, adopt the right attitude, and make something work even when you think the situation is hopeless.

The same is true in business. There will be times when no apparent progress has been made for months. A deadline looms and everything comes together.

The story of the development of India's services industry has elements of that spirit – the entrepreneurial, trading mentality. It also has another basis, in foresight, planning, and execution. It is that paradoxical relationship between apparently chaotic innocence of time constraints and a determined strategy that will baffle you as a westerner – and it will keep you on your toes.

Some 30 years ago, India worked out that if it was ever to become a developed country, it first had to be an information technology country. The future lay in information processing and services associated with information of all kinds. As India has always had a deserved reputation in mathematics, the step into this new world was not as great as it might have been.

This industry is often referred to as the Indian software industry. Software development is where it started, but it was only the beginning. It is not for nothing that the national body that represents more than 800 companies engaged in this field is called the National Association of Software and Services Companies (NASSCOM). Its roots lie in software and software development, but the industry today is about the whole field of IT services.

Out of the success of the IT services industry, the development of the World Wide Web, and faster and more reliable communications has come a new industry, often developing with the same Indian companies: business process outsourcing offshore.

Most people are aware of the cost savings involved in taking work offshore to India in the IT services arena. There are similar cost advantages in taking BPO offshore. The figures from management consultancy McKinsey that follow should be treated with the usual skepticism about statistics and India, but the general thrust is good enough for most people.

In mid-2003 the annual cost of an experienced call center agent in the US was about $43,000. In India, the direct equivalent was about $6,200. The full cost of the US employee was of the order of $58,500, but the comparative person in India cost $12,000. These figures are for direct employees of large companies without start-up costs, but include the office buildings, for example. If you add, say, 100 percent to the full cost of an Indian employee, to include your Indian supplier's margin, you have still got nearly a 50 percent saving over employing the equivalent American. If you then factor in the difference in educational achievement, which will probably be far higher in India, there is a compelling argument to consider outsourcing at least some of your business processes to India.

To quantify the savings, GE Financial Services and American Express claim to have saved over $450 million by taking BPO offshore in 2002 alone. The satisfaction rating for GE call centers in India was 92 percent. Its US-based call centers averaged 85 percent.

The Indian IT services industry

In order to create a world-class IT services industry, a development program was planned, focused at the beginning on education and training. The central planning that India used in the 1970s meant that this long-term plan was implemented with remarkable impetus.

It is still quite astonishing how progress can be made almost instantaneously in India if it is decided that it is now absolutely necessary, even when the existing situation is apparently a world-class muddle. There is no luck involved, as the process is repeated so often. Sometimes how it is achieved remains a mystery, but in this case there was a clear vision and determination.

India established, or developed, the Indian Institutes of Technology mentioned in Chapter 1, which turn out huge numbers of graduates and postgraduates. More than 2 million people graduate from higher education in any one year, and more than 250,000 of these will be IT graduates. That sort of figure leaves most people astounded, but the more impressive attribute is the extremely high standard of these individuals. As a group, they have world renown.

At state level, you will also find a commitment to excellence in information technology that is astonishing. Not all 28 states are equal in this respect, but the ones in the forefront are at least on a level with anywhere else in the world. The choices available are more than Bangalore, which is often regarded as the silicon valley of India, Mumbai, and Delhi, where the main centers of the IT industry have been. You should now be aware of Hyderabad, Calcutta, Pune, and Chennai, among other places. There will be competition between the various states and even the metros for any business that is put offshore in India, which is another reason to visit.

Having ensured the human resources to address the global IT market, the Indian government created a business-friendly environment for the IT services industry, in many ways different from the strangling bureaucracy that sometimes characterizes the rest of the country. If you have to import capital goods into India you will find it a challenge, even today, but there are special dispensations for the IT software industry. As part of the Union government's farsighted and successful information technology strategy, it established fiscal advantages for Indian companies to be in the offshore IT market. These include exemption from all company taxes. These taxes can run as high as 48 percent for a foreign-owned company in India, and so to have a tax regime where they are removed entirely created a powerful incentive.

Most Indian software companies will admit to 40 percent margins on offshore IT services work conducted in India, and somewhere near that for work carried out onshore in the West. The tax advantages of offshore as opposed to merely domestic work are therefore considerable.

If you factor in the fact that India's domestic market is so sharply price sensitive that analogies with razors can't hope to do justice to reality, there is even more reason for Indian companies to look for offshore revenues. That is why any Indian IT services company with more than two people on its books is hardly interested in the domestic market and has probably already approached your company several times marketing its capabilities.

These factors – a well-trained and educated work force, a friendly tax regime, and a home market where making even a miserable profit is difficult – combined with a growing worldwide demand for IT services that was correctly anticipated by the Indian government, have led to explosive growth in this industry in India. As a result, according to NASSCOM, 70 percent of US CIOs spent at least 15 percent of their budgets on outsourcing to India in 2002.

The Indian business process outsourcing industry

Once Indian business people started selling to the US and Europe, they became aware of other opportunities where a low-cost work force would be a major competitive advantage. As these Indians were naturally IT aware, they looked at the many areas where IT could be used to shrink the distance between the West and India and allow the transfer of services offshore.

India's Union Communications and IT Minister Arun Shourie gives some idea of the range of activities that are now involved: "A series of new disciplines is about to break out in India for which IT will be what arithmetic is to calculation. Biotechnology, nanotechnology, telemedicine, telesurgery, distance learning, products with embedded software, automated production processes, product design – and many more. Each of these will see a leap in the coming years in India, and in each of them IT will be a basic ingredient."[1]

BPO was an established business in the West by the mid-1990s, with some 30 years of history in the US. One of the first examples was the outsourcing of some of the Medicaid processing to EDS in 1966. In the UK, and to a lesser extent in mainland Europe, BPO was already a fact of life as well. The combination of an established business activity and a new focus on it by Indian entrepreneurs, who were acutely aware of the benefits of using IT to shrink distances, meant that there could be a major new industry: BPO offshore.

BPO offshore itself started properly with medical notes transcription and India was ideally placed to provide the service. After a day's heavy dictating of notes on consultations with patients in the US, an American medical practitioner, probably to avoid or limit litigation as much as anything, transfers the tape electronically to India for what will appear to be an overnight transcription service. During the night in the US and the day in India – with India between 9.5 and 13.5 hours ahead of the US – the tape is transcribed and sent back. First thing in the US morning, the notes of yesterday's consultations are available.

The rates for this service were well below comparable US rates even initially and they have reduced since then, as it has become commoditized and there is more competition in India. The result is that rates, even by Indian standards, are now pretty low, but it is still a high-value service, partly because it is so timely. Using a US transcription service, the delay before the notes were ready could previously be more than a day.

In-bound call centers were also established at about the same time. They started essentially with answers to the question "What?" and provided fairly basic information about products or services, such as how to return goods that were faulty.

Over the years call centers have migrated into more and more complex services. They became capable of providing the answer to "How?" and lately have become capable of taking callers throughout the world through particular application forms and giving advice. An even more recent development has been outbound call centers, where direct marketing and sales can take place, but so far these have usually been confined to querying responses already submitted.

A call center agent in India will cost you in total somewhere around $10 an hour. Just as significantly, they may have a world-recognized PhD, be actively involved in self-learning and self-improvement, and be willing, regardless of sex, to be called Chuck, Ellie-Mae, Tracey, or Jean-Paul, depending on your nationality. Impressive as this is, it is only part of the story.

The stories about how call centers work in India are legendary – and probably mostly apocryphal – but cultural matching does occur, particularly where Indians in India are said to keep up to date with events local to the market they are serving. On the other hand, I've not yet met anyone, either Indian or from the West, who has discussed the latest episode of a television soap or even talked about the weather in the client's own region.

It is true that Indian English speakers are trained to talk in less obviously Indian accents so that they have an acceptable, neutralized pronunciation for Wisconsin or Durham, and there are language trainers who claim to be able to get Indian English speakers to talk in various local accents.

It takes about six weeks to take an educated English-speaking Indian and train him or her to deal with callers in an appropriate accent. I have seen examples, and it is astonishing for a different reason than might be obvious. One aspect I noticed when watching an agent in a call center was that as it is the telephone voice that is important, the body language is unaffected and remains Indian. It is absolutely fascinating to listen to a rather refined English accent while watching hands moving and the head rolling in a typically Indian way.

The real emphasis on accent training is, in fact, on listening skills. All of us will have difficulty with various accents in our home country, and understanding what a caller is requesting is vital to providing appropriate customer service and precedes any requirement to speak back.

Languages, other than Indian languages and English, have not been a focus of Indian education, but there are the beginnings of German, French, and Spanish language capabilities in India. Portuguese – remember that Goa, a small enclave on the west coast, was a Portuguese colony – is also spoken by a small number of Indians.

Call centers are the fastest-growing market sector in India, even though manufacturing, pharmaceuticals, and primary energy sources are all growing astonishingly fast. At the same time, call centers are becoming commoditized as a service, and the rates that Indian companies can charge are under attack. The margins are still healthy enough, nevertheless.

ITES

One incentive for the growth in call centers and BPO offshore reveals another aspect of that Indian ability to find just the right solution to a particular problem when there is a trading advantage to be gained. Many of the original companies who got involved in BPO offshore were, as we have seen, connected initially with IT services.

This created a real dilemma for such companies. IT services exported from India were in a zero tax regime. Potentially BPO offshore would be treated as just another Indian industry and would have to pay tax. It was therefore far less attractive. Thus, when India started to move into offshore BPO, the Indians involved had to come up with a way of enjoying the tax advantages they already secured for IT services. The answer lay at hand. It was a four letter acronym, ITES. This handy little collection of tax-avoiding capital letters actually stands for IT Enabled Services.

The argument was succinct and persuasive. If these services were enabled by information technology, which they undoubtedly were, they had to be information technology services, and therefore qualified, as of right, to be tax free. This was neat and effective and has apparently been accepted in its totality.

In other countries, this type of logic might have created enormous opportunities for further exploitation of a reasonable loophole – it is probably doing so in India, but since the results are seen as beneficial to the country, no one appears too bothered.

There is an unexpected downside, however, for Indians addressing western businesses when they use the acronym ITES. The initial two letters, IT, have confused matters, and ITES is often mistakenly thought of as purely to do with IT.

So BPO offshore – or, to preserve the tax advantages, ITES offshore – is where the fastest-growing element of India Ltd. or India Inc. is going to be in the near future. Whereas you cannot now be an early adopter of IT services offshore in India, you can be a relatively early one for BPO offshore – and you can gain a significant competitive advantage.

Quality

Most western companies of any size have been involved with quality and quality initiatives for years. The Indian approach will simply amaze you, however. It is not superficial, not an add-on, not something that head office has imposed, not this week's CEO-inspired radical new approach, not number one in a series of key measures where there is never a number two. Quality to the Indians is all the things we used to say: it is inherent, it is the process, it is what we are about, it is a way of life.

The most significant measure for software development companies, and it does spread wider as those companies move into BPO, is the Software Engineering Institute's Capability Maturity Model, which gets reduced to SEI CMM, or even CMM.[2] There are five levels of maturity, with a maturity level being a well-defined attainment that points toward achieving a mature software development and support process. The five maturity levels provide the top-level structure of the CMM.

The first is *Process capability*, which focuses on achieving expected results every time. *Key process areas*, which group together related processes, are focused on gaining a solid process flow. Then there are *Goals*, related to effective implementation. *Common features* are identified as five further areas: Commitment to Perform, Ability to Perform, Activities Performed, Measurement and Analysis, and Verifying Implementation. These are concerned with ensuring that a process is effective, repeatable, and lasting. There are also *Key practices*, which describe the infrastructure and activities that contribute most to the effective implementation and institutionalization of the key process area.

As organizations establish and improve the processes by which they develop and maintain their software, they progress through levels of maturity. Each maturity level provides a foundation for continuous process improvement.

The highest level is SEI CMM Level 5. India claims to have had the first companies to achieve that level of maturity, and still has the highest percentage of such companies. In my view the differences are not marked between companies at Level 4 and Level 5. However, at gatherings of interested Indian companies such a view is rebutted firmly, and there is almost a religious element to the discussion. These companies tend to be zealots and evangelists for SEI CMM Levels, Level 5 especially.

The use of religious language to describe the attachment is deliberate, because it is the only adequate vocabulary to convey the intensity of the focus on quality in India. The commitment is passionate. This is, of course, a reflection of how Indian companies have judged what has impressed western companies in their presentations, and a virtuous circle has been created. Western companies like to see such quality certification and Indian companies have responded and made the subject their own. Western companies have responded to this enthusiasm and the Indian companies have redoubled their focus.

The second quality measure or approach – it is both, as the best quality instruments have to be – revolves around Six Sigma, the concept that originated with Motorola and its zero defects program over 15 years ago. Six Sigma emphasizes setting extremely high objectives, collecting data, and analyzing results to a fine degree as a way to reduce defects in products and services. The Greek letter *sigma* can be used to identify variation from a standard. Six Sigma proposes that if you measure how many defects or variations there are in a process, then you can figure out how to eliminate them and get as close to perfection as possible. In order for a company to achieve Six Sigma, it cannot produce more than 3.4 defects per million chances for a defect to occur. That is challenging.

There are two Six Sigma processes: Six Sigma DMAIC and Six Sigma DMADV. Six Sigma DMAIC is a process that defines, measures, analyzes, improves, and controls existing processes that fall below the Six Sigma specification. Six Sigma DMADV defines, measures, analyzes, designs, and verifies new processes or products that are trying to achieve Six Sigma quality.

Not surprisingly, the images and language used in Six Sigma discussions tend toward the martial arts, which can create a fanciful picture of opposing camps within a Six Sigma-focused organization squaring up to each other at the end of every day. All Six Sigma processes are executed by Six Sigma Green Belts or Six Sigma Black Belts, which are then overseen by a Six Sigma Master Black Belt. These terms were created by Motorola and clearly had a purpose.

Six Sigma proponents claim that its benefits include up to 50 percent process cost reduction, cycle time improvement, less waste of materials, a better understanding of customer requirements, increased customer satisfaction, and more reliable products and services. It is acknowledged that Six Sigma can be costly to implement and it can take several years before a company begins to see bottom-line results.

Indian companies have taken to Six Sigma, of course introduced by US companies like GE, as if it were part of their immediate life support system. The focus on variation and unexpected results is intense and amazing.

Don't judge Indian companies against their western equivalents when considering quality, nevertheless. It is easy, as we will see, for a western company to experience its first presentation by an Indian company on its approach to quality and simply be overwhelmed. Judge your Indian company against other Indian companies – the standards are higher. On its own this commitment to quality and quality measures is not a differentiator between Indian companies, however much it differentiates Indian companies from their western equivalents.

Other countries

Because of India's significant advantages in language, education, culture, and entrepreneurship, choosing another country for offshore work has to be a deliberate, fully conscious decision. By the time you have finished this book, you will be in no doubt that Indian business will be able to provide you with the services you need. If it can be done in a separate office locally, it can be done in India.

That doesn't mean to say that India is always the right choice or the only choice, although it is the obvious yardstick or benchmark. You will find places where the wage rates are lower. Some countries have a better infrastructure, such as roads and telecommunications and power supply. There are countries with universal primary education that is used. There are places where the cultural issues are less daunting. There are certainly other countries in the same state of development as India that have better domain skills in some commercial activities. Indians and Indian business people in particular can be quite complacent about the unique qualities India has in this market, and there are more aggressive countries that will offer you apparently much more. If any of these factors outweigh the advantages that India has, then the answer is obvious.

While India is not always the right choice, it is always a good place to start. The long list of other countries can then be properly assessed.

One country that everyone mentions and that must be considered is China. So much western manufacturing has gone to China and there is so much interest in this vast country as a home for offshore business processes that it is a clear competitor to India. Indeed, Indian companies are themselves investing in China as a low-cost alternative for IT development! NIIT, an Indian company specializing originally in training, announced in 2003 that it will be developing 150 training centers in China, probably as joint ventures.

Wage costs are generally lower than in India. The use of western languages, including English, is improving from a low base. There is enormous government support for foreign direct investment. The infrastructure will often put India at a disadvantage. On the other hand, China has an aging population, thanks to the one child policy. The cultural differences are in another league. The political structures are challenging.

You can probably appreciate that there is absolutely no single, clearly correct answer, as each country will have advantages and disadvantages. Whether you consider, among the many tens of candidate countries, Brazil, the Philippines, Hungary, Vietnam, Bulgaria, Mexico, Ireland, Canada, Latvia, Malaysia, South Africa, Korea, Russia, Indonesia, Mauritius, Botswana, Kazakhstan, Poland, or even Spain, part of the answer you come to will be impossible to support with objective logic.

More emotion can be generated by these choices than could possibly be justified in the cold light of a business day. By using India as your touchstone, you can at least guard against some of the excesses.

With this in mind, the next chapter will consider how to identify and choose between different Indian suppliers or partners.

4
Where to Start

Once you know what you want to take offshore, you need to work out how to do it. You could simply use an international outsourcing company established in your home market and allow that company to make all the decisions. While this will initially simplify matters, it may well prevent you from taking full advantage of the further opportunities that India offers in the longer term.

If your scale justifies taking more direct involvement in India, it is, of course, possible to manage the whole operation yourself, basing a team in India and employing Indian companies as subcontractors for individual elements of the development of your service center. As a variation, you could have the assistance of an Indian consultancy and a smaller team from your country.

Managing the activity yourself nearly always ends up being much the most expensive option, and will inevitably take more elapsed time. I can't recommend that way of offshoring for your first project, though many companies do. In making the decision about whether to adopt this method, analyze in detail why you are taking that step. More often than not it is because control seems to be at risk. Sometimes, and more validly, it is because your company has a culture of doing it this way, which is true, for example, of one of the world's largest retailers.

This chapter is written mainly from the stance that you will employ an Indian company at the very least to advise you on the various steps, but more probably to set up an operation for you that you will then take over and run, or that you will buy a service from an Indian company. This doesn't presuppose what the contract will look like. It may start off as a purely commercial transaction, be initiated as or evolve into a partnership, or even be a joint venture.

Some space will be devoted to pitfalls in assessing which companies to contract with, especially if the usual western perspectives are employed as part of the procurement cycle. To broaden that out, there are insights into how Indian services companies approach western businesses. This is a context worth bearing in mind. Both aspects of any such business relationship have evolved together, as Indian companies respond to western expectations and western companies have had their perspective altered by the way Indian companies present themselves.

You will almost certainly be relatively successful against your own expectations if you have a well-founded project going offshore, and that confuses matters. The real issue is taking a more objective view of your success, which requires more depth of analysis. The key is whether you are more successful, or at least as successful, as the people who make the most out of their commercial relationship with India.

Identifying suitable suppliers or partners

When you start trying to work out which companies to work with, don't employ the standard questions that a procurement department, well versed in US, UK, or European approaches, would use. A western approach will sometimes generate more heat than light. Such assessments generally rely on weighting answers, with, say, the company with the lowest cost receiving five points and the next two or three companies receiving four points. When cost savings are a given, this kind of scoring becomes less informative.

When thinking about which companies to select, it is obviously a good idea to take a rather more considered view than merely reacting to the unsolicited mailings that many Indian services companies direct at their targeted companies. In the UK even medium-sized software companies receive one or more unsolicited offers a week from Indian companies, major accountancy practices receive one a fortnight, and many commercial firms are also under siege.

Therefore, in addition to the usual considerations when choosing a supplier or partner, this chapter presents seven criteria that I have identified over the years as particularly important when dealing with Indian services companies. These criteria are interlinked. Each informs and counterbalances the others, and while they vary in importance, that interplay will help you judge more accurately whether your assessment of your potential suppliers is valid.

You may find that the criteria presented here have varying degrees of appropriateness for your own business. You alone can assess that, but they do

provide a reliable and objective way of assessing potential
move well beyond pure cost advantage and the criteria tha
expect you to apply.

Fact finding in India

There is absolutely no substitute for going to India at a very early stage if your
project is of any size or has the potential to become a significant element in
your business, even when you can get knowledgeable and experienced advice
in your home market.

Some companies believe they have moved work offshore successfully
without taking that step. It might have been a successful move in terms of
reducing costs, but it probably wasn't anywhere near as successful as it might
have been. You will gain a really clear series of insights into Indian business
and its methods by going to India. What you learn will stand you in good
stead and allow you to understand the risks and benefits much more
immediately.

At a formal level, you can get help setting up such a trip from consultants in
this field, NASSCOM, any of the Indian companies established in your domestic market, and the Indian High Commission or Embassy. Recently Indian
diplomatic staff have become far more responsive.

There are many reasons why going to India is important, which will become
clearer in this chapter. You might also enjoy the trip!

The tender process

Indian companies in the software or ITES markets really don't conform to
western tender response sheets. Such tenders are usually scored in terms of
compliance with some preconceived view of the required capability and the
market being addressed. In one particular evaluation, the two companies that
came out best were almost entirely unsuitable for what was required, even
though their answers scored best against the procurement criteria. What went
wrong was that the invitation to tender didn't use the right criteria when dealing with a shortlist of Indian companies.

The companies that scored so well could provide the service required. The procurement department was experienced and knowledgeable. The problem was that the tender document wasn't focused on the real issues. The areas that the tender process *didn't* consider were more important than the procurement people realized, and this limited the advantages the US company could gain from taking the work offshore. What was finally produced was an apparently objective assessment that didn't address the specifics of India and Indian companies and, more importantly, didn't comprehend the business advantages that Indian companies could produce above and beyond the more limited view the questions took.

These questions were quite logical: "How many staff do you have with experience of insurance administration?" or "How many staff are trained in using office automation tools?" And the answers supplied weren't suspect in the usual western sense. You will probably have had the experience of reading answers from domestic suppliers that have a hidden argument or subtext, which either says "It depends what you mean by…" or suggests "We've made an assumption that what we've got matches your requirements." You may even have responded to tender invitations with just the same words in your mind.

However, the questions bemused the Indians who had to try to answer them. They were written in a way that is simply not how the services industry works in India. As we have seen, it's a large industry, with a large number of people in it, scattered over the face of India, and with large concentrations in, for example, Bangalore, Chennai, Hyderabad, Mumbai, Delhi, and even Calcutta. On the other hand, it's a very small world.

In any meeting in India, you have only got to ask whether anyone in the room knows someone who has worked in a particular vertical industry call center or can talk with an East Coast accent, and there will be a reasonable choice of names. Ask whether those present know anyone who has got more than a smattering of knowledge of an obscure software package that's been out of fashion for years, and about half a dozen names will appear like magic. Very often, the names given by different people will overlap, and that is the clue you need.

The point is that if you need a certain kind of expertise, it doesn't matter that much which company you go to. The company you approach will locate a good practitioner and if necessary recruit him or her. I have seen this done many times and overnight a first-class professional has turned up for induction in the appropriate business requirements. In one extreme example, during the actual procurement process a particular individual was located, employed by the Indian services company, and became the lead presenter, precisely because the potential supplier hadn't previously had that particular expertise in house.

If an Indian services company had a large number of people hanging around just waiting for you to pop up with your arcane request, how efficient could it be? Yet this is the apparent expectation of some western companies. Existing resources may well be appropriate in the West, but in India they are definitely of lower importance.

One major advantage of offshoring to India is the extra flexibility it will give you, on top of the cost savings. It is easy to eliminate that advantage by using an inappropriate tender process. Going to India and seeing how companies operate for yourself will help you avoid that trap and the many others that defy western logic but are nonetheless true.

It may be that you will then decide to employ an adapted tender process. If you must, use it only to create your long list of potential suppliers.

The Indian company's presentation

Indian services companies use a standard format for presentations to potential western clients. The presentations may be superficially different, but their content is almost guaranteed. There is probably a special part of Indian IIT or business college courses that covers this.

Many elements of the presentation will be familiar and even common to those given by western companies, and as presentations go, there won't be much wrong with what it contains. The graphics will be excellent. The structure will be clear. In fact, it will be a professional and convincing experience on more than the first occasion. Slick, effective, and informative though these presentations may be, they all miss the same issues.

While the order of the slides is not sacrosanct, the presentation will probably start by majoring on references – which is no bad thing. It will next stress the extraordinary lengths the Indian company has gone to in order to achieve compliance with whatever quality measurements are in vogue this week – still no bad thing in itself. It will then give a view of the amazing premises the company is housed in – well worth stressing. It will focus on the uninterruptible power supplies that ensure continuity of work, which is important as power breakdowns can be frequent in some states. The fantastic communications capabilities in each company will be detailed, looking at satellite links, leased lines, and any other applicable technology. The presentation will talk about people's willingness to go the extra mile and their flexibility. It will include a picture of staff attrition rates that will reveal that virtually nobody has ever voluntarily left the company – an excellent recommendation, of course. With that one exception, all of the statements in the presentations will be verifiably true; the claims for low attrition rates are unbelievable in most cases, since the industry works at many levels in a way that requires attrition.

When you have seen one, you will have grasped the whole nature of these presentations. If you have seen one already, you will recognize the pattern.

Western business people generally react very favorably to such a presentation. More than that, the standard western newcomer's response is to be overwhelmed. The response can be so total that there will be immediate suggestions that this is the company you have to work with. The net result in a reasonably large company is that by the time you start looking for an Indian supplier or partner, you will find that nearly every manager who has any sort of responsibility at all, not necessarily in any relevant discipline, will have a pet Indian services company that he or she wants to add to procurement's list.

These presentations have been honed into their present form by years of presenting to westerners. Indians, inveterate traders, study very carefully which messages create impact. They then concentrate on these commercially and psychologically important statements. It is no wonder they are so effective.

However, there will be at least one massive gap. There will be virtually no differentiation from other Indian companies – except a slide saying that this particular company, unlike every other Indian company, has tremendous references, is committed to quality, has better office space and facilities, is very flexible, has installed uninterruptible power supplies and every communication device known to humanity, has virtually no voluntary attrition, and is remarkably cost-effective.

In short, there is no differentiation at all. When questioned, nevertheless, all Indian companies agree how important differentiation is, and most point to this particular slide in their standard presentation as proof of their understanding.

If you do look at more than one Indian company's presentation, you may be left to choose between companies that appear to have exactly the same qualities and capabilities. Your procurement department will get hold of the opportunity, and it will go the way of all such things and turn into a score sheet. And if the Indian companies have anything to do with it, and can take the minds of procurement off the number of under-used call center agents in the relevant companies who speak with a Southern accent, you will get an objective assessment of just what the presentation contains.

There are other issues with these presentations, particularly the type of response you will get to any questions you ask. In too many cases the answers will be designed to steer you back to the criteria that the Indian companies know are their immediate strengths. There will be little engagement with any serious issues you raise.

Therefore, differentiation between Indian companies is what the seven criteria that follow are focused on. You absolutely do need to be able to distinguish between companies, because while all may be able to deliver the service, not all will be able to work with you effectively.

Seven criteria for choosing a supplier

While dealing with Indian companies over time and in different contexts, I have gradually worked out the criteria that need to be satisfied and their hierarchy. It may seem that in stressing these criteria, issues like quality are being overlooked. Certainly you will need to address all such issues, but you need to move beyond them as well and look at some underlying concerns.

You may find that the scale of importance attached to these criteria doesn't match your needs. Although that is quite likely, remember that the seven criteria have been created out of direct experience over a number of years and they do offer a good starting point. They have also been tested in live projects and have been altered and their hierarchy amended to take account of what was learnt.

Management capability
The first criterion for selecting an Indian company as a potential supplier is focused on management capability. This is more than merely identifying a

good manager, though that is important. What is required is a company where there is an effective management structure, an effective management culture, and an effective management. This doesn't sound earth-shattering, yet it is rarer than you might expect.

Many, perhaps even most, Indians who have any management capability at all either set up their own companies, thereby depriving established companies of the right caliber of people, or they have already moved to the US or Europe. There are enough exceptions, but you will have to look quite deeply into companies to discover them. More importantly, however, the lack of suitable managers affects the management culture inside Indian businesses. Not only are effective middle managers a rare breed, it is even rarer for them to be accorded the right degree of respect.

Companies with an effective management culture are not only worth looking for but are the ones to deal with. If you don't have that management capability throughout the organization you are attempting to work with, no matter how many potential call center agents with particular attributes are on its books, you will be at least relatively unsuccessful.

To comprehend the real difference that management capability can give you and its overwhelming importance, all you have to do is discuss the subject with those who are looking to do business with you. You won't necessarily know whether the company you are dealing with possesses what you require, but you will soon learn if it doesn't.

To be fair to the people you question, this will usually be a surprising line of inquiry. Questions about management style, culture, or capability may well not have figured before in their discussions with potential clients. They don't fit in with what Indian management schools teach. Indian companies are often not that aware of what management, especially middle management, capability brings. This is, of course, the corollary of the Indian entrepreneurial culture that is always looking for opportunities rather than consolidation.

Management capability in this context includes elements of emotional intelligence – particularly the ability to understand the motivation of the people working for them. It encompasses the ability to understand the difference between a written specification and what is actually required, and, by extension, between objectives and assessing what has actually been achieved.

A further crucial middle management ability in the Indian hierarchical context is for a middle manager to hold his or her ground against a director and have the tenacity to insist on completing the work in the way actually required.

Incidentally, you might be appalled in India by the lack of respect shown by a minority of company directors to people working for them. The employees concerned are not usually their direct reports, but those, for example, who provide tea and coffee in the meetings. Watch carefully, as this will usually provide a good insight into how people higher up the hierarchy are treated behind closed doors.

You should apply the concepts of management that you have in your own company to the management culture in any Indian company with which you are considering working. This can be assessed quite reasonably even at senior levels, and certainly in the structure of the company. If the company is set up with due recognition of how project managers need to function, or, at another extreme, is set up as a partnership, you will be getting close to seeing a company with the important management characteristics.

Alignment with western business practice

Another way of assessing management capability in this context would be how aligned it is to western business practices, rather than simply being aware of them.

Real alignment is more than the ability to use western management speak. Indian management schools are well ahead of this game and their alumni are more than able to pepper their conversations with terms like key performance indicators, SMART approaches, unique selling points, and lean development.

Try to get an understanding of the way the internal budget round is conducted in your selected Indian companies and you will soon see whether they will be able to deal with you effectively, by understanding your issues from your perspective. This means, for example, whether the Indian company will be able to understand your decision-making processes and their sequence, and be capable of working with you on that basis.

Competitive threats

You do need to analyze what competitive threats may arise out of the relationship with any Indian company you are considering and how they will be dealt with.

Some people would place even more emphasis on this. The argument for putting it third is that you will need to be able to appreciate the Indian company's intentions before you can fully comprehend what sort of competitive issues will arise, and you won't understand those intentions until you have a better view of how the company in front of you actually functions.

Competitive issues will inevitably arise between two companies trying to partner or even trying to sell and buy services from each other. As always, the essential element is to understand these competitive threats and judge whether they, and the risks they pose, are acceptable.

Let's examine this from the perspective of a large western company. The hardest competitive threats, and the most insidious, lie in the simplest areas. If the western company contracts with an Indian company for services, whether it is development of software, maintenance of an application, or providing a complete business process outsourcing facility, a successful project will be a feather in the cap of the Indian company. It will quite properly use the project as a reference, and the western company may find that its own enterprise and competitive edge in establishing itself in the market are devalued.

It is not necessary for the Indian company to go to the western company's customers directly or for those customers to go directly to the Indian company. Both may well happen. The real threat, however, is that other potential customers for the service or products you have to offer in your domestic market will look at how you are providing the service and wonder why they should come to you at all.

There is no comprehensive solution, but this is a fact of business that needs to be addressed, not hidden or ignored or solved with a quick pen stroke. You cannot rely on a non-compete clause, though examples abound. One ludicrously established a capped financial penalty for any infringement of intellectual property. The sum of money was substantial: $5 million. In practice, that only made the cost of entry to the market quantifiable. While the market potential was less than the financial penalty, everything was hunky-dory. After that, it was a sea of sharks.

Some smart people advise you to avoid getting into a situation where this is possible. That is scarcely practical when business works so frequently through partnership or cooperation. You cannot altogether avoid it.

Nevertheless, there are palliatives where there isn't a straightforward solution. The key issue is the relationship between the two companies.

First, it will help if you create a contractual relationship that blurs the buyer and seller issues. Some form of partnership and longer-term commitment will help, as the balance of short-term advantage and longer-term results is a key driver. This emphasizes the importance of the first two criteria, management capability and alignment with western business practices.

Secondly, you can look at the structural elements in the relationship. To do this you have to understand whether the company you are looking to work with is likely to want to move into your market space. Even if the answer is that it may, that will not necessarily rule out working with it. It might give you reason for caution, however. It is also worth considering how the Indian company goes to market. If it is trying to get as many customers as possible and grow even faster than other Indian companies, you might feel there is more of an immediate danger. If the go-to-market model suggests it wants a small number of large accounts, there may be less of a competitive threat.

You need to consider competitive issues from all angles – not merely in the short term – and define a risk-mitigation process that will work over years.

For small and medium-sized western companies, the competitive issues are less important and certainly less clear. My advice is that you still need to be aware of them. Contracting with a large Indian company won't present as many issues for you, especially if pricing is the most important factor in the short term.

Whether you are a large or small company, you can probably look at the potential issues of exposing yourself to competition in a more positive way. It might be that a reciprocal arrangement, of the type I discuss in Chapter 15, could have real benefits to both sides. Such an arrangement probably won't occur to your Indian supplier and your suggestion may be met with surprise. Nevertheless, it can present a real opportunity – and you will also see how well your Indian opposite numbers think on their feet.

Size

The ideal size of company for you to work with will not be immediately obvious.

If the Indian company is large, many large western companies will be much happier, as such companies provide stability, a track record, established procedures, and a sales and marketing capability that you can understand. If you can understand it, however, so can your potential customers and your competitors.

That large Indian company, no matter how important you are to it in revenue and profit terms, will also have its own agenda and strategy. Over the longer term, a large Indian company may well pose a larger competitive threat to you.

If the company you choose is too small, however, it probably won't be a success either. Small is a relative term. It is the relationship to the size of your company that is important. This is where the significance of size moves beyond the competitive issues and is properly a criterion in its own right.

One large western company selected a comparatively small Indian supplier for services. The decision was based essentially on price, once the usual criteria of quality and ability to deliver were met. The Indian company, curiously as far as the large company's procurement department was concerned, had already worked out that the decision was completely focused on price, despite the protestations of the procurement team that it was a well-balanced assessment.

Six months on, the contract was in place and everything was fine. The Indian company's annual revenues had doubled in less than a year; still nothing to worry about, since Indian companies can work very successfully like that. The large western company decided that it had been so successful in beating up the small company over price, it could get more. With some $40 million of services underway or earmarked for the Indian company, how could a small organization stand up to Goliath?

Having been used as a punch bag and had its owners treated with apparent respect at meetings but obvious and total contempt behind their backs, the Indian company was waiting for the right moment. Because it regarded what the western company was doing as bullying, it planned to apply a ratchet to the pricing just at the moment when the large company could ill afford any break in the continuity of supply. Being an Indian company, it was also prepared to walk away or lose the business.

The smaller company had initially worked on the basis that once the western company realized the substantial gains to be made by working in partnership, there was the foundation for a long-term relationship. This was naïve in this case, but well-meaning and a good indicator of the qualities of this specific Indian company, which I rate highly. The bigger loser was the large western company.

Of course this is bad business practice, but the mismatch in size actually encouraged it. The large western company was not staffed by rogues and adhered to an ethical code. It merely took advantage of what seemed like an opportunity. Though it was the result of arrogance, senior management didn't even think of it like that. I have seen large companies try to take advantage of small companies too often for it to be a one-off and it is likely that no safe-guards will actually work.

The key is for western companies to work with companies that are neither too large nor too small and to remember that there is a huge premium on achieving a win–win solution. The right size of company as a supplier, partner, or joint venture partner, in order to reduce any competitive threat and gain real added value together, is one that you find a challenge to negotiate with. As soon as there is a sticking point or disagreement, you can judge if the company is large enough to deal with you. You don't want obduracy, but nor do you want servile agreement.

Smaller western companies face fewer pitfalls than larger ones in working with certain sizes of Indian companies. The main issue, which you will proba-bly not need too much reminding about, is how much attention your modestly sized project is going to receive. If you represent a very small project to a large company the answer is obvious, especially if there is little potential for growth in the size of project or the relationship. You may feel commercially more com-fortable working with a larger company, but don't rule out the many excellent small companies who may want to grow with you rather than just from you.

Size may have one further significance. An enormous number of Indian companies have entered the offshoring market, and more do every day. There will inevitably be a shakeout in the industry by mergers and takeovers. If the experience in the IT outsourcing industry is any guide, this will have little effect on western client companies. Nevertheless, do be aware of the potential for this to happen and consider whether the size of your supplier or partner is likely to make a difference.

Understanding each other's strategic objectives

The fifth criterion is some sense that both sides understand each other's strate-gic objectives, beyond the immediate contract or issues. This is the same as you would expect when dealing with a western company for any contractual agree-ment, partnership, or even joint venture, but it is a particular requirement when dealing with India and Indian companies. Even if the agreement is one that accepts the two companies will go in different directions at the conclusion of the work, there needs to be a firm understanding of the strategic aims.

The business environment in India is changing so fast that you will need to know where the focus in your chosen Indian company is going to be over the short and medium term. While the factors influencing the changes include deregulation and liberalization, the most important issue is the one you will be contributing to. Business process outsourcing is growing so fast, it is distorting the plans that Indian companies are making. Because Indian companies are remarkably fleet of foot and agile, they will be able to change direction in the time and space it takes a large western corporation to appreciate that it needs to change direction. You will have to have a firm grasp of the Indian company's strategic thinking about its future directions.

If you don't have that reassurance, there will always be a concern in your mind that the Indian company is going to change direction without giving you too much warning. If that comes as a surprise to you, there is every possibility of at least a misunderstanding and a loss of confidence in each other, which would be disastrous.

Shared objectives

The ability to share objectives is lower down this list, but its position depends on what sort of relationship you want with India and Indian companies. You may want it higher in the list of criteria. It is also related to many of the other elements in the relationship.

Having shared objectives requires a commercial relationship that is difficult enough between two western companies. Across two different cultures, the most extreme example, a joint venture, is extraordinarily difficult to create and develop successfully. It may well be that despite all these difficulties it will prove to be the most successful model over time for offshoring. There is an attractive quality in marrying together Indian trading capabilities based on attention to detail and delivery with western lateral thinking, buttressed by the margins and the helpful fiscal regime.

This is not to underestimate the huge difficulties and it may be that a better solution is to take a percentage investment in an Indian company. GE has certainly started to consider that and is already taking stock in companies that are heavily involved in India. If you have 26 percent of the shares in an Indian company, you have an effective veto. That may be all you need.

Indian companies still enjoy what Indian owners would call a healthy valuation, despite such factors as the end of the dot-com boom, the conflicts in

Afghanistan and Iraq, and protectionism. Nevertheless, Indian share prices are not formed in a vacuum and there will be swings in company valuations. Achieving a fair evaluation of the worth of an Indian services company is not going to be easy and several deals have fallen through at quite a late stage.

Other issues may affect pricing in the short and long term. For example, the US is starting to consider various protectionist measures, including not wanting government work taken offshore. There is some alarm in the UK over services increasingly moving offshore, and even more alarm in continental Europe. It is worth bearing these points in mind, especially when attempting to put a value on an Indian services company. (There is more discussion of these issues in Chapter 16.)

A better way of attaining shared objectives in a joint venture might be to start a new company between you from scratch. At least both sides then have similar problems. You may want to consider this approach seriously, as the margins on offshore work are still healthy. On the other hand, as with all joint ventures, you need to consider the management costs that will be involved.

Intention

My final criterion is closely linked to shared objectives and it revolves around intention. You cannot, of course, judge other people's intentions with any degree of reliability. There is a way of dealing with the issue, however. If you can see that your potential Indian supplier or partner is trying hard to understand *your* intentions, that is generally a good sign.

You can judge that by the usual standards. If the answer to everything is that it is no problem, if you are told things that are not relevant in response to questions you have asked, and if you can see the other person's agenda far more clearly than your own, you are probably doomed to failure. I have seen all of these behaviors when dealing with all sorts of companies, not just in India. On the other hand, the reluctance to say no to any request, an integral part of Indian culture, does mean that the first response – that nothing is a problem – is far more prevalent. It is quite proper to distrust anyone who cannot, or claims not to be able to, see where any problems might be lurking.

This may appear very one-sided, putting all the onus on the Indian company. You need to remember that the Indian company is marketing and selling to you in most of these situations and it is entirely appropriate to expect the focus to be on your needs. If you detect any lack of focus on you, it is likely that the intention is not quite what you want. The normal rules of sales and marketing engagements are not suspended in this context.

Whether the Indian company you are dealing with is trying to understand your intention is not my most important criterion – but it is a very good test of whether what you have decided so far is likely to be successful.

Summary

The seven criteria that will help you assess the suitability of an Indian supplier are therefore:

- ❑ Management capability
- ❑ Alignment with western business practice
- ❑ Competitive threats
- ❑ Size
- ❑ Understanding of each other's strategic objectives
- ❑ Shared objectives
- ❑ Intention

The qualities that Indian companies will present to you, including quality, cost advantages, and flexibility, are still vital, but you need to be able to differentiate between the Indian companies in terms that reflect your business needs.

Language and communication

Underlying many of the seven criteria is a major issue: the use of language. In order to grasp what lies at the heart of these criteria, especially the issues of management capability and business alignment, it is necessary to have a common conceptual basis with Indian business people. At root, this is some form of western understanding.

Put this way it seems arrogant, because it apparently places all the hard work on Indian business people again. Yet because of the global spread of western business models and methods, the greater exposure of Indians to western business than the other way round, and the influence of western media, there is more chance for Indians to get inside western minds than the reverse.

My essential test of whether what has been agreed in a meeting is commonly understood is to get the other person to tell me in their own words what they think was the result. That isn't foolproof even in the West.

On one particular occasion, this apparently worked very well. What the man said back to me accorded very closely with what I had said. Everything appeared fine.

Yet I was aware of a nagging doubt as I left the meeting and adopted my usual position in the back of the car, threading through the Mumbai traffic. Thirty minutes later I realized what was worrying me. The Indian businessman had given his understanding of the position in my words. He had felt that using what I had said in the way I had said it would be both polite and far more reassuring.

It was just the opposite. Unless he could tell me what we were agreeing in his own words, then we had no chance of knowing what our position was or whether we had agreed anything.

As it was India, I was able to phone him and go back and see him later the same day. I found that we were pretty close, but did not actually have the same view of what was deliverable.

This is common sense, based on emotional intelligence, and quite straight-forward, but you cannot ever merely assume that communication is working across cultures.

International Indian companies

Whatever criteria you have used to decide on your supplier or partner, there are a number of other considerations. The most important concerns how *Indian* the company you are dealing with is.

A significant number of Indian companies have developed, or have become, US or sometimes UK companies. Many have UK, US, or European subsidiaries. You might think this makes them easier to deal with, especially if they have an American, British, or, say, German, team at the head. Having a western presence in your country may help but it isn't the complete answer, even though there are excellent westerners managing Indian companies in the West.

Indian companies that are international are in fact mostly just that. They are very obviously Indian companies, with Indian perspectives, working in an international arena. A frighteningly small minority of them, from the largest to the smallest, are international companies that happen to have Indian roots. That may sound a clever play on words, but it is important. It is significant not only in terms of how successful a relationship you can have, but in understanding the cultural, psychological, and business imperatives.

What is significant is not the fact that the company has gone international and yet is still Indian or exhibits peculiarly Indian quirks. US companies that are international do remain distinctively American. International British companies may not serve tea on a silver salver at 4pm wherever they are in the world, but they do retain a different approach from other nations' companies.

These distinctive national qualities become heightened at times of stress. As the Americans recoil from being part of a world that seems hostile, they interpret the world more and more as being a subset of Anaheim. As the Brits find that there isn't a soul in these far-flung parts who went to their school, they become even more convinced that Berkshire is the essence of normalcy.

Even in the most command-and-control American company, however, there is always a residual commitment to thinking global and acting local. The same is true for European and British companies, which do have an international perspective although they remain ultra-typical representatives of their original country.

Indian companies that have gone international still revert to type much more quickly even when they have absorbed the maxim of thinking global and acting local. The reasons include the fact that if you move from a high-wage and high-cost environment like the West to a much lower-cost one, the stresses are all focused in the easiest direction. Moving from a lower-cost economy to a higher-cost one is much more daunting. Even Indian entrepreneurs who have the greatest insight into cost structures outside India often cannot cope with salaries that seem normal in the West.

Secondly, Indian companies are only now moving successfully up the services value chain. This isn't generally understood in the West. More than one western company has entered the offshore BPO market thinking that we still live in a world where India provides "techno-coolies." Even in 2003, a senior vice-president could say openly that all the design, architecture, and domain expertise would remain in the US. Some high-tech sweatshop over there – an arm waved vaguely toward the outside world – would do the grunt work.

We have moved on from that, of course, as he discovered in quite a rude awakening. Yet we haven't got to the point where the management consultancy expertise that initiates – or at least used to initiate – major projects can be provided by an Indian offshore company in a way that western companies will accept easily. Indian companies are apparently desperately trying to move into that space. It is, at this moment, only an intellectual move.

As a result, what you will see if you are dealing with an Indian company in the West will at best be a veneer on top of the real entity and you will not be able to judge the criteria that I have suggested are important. I know several Indian companies with offices in the West managed by westerners who endorse my view quite willingly.

You have to remember that Indian companies, no matter how international they appear, are still Indian companies, and you have to judge them in India.

Outside of India, you need to be aware that even though the chief executive is a Person of Indian Origin (PIO) and possibly the third richest man in the world, or even a Non-Resident Indian (NRI), a major part of the reference framework will still be Bangalore or Delhi. This may not be obvious in the West. In the Indian locations of most Indian companies, you can be sure that this focus and set of assumptions will be much more pronounced – and as you need to be able to judge that accurately, India is the place to do it if your project has any size that justifies going there.

Make any decisions either in India or after you have been there – which is where we turn in Part II.

Part II

Welcome to India

You have to experience India and Indian business at first hand to be able to make your decisions about offshoring with confidence. By going to India you will appreciate the scale of what you need to do. More than anything else, I want to persuade you to go to India because it is the fastest way of coming to terms with what is happening in the services revolution.

India is exotic and different for westerners in a kaleidoscope of sensations. It is also often daunting. It is a challenge, culturally and in business terms. India has a heritage of learning and academic success, particularly in mathematics where some fundamental discoveries, such as the use of the number zero, are attributed to Indians. The country is full of pragmatic people, who have built an economy out of trading and deal making. India is, in short, a country of contrasts and paradoxes, with the latest electronics existing in immediate contact with bullock carts.

None of these, of course, make it essential for you to go there for business.

But stand in New Delhi and try to take in the surreal quality of government buildings designed by British architect Sir Edward Lutyens as a classical monument to the permanence of the British Empire, and you will feel the timeless quality of India.

Drive along the road in Mumbai, your eyes battered by hand-painted bill boards advertising internet connectivity, cellphones, and the latest electronic gadgets, and you will be even more bewildered by the cows wandering in the road, the bicycle rickshaws, and food sellers doling out unfamiliar liquids into plastic cups.

Observe the hand-swept roads in Hyderabad leading to new construction after new construction, the greenness of Bangalore and its energized, frantic activity, the new high-tech parks in Chennai, the dynamic towns round Delhi such as Noida, the offices like palaces, resplendent with marble in Bandra Kurla, Mumbai – and you will see the intensity of a country that is not only grasping the future, but creating it in front of you.

When you meet Indian business face to face in India, so different from its adopted western face in the US and Europe, you will be bowled over. It won't be easy to take in and understand, but you will either be part of that future or part of the past.

There is one further, related reason why you have to go to India – and this will be the least comfortable but by far the most important. Only by going to

India will you remove the security blanket that so many western business people are still grasping about the future that India holds.

This security blanket of established ideas can be heard in the suggestion that just saving $30,000 per year is not worth the extra risks. Business managers object that you have to consider all the extra checking that will go on – because, in their opinion, you can't simply transfer business processes offshore and not check everything rigorously when it comes back. At another level, you will hear people say that as they are a tightly knit team, it would be impossible to put such a business process offshore.

It is worth recognizing that there is often more than a grain of truth in each of these statements. Intelligent people would not say them otherwise. Yet you will find that these threads in the security blanket are just that: apparent common sense masquerading as facts that might make you feel better and more comfortable.

Then, when all else fails, there is one final thread left in the security blanket. Somewhere in the western collective consciousness, there is a comfortable feeling that India and Indian business are really at the low end of the value chain. When it comes to the high-end processes, well, of course, they simply can't go offshore to India.

By going to India you will see how much truth there is in these statements, and you will also be faced with the glaring contradictions that mean whatever value such nostrums may have is being eroded every day.

BEFORE YOU GO

Before you go to India you will need to obtain a visa, the application form for which can be downloaded from your local Indian Embassy or High Commission website. It takes a few days to process, but a visa can be obtained inside 24 hours if necessary. You will need an invitation letter from an Indian company and a letter from your own confirming that should you become destitute in India the company will get you home.

You will also need medical advice some time before you leave. Malaria, hepatitis, typhoid, polio, and tetanus all need to be dealt with. Most Indians will be astonished that you bother taking anti-malarial tablets, even though you will meet Indians who have suffered from malaria in the last year or so.

Their astonishment will be as nothing compared to yours when you read the list of side-effects, which can include hair loss, insomnia, stomatitis, tiredness, weakness, giddiness, anemia, nausea, and diarrhea, although I find it hard to understand how in India the last two can be definitively related to the tablets.

5
Your Arrival

Most international flights land in India at around midnight local time. Although that will be about 1.30pm EST and 6.30pm GMT, it will seem very late at night even to your body clock. It will be hot and dark and assault your nostrils, and that's just taking the air bridge from the plane.

It feels as though the whole of India arrives every night at the country's international airports, an impression reinforced by the darkness, the heat, the absolute mass of humanity, and the pools of light that create a world of their own. In fact it is only about five jumbo jets' worth of people, but since the planes are invariably full and they all land within two hours, and about the same number of people are leaving India at the same time, the crush and the sense of urgent purposelessness are overwhelming.

During the many other hours of their existence the international airports are relatively deserted and perfectly able to cope. Some sort of bureaucratic averaging seems to have determined the facilities that are required at any time; unfortunately, around midnight is not just any time.

The air will be alive with an urgency that you won't experience again until you return to the airport to fly out. As you stroll into the corridors on your first visit, you will be amazed at the speed with which everyone else is charging through the terminal.

Immigration

On your way to Immigration, you will be watched with a kind of weary fascination by an absolute army of people who are there for some other purpose. That's your first insight into India: I've still no idea what that other purpose is.

Follow the hurrying crowd – you'll be hard pressed to find any definitive signs pointing you the right way to go, so you'll have to – and you'll eventually get to what seems like a subterranean cavern in Mumbai or quite a pleasant, high-ceilinged hall in Delhi: Immigration. I was once part of a mass of people leaving an airplane who were led the wrong way by one baffled soul, probably on his first visit. I followed blindly. Getting out of that mess was extraordinary.

When you arrive at Immigration, you'll understand why everyone else was rushing: the queue or, more properly, queues.

Over the last few years the immigration facilities in Mumbai have improved, and nowadays there's a sort of Disneyland arrangement of ropes and paths. When the officials forget to set them up properly – and I've seen the odd cul-de-sac – the queues can stretch back almost to the planes. Delhi, in contrast, still has one of those guessing games where you try to judge which queue is going to take the least time.

The Immigration queues in both places used to be easy places to pick out the Brits. They were the lost creatures at the back, while the queue grew from the middle – well, actually the front.

After wrestling with the main queues in Mumbai – in theory one for Indians, one for foreigners – you will be directed to form a queue for an individual immigration officer. Invariably you will find yourself rather forcibly sent to join the longest queue.

You will, I swear, end up in front of an immigration officer's desk. Eventually. You hand over your passport, your entry form, and your customs form. At this point you will usually find you have forgotten to sign the form twice.

The official will look at you many times before stamping the various pieces of paper, some of them twice, handing back your passport, and rolling his or her eyes at you. This isn't an invitation, except to go to the next queue. You will then queue to have your luggage x-rayed on its way into the country and then queue to go through customs. You may not notice you've actually been through customs; it was two or three trips before I did. As you pass out of the airside part of the airport, someone will take off you the small piece of paper that was at the bottom of the immigration form. I think that's the form for customs.

You will then queue to leave the terminal.

Trying to get to the front of those queues is what all that leaping off the plane and rushing is for. I've timed it – it makes a huge difference. Treat opening the plane doors as getting onto the starting blocks. Rush!

CURRENCY EXCHANGE

If this is your first visit, you will need to obtain a small amount of rupees. The Indian rupee is not a properly convertible currency and it is usually not possible to get rupees before you arrive. Nevertheless, you will need some immediately for a tip after the trip to your hotel. There will be exchange facilities on the landside of your airport, and I suggest you change $20 or £20 and ask for 50 and 100 rupee notes.

A rupee is worth about two European or American cents or about 1.25p in UK terms. It's now divided into 100 paise, although it used to be 16 annas.

I've found that carrying foreign bank notes for exchange is best, especially as the amount of cash you will need is limited. There appears to be no penalty for small purchases of rupees. Exchange rates will be OK at the airport, although not the best.

Depending on your hotel chain, you may find you can get a really good rate at the cashier desk. Certainly at Sheraton hotels the rate is at least as good as the best bank rates, but the Marriott exchange rate is just the opposite. In between there are all sorts of varying rates.

LAKHS AND CRORES

Here I need to introduce the two number words that will enrich your life if you try to negotiate anything in India: lakhs and crores. Both are part of the old Indian numbering system, which is focused on hundreds rather than thousands; apart, naturally enough, after the first thousand. These words are in common, everyday use and are just as natural to Indians as our millions. You will need to understand them if you want to make large transactions in India.

A lakh, pronounced almost as "lack," is one hundred thousand. One lakh rupees, depending on currency variations, is about $2,000 – and is certainly that when the exchange rate is INR50 to the US dollar. That is about £1,200. A lakh is written in numbers like this: 1,00,000.

A crore, pronounced "craw," is a hundred lakhs, or ten million. A crore rupees, at INR50 to the dollar, is therefore $200,000 or about £120,000. A crore is written thus: 1,00,00,000.

So far it looks deceptively easy to work out what any number of crores and lakhs represent as a dollar amount. I can only tell you that in the heat of negotiation sorting out what 50 crore, 20 lakhs – that is, INR50,20,00,000 – means in US dollars has made grown people weep. The main number is generally straightforward: it is obtained by multiplying the crores and lakhs by two. Establishing the right number of zeros can while away a whole afternoon unless you write it down.

There is a real benefit, however: you know instantly which currency you are talking about. If it's lakhs and crores, you're in rupees. If you're talking thousands and millions, you're in a western currency, usually the dollar. This does rule out a great deal of potential confusion while, of course, creating its own as well.

FROM AIRPORT TO HOTEL

Back to the terminal, where if you only have one suitcase you will be in a tiny minority. The amount of luggage associated with any individual must multiply during the journey. And most of it is usually being handled by an indomitable old lady, no more than about five feet tall. She will be perfectly capable of getting her equivalent of a camel train out into the open, but she won't necessarily go in a straight line. It will be a formidable test to see whether you can get by her!

Before you leave your home country, arrange for a car and driver from the hotel to pick you up. The driver will find you in the middle of the next seething crush of people, those outside the terminal. His detective work will usually be accomplished despite the impressive board he holds up, which will have the name of the hotel and an anagram of your name. Once you have exchanged pleasantries over the fence, your driver will disappear completely. Keep walking. As you turn into the main crush of people, someone in white will nip up and rush off with your suitcase.

Armed with your rupees, follow him. He will move at a cracking pace, designed to remove any lingering fear of deep vein thrombosis from your long-haul flight, across paths and roads that seem to have been made up at some time, and you will find the car.

On your first trip, especially in Mumbai, get in the car and close your eyes. This is nothing to do with any need to avoid seeing beggars, shanty towns, bizarre acts of human life being conducted in public, wandering cows or goats (sheep are tethered because they wander too far, an interesting concept when you consider where the cows and goats are), and a whole city alive and vibrant at one o'clock in the morning. Nor should you keep your eyes shut just because you may be unused to people driving on the left – or, in fact, on both sides of the road at once.

The object of closing your eyes is first of all to avoid seeing how your driver extricates the car from the car park. And then to avoid seeing how he negotiates his way through the traffic.

This is not because the driver will be a poor driver. It is my contention that Indian drivers in Mumbai, who differ markedly in style from those in Delhi, are the best in the world. The traffic in Mumbai is about half the speed of the traffic in Delhi. Driving in Delhi is a sort of urban-wide chicken run. In Mumbai it is a game of poker.

Just watch, if you dare, what happens in Delhi at what the Indians call a circle and Brits call a roundabout. In the UK, priority lies with the person on the roundabout. In Delhi, the concept of priority is not one that makes sense.

So if you do bravely keep your eyes open, you will find yourself saying several times a minute, in a voice pitched at an astonishingly high frequency, "There isn't room, we're going to cra..." followed by "Oh, I see, there was room."

You will soon realize why external rear-view mirrors are always folded flat – doing so could give you the vital extra few millimeters. There is also a prevalent bewilderment in India at the concept that anyone needs to know what is behind them.

I was once astonished to hear my companion call out to the driver in English, having shouted something at him in Hindi: "Use the mirror!" I turned to him with real surprise and congratulated him on adopting western approaches to what was behind us. He couldn't work out what I was on about. "I don't understand you," he replied, somewhat shamefaced. "I meant that the driver should use the mirror to give that pedestrian [who had been holding us up] a knock as we went by."

My companion was also the person who told me that jumping a red light in Delhi could always be explained away as a marginal case, on the basis that he had thought it was green.

You will see on the back of most vans, buses, trucks, and lorries of all sizes: "Horn, please." After a few hours in India you will wonder why on earth anyone needs such an invitation, since the horn is what you press with your right hand continuously. As a result, no one takes the slightest notice of it.

Before you leave the car park you will experience a series of sharp movements forward and back until the car is catapulted onto the highway out of the airport. It's probably advisable to continue to keep your eyes closed, but you won't be able to resist looking, especially when you suddenly stop for the first time.

Traffic lights are one of the wonders of India. Some of the lights are controlled in a sophisticated and challenging way, in that at certain points in the night – and possibly in the day – they change to flashing amber, meaning that anyone can cross them, as long as they take care. (I added that as a sop to road safety experts, I didn't really mean it.) Since in Mumbai at least this seems to be what happens anyway, even if the lights are solemnly changing with relentless precision, you may wonder what the point is.

I did ask an Indian colleague what those pretty red, amber, and green lights at road junctions were for. He replied: "Not entirely sure. I think the Brits left them behind and we've never had the heart to take them down. They don't interfere at all and perhaps they add to the color of the place."

Even in the early hours of the morning the traffic will be quite heavy. This means that the roads will be full, at least to western eyes; that is, two lanes of traffic in each direction on a two-lane road. In India, this is tantamount to being empty. Here, a road with two lanes each side can cater for nearly eight lanes of traffic. The middle lanes are usually full of cars trying to travel in both directions, which normally form a completely stationary line of tussling traffic.

In addition to the four-wheeled traffic there are the three-wheelers – motorized rickshaws, commonly known as cockroaches in Mumbai – bikes, motorbikes, tractors, bullock carts, and the occasional elephant.

Elephants have right of way. There is nothing about this in the highway code apparently, but at crucial moments it seems an obvious fact of life, even if they are in the middle of the wrong side of the road coming toward you. In Delhi you may even catch sight of troupes of monkeys living and playing by the side of the road.

The best illustration of why you may sometimes want to open your eyes comes from a rare experience. On my only day off, I went to Agra to see the Taj Mahal.

I had stayed overnight in the Sheraton, in a Taj View Suite, previously occupied by "Lady Hilary Clinton." In the true UK boarding-house tradition of rooms with a sea view, if you stood on one of the many tables and peered round the curtain at risk of life and limb, there was indeed a minuscule white image of a cupola that might have been the Taj.

At 6 o'clock in the morning, standing in front of the Taj as the sun came up, watching the changing colors on the marble, I was blown away. It is beyond words. Whatever else you do, go to Agra.

On the road journey from Delhi – not recommended, take the train – the driver had been remarkably adept at keeping me on the edge of my seat, even though I was a seasoned Indian hand. The moment that stays in my mind, and when I reached top C above the highest C on a piano, was overtaking a tractor that was overtaking a bullock cart, on a long left-hand bend, on a dual carriageway. We were naturally and properly in the outside lane. Coming toward us, however, was a very large truck, on our side of the dual carriage-way, in our lane. I can remember my exact words, which lacked in variety what they made up for in urgency: "Brake. Brake! Brake!! Brake!!!"

Nevertheless, the correct procedure in these circumstances is to acceler-ate. I am here to tell the tale: there was room, apparently. You can now fur-ther understand the importance of folding back those external mirrors.

Anyway, we reached a railroad crossing, the gates of which had come down too fast for even our driver to nip across just in front of the train. As the road could accommodate about two lanes of western traffic each side, our side of the crossing filled up with four or so lanes of cars and a few lanes of other vehicles, plus the all-important cows. What happened then was why I suggest opening your eyes.

The inviting open space represented by the two lanes coming the other way was too much for Indian drivers to bear. Within two minutes, this too had filled up with four or five lanes of traffic. (More cows also arrived, but you'd expect that.)

The intriguing issue was that, of course, the whole process was repeated on the other side of the crossing. We now had more than eight lanes of traffic, plus cows, at all sorts of angles, facing each other, waiting for the gates to rise.

In the UK or the US, there would have been carnage. Road rage would have engulfed 200 yards of stationary traffic. It being India, the traffic carried on forward, sliding through impossible gaps, lurching to a halt at uncomprehending cows, and generally resolving itself and getting on its way within minutes. The whole range of issues was resolved with no anger – anger seems to depend on people doing something unexpected to you, and in India you expect every inch of road space to be occupied. Where was the problem?

Meanwhile, back on your journey from the airport, your driver will offer you water and ask you whether this is your first time in India. This happens no matter how many times you have the same driver.

TIPPING – AND BEGGING

When you arrive at the hotel, you need to decide how much of a tip to give the driver, depending on the distance you have traveled. I'd probably give INR100. (Actually I always give INR100, but I like to think there is some sort of rational process behind what I do.)

You can merely leave the car and your luggage, walk into the hotel, and register. Miraculously, the luggage will find you in your room. I always tip the person bringing the luggage another INR100. I think this is probably over the odds, but, unlike some countries, no fun is made of you for over-tipping. Tips in five-star hotels are shared out among all the staff anyway.

This one minor issue of tipping is always a cause for concern. I've seen even grizzled business travelers reduced to quivering wrecks by the questions you need to consider, even though they're simple enough: Do you? Whom do you? When do you? How much?

In India, the answers are also relatively simple in the most broad and general terms: Yes. Anyone. As often as you like. Whatever you think.

At that point you might need a little more insight, but that was the advice my Indian colleague gave me on my first trip. I was then faced on my journey into the office with a taxi bill that looked suspiciously like INR13. (It wasn't, but I was going by the taxi meter and didn't know any better.) That's about 25 US or European cents, or 15p in the UK. Doing a quick European calculation, I worked out that was INR14.5 including tip, and brandished a 50 rupee note. Thankfully, even I realized that $1 for the fare was probably nothing to worry about and managed to brush aside the genuine difficulty the taxi driver had with finding change.

If we address a few economic facts, you will understand the scale that needs to apply. A driver working for you full-time in Mumbai or Delhi will cost you about $100 a month for about ten hours a day, six days a week, before overtime. Even with the cost of a car, this will be considerably less than hiring a taxi for the month, but if you work for an American corporation you will probably find that no one below the rank of senior executive vice-president is entitled to a driver. The wages will therefore probably be recorded locally as stationery. (I love the pun.) This may seem an excessive amount for envelopes every month, but you have to translate the expenses into something head office understands.

An excellent programmer/analyst will cost you something like $500 per month or $6,000 a year. A night in a five-star hotel will cost you up to $200, including a range of taxes that rival ancient Egypt for ingenuity. An excellent dinner will cost as much as $30 a head in the same hotel, but only if you go mad on the drinks.

A tip, therefore, is not going to be merely the European 10 percent or the American 20 percent calculation. I work in multiples of US dollars, or INR50 at a time. I'm not saying I'm particularly generous or stingy, but it seems to be about the acceptable level. The guiding number is around $2, or INR100.

Indians will tip a good deal less, but that isn't important. Your Indian colleagues will also perhaps regard you as crazy, but the faux pas isn't that great. And you do have the excuse that you are a foreigner.

That isn't the end of the story, however. I don't tip the doorman every time I leave the hotel. I do a rough calculation, and usually hand over INR300 at the end of the week. Most of my colleagues seem to give more than that, but it is very difficult to get real figures from anyone. If it costs between $20 and $30 a week in tips all told, I think it's about right.

If tipping seems more straightforward than it might be, the really diffi-cult issue in India is begging. I have steadfastly taken the advice of the Save the Children Fund and other charities, though I haven't tested it. Their advice is not to give handouts to beggars. If your conscience is pricked – and it will be – make a regular donation to a registered charity of your choice. This might be self-serving of the charities, and it is very hard advice when faced with what you will see every day – I defy parents to look at the tiniest of children at road junctions going slowly between the cars and not to think how they would feel if they were their children – but it's the only way to stay sane.

I guess I also salve my conscience with, or hide behind, the fact that I have promoted the concept of corporate social responsibility, so the company I worked for had to see itself as part of the development of India. We developed a sustainable, demand-led initiative that could achieve some good. Like trickle-down economics, which seems to me to be a justification for trickle-up economics nine times out of ten, I cannot say that corporate social responsi-bility necessarily has any validity. However, I believe that at the very least it is better than nothing, and it might make a difference. (There is more on this in Chapter 16.)

HOTELS AND OTHER EXPERIENCES

After surviving the white-knuckle ride from the airport, you will be at a fan-tastic hotel, if it is a five-star hotel in one of the metros. Indian hotels are just magnificent. I haven't been to every five-star hotel in the country, but I have stayed in a good few and without exception they have been amazing.

It is quite invidious to choose one above all others, but why not? If I had to choose, it would undoubtedly be the Maurya Sheraton in Delhi. It is like a pastiche of a customer service training film, with one quality above all oth-ers: it isn't at all intrusive. The general manager, Gautam Anand, is aston-ishing. His eye for detail, focus on customer service, memory for names, and the respect he gains from his staff are qualities that you'd earn an absolute fortune from if you could bottle them.

I generally stay in the Towers part of the Sheraton, where the staff are amazingly friendly and helpful. At one time, because I stayed so often, I got an automatic upgrade to ITC One, the premium of premium places. That was completely and sublimely over the top – marvelous.

Almost before I got out of the car, I was greeted by a besuited and extra-ordinarily polite young lady. She escorted me through the lobby, followed by one person to organize my extensive luggage – one suitcase and one laptop case – and two further people to carry them individually. This entourage slowly and elegantly made its way to the ITC One check-in.

Virtually no formalities later I was shown to my room, where I was given a demonstration of the extensive toys, including the massage chair. You can imagine that as a Brit I wouldn't not feel entirely comfortable with a device like this. Being asked to sit in it while the various knobs and handles were turned to let loose the electric motors, and then having to writhe in some comfort at the strange things this chair was doing to parts of me I rarely take with me on a business trip, was excruciating. I was so acutely embarrassed that I haven't dared sit in one since, but I'm told they are relaxing.

Arriving in the hotel's special ITC One executive lounge is like one of those magic games where even before you've realized it, you've been provided with the drink you might have ordered. Amazing. Fantastic.

Most hotels don't get to this level, but I'm staggered how your standards change after being in such a hotel. The only pity is that the working day is so long in India, you will hardly ever spend any time at the hotel. Without exaggerating, I have made appointments – and been taken seriously – for midnight.

THE PHONE SYSTEM

Before you go to bed on your first night, you'll want to phone home.

The improvements to the phone system in India over the last few years have been staggering and the network coverage for cellphones is very good. There are fantastic communications systems, including satellite and leased lines of enormous bandwidth for business use, ensuring that communications are efficient, effective, and relatively inexpensive.

Nevertheless, the telephone system is a challenge. Four simple pieces of information are necessary to limit some of the frustration and eventual upset.

If you dial a number and you get a short, continuous tone – about half a second – followed by a pause of about three seconds, and then the sequence is repeated, this isn't an engaged tone. It's the telephone exchange hunting for a line to take your call. You may get through after a wait of up to 20 seconds, which seems like a lifetime. I didn't know on my first few trips what the signal meant and thought it was telling me the number I had dialed was engaged. In retrospect, especially a few years ago, that was probably a good outcome, as it prevented me from the next two frustrations and eventually discovering the final one.

Secondly, beware of the time lag between someone speaking and you hearing them. I know it's entirely possible to bounce telephone messages off the moon, I just wish it wasn't necessary to prove it so many times when talking on an ordinary phone system between India and the West. It is a special skill to be able to carry on a conversation if there is a three-second pause between speakers. The moment you know it has moved from farce to tragedy is when both of you say, apparently together: "No, you speak." I say "apparently" because the synchronization required to achieve this effect must be difficult to engineer. I make no reference to the echo that is sometimes present, as I always think it's pleasant to listen to someone intelligent for a change when it's your voice that is echoing backwards and forwards.

Thirdly, if you receive a spoken message after dialing a number, test its validity several times. This will take some doing, as the voices have obviously been chosen with care to rile even the most placid soul. When trying to redial a number that you have just been talking to, it is more than annoying to be told: "The number you have dialed does not exist." There are variations on this, including the more direct and as annoying: "No such telephone number exists."

The real irritation, however, lies in the delivery and tone of these announcements. The first message is vouchsafed by a very superior and smug female voice. You can feel her pleasure at knowing something you haven't the wit to comprehend. The message is really that it is a pity there are such simpletons in the world as you, when there are such amazingly haughty and self-satisfied beings like her. Pooh Bah in *The Mikado* has met his match.

Yet the tone is as nothing compared to the delivery. If you can manage a sneer of the most extraordinary virulence – and I promise you won't match this voice – read the following, with the appropriate pause and stress, and imagine how you feel when you have just been talking to the number in question and you know it is valid: "The number [one-second pause] *you* have dialed [three-second pause] does not [one-second pause] exist."

In terms of the Indian telephone system, procrastination is not the thief of time, repetition is. You can tell it's endemic because watching local Indians making phone calls gives it away. They will instantly redial without a moment's hesitation or thought.

The fourth simple fact, which has lessened in significance over the last few years, is rather delayed in impact. It is the cost of the calls, an element that you will probably only appreciate when you receive the bill. If you remember making international calls in the 1980s, this will take you back. The cost of each call is at a level that says you are a person of distinction and choice, with no idea about the value of money. The GDP of a small republic pales into insignificance beside the roaming charges if you leave your mobile on in India – and that's without using the handset to dial out.

If you have a US cellphone, you will need to get a UK or European phone, or switch to using a tri-band phone. Since the latter won't switch automatically from the US frequency, however, you will have to remember to switch bands when you arrive in India.

You will obviously want to recharge your cellphone or laptop. The electrical sockets in India are what an elderly Brit might recognize as 15 amp round pin. You can usually find a socket that takes European two-pin plugs, there might even be a UK 13 amp square socket, and in most hotels there will be a socket for a US blade plug. The voltage is said to be circa 230.

SETTLING DOWN FOR YOUR FIRST NIGHT

Your watch will be telling you it's either about 3.00pm EST or 8.30pm GMT, your body clock will be telling you it's well past your bedtime, and the clock in the room will tell you it's about 1.30am IST (Indian Standard Time).

The worst part of all this is that when your trip to India was being arranged, it probably seemed entirely reasonable to be getting up for a 9am meeting. It's very likely that the person arranging it will have made it sound even more thoughtful, by saying that normally they'd meet you at, say, 8, but since it's your first day you can have an extra hour.

Since 9am IST is 3.30am GMT or 10.30pm EST – if you've come from America, you'll be getting up before you would normally go to bed – your appreciation of this sensitivity may well be stretched a little as the reality dawns on you. There is nothing specific to India about this, but it will be much harder to deal with, since you will probably receive a call at 7.30am from the person meeting you, just to check that you are all right and still expecting to meet at 9. The other person won't, of course, turn up until at least 9.30.

So apart from having a body clock out of sync with your local time, a bewilderment about which meal is next, and a general feeling of not being quite right, you will retire to bed in a state of some agitation. You will be upset if you haven't been able to call home and probably irritated by the process if you did.

Just the recipe for a good night's sleep – which you will definitely need.

6

PREPARING FOR DAY ONE

After the solicitous call at 7.30am – if you are anything like me, only minutes after you finally got to sleep – you may fall into a heavy doze, to be woken at 8 by the wake-up call you arranged the night before. (Ten minutes later you will get a reminder, even if you have declined one both before you went to bed and when you woke up.)

DRESS CODE

Ablutions over, it's time to consider the dress code. Trust no one on this, especially not an Indian. They will simply be excruciatingly polite, until after the event when they will say something like: "I suppose it didn't matter too much that you weren't wearing a jacket."

This is one of those areas where Americans find it harder to adjust than Brits or most Europeans. Being overdressed is never a problem in India. If you are comfortable in formal business wear, a suit and tie for a man or the equivalent if you are a woman, you may get warm walking from the freezing air-conditioned car to the polar air-conditioned office, but you will be perfectly comfortable otherwise.

This is so completely different from the US, where I have struggled with the dress code, and is one clue to why India poses more challenges for Americans.

Every six weeks I used to have to visit Microsoft in Redmond, which I accept is extreme even by US standards. Being overdressed there is tantamount to an insult; worse, it is a mark of disrespect. I did realize this even the first time I went, and made an extraordinary effort for a Brit: I turned up in a shirt with a collar, no tie, chinos, and leather shoes. As the Americans were expecting a Brit with his no doubt curious sense of what was appropriate, they had all made an effort to dress up, which consisted of ironed shorts and T-shirt, socks, and trainers. They looked so uncomfortable I wanted to ask whether someone had put too much starch in their clothes.

The following day, I thought I had better make more of an effort. I had a limited repertoire with me, but I managed to throw together a less formal shirt, the same chinos, and trainers. (I couldn't have actually managed to wear shorts, had I had the wit to bring a pair with me. The thought of exposing my knees in a business meeting is rather daunting.) My hosts had decided that they had made the effort the day before, and were back in shorts that looked as though there were pizza stains on them, rather scruffier T-shirts, no socks, and their third-best trainers. They were a good deal more relaxed.

For the next day, I decided I couldn't chase them down that route, because I'd gone as far as I could and there was no telling where it might end. I had to give up.

In India, then, if in doubt err on the more formal side. Most of the time, what Brits know as smart or business casual will be perfectly appropriate. If you can wear relatively smart casual clothes in business meetings without too much angst, then the equivalent of a reasonable shirt and pressed trousers, with leather shoes, will suffice most of the time for both men and women.

Whatever you expect to be doing during the day, and however casual a program you have, I would always take a jacket and tie, and a woman should take the equivalent. As you will see when we consider time in Chapter 8, you will always need to be prepared for the unexpected, including that level of formality.

Most western women I have worked with in India say that a long dress or skirt is the most appropriate to wear in the evening and what they feel most comfortable in. This will mean that you will complement any Indian women present, who will be more inclined to wear a sari in the evening if they haven't during the day. A sari is a long piece of cloth that is wound continuously round the body, stretching from the left shoulder to the ankles.

By the way, it's a good idea to take a jersey when going to business meetings in India. Virtually all the rooms you enter will be air conditioned. You will step out of the very damp heat, especially in Mumbai where it's like taking a warm bath with all your clothes on, into a refreshingly cold atmosphere.

You will then freeze. It seems to be a mark of sophistication to run all air conditioning at the level where cryogenic experiments can take place. Requests to let a bit of warmth in are usually greeted with knowing smiles by all those used to irony. I have been colder in India than anywhere else in the world.

Once you've put on the right clothes, it's time for breakfast. Just walking along the hotel corridor, being greeted by a smile and a reasonable and friendly question by all the staff, is fantastic. Yes, it's training. Yes, it could be artificial – and it is. But it's carried off with such ease and friendliness that it certainly lifts any jaded business trip. It's worth going to India just to experience that.

EATING...

In general, Indians don't go in for business breakfasts. The day starts much more leisurely – as it has to, since the previous day ended so late. The person you have arranged to meet on your first morning will turn up around an hour late, say about 9.30, and will have a cup of coffee or tea with you over breakfast, although there will be as many individual variations as there are individuals. One of my team would always start by declining anything to eat at breakfast, but by the time we finished he had always made a fair impact on the hotel's food stores.

Business meals are tricky in any culture. I might have unconsciously fallen into every pothole there is, but I am not aware of any particularly difficult issues in India. Most western countries are used to the idea of Indian food, especially because of the Indian diaspora.

The food served is usually Bangladeshi or Bengali. However, there is a great deal more to Indian food than the top right-hand corner of the country.

It's a general rule that the further south you go, the hotter the food. Like all rules in India, it is partly true. Your fellow Indian diners will be solicitous about how hot the food is, regardless of where it is from, but especially if it is from the south.

My first experience of this was with a colleague originally from Goa, sort of halfway down the left-hand side. We were in Hyderabad, which is toward the south. He warned me about how hot the food was, but I plowed on. I found it great, but when I looked across at him he was sweating and drinking water at a furious rate. (To be fair he could have come across a really hot chilli, but I don't like to believe that.)

Not much problem with the food, then, as long as you like spicy or very spicy things. If you can't bear spices, I'm afraid it's usually omelettes. Of course, they will come with some spice.

There is one word of caution. There are two categories of main course: veg and non-veg. I always find these abbreviations rather offputting for some reason, but they mean what they say. Indians classify food the other way round from in the West: the norm appears to be vegetarian. As far as I am aware, however – and bear in mind my later strictures about how polite Indians are, especially as hosts – I don't believe any offense is given or taken if you have a non-veg meal when your companions are having veg.

Outside of Calcutta and Bengal, you won't usually find much in the way of Indian puddings, though there will be some western cakes and perhaps a trifle. Some of the fresh fruit is amazing. In Calcutta, there will be a selection of already incredibly sweet things doused in treacle. You can feel your arteries harden even before you put any in your mouth. About the only universally available pudding will be *kulfi*, a form of Indian ice cream, which is very sweet.

Starting to eat isn't the nightmare it is in British entertaining. Brits are told to wait until other people have started eating before they begin. Work that one out – and wonder whether a table of Brits will ever manage to eat! I've known food get so cold at corporate dinners that it was practically inedible, since no one wanted to be the first to start. It's not for nothing that the Brits don't have an equivalent of *bon appétit* or *eet smakelijk* to indicate that this is the time to get the nosebag on.

The general rule in India is, apparently, food arrives, start, and let the devil take the hindmost. It's not aggressive at all, but it is even brisker than the American sense of getting on with the meal while it's hot, which I've always admired.

It's not that simple in India, naturally, and it has become trickier, I suspect mainly because of western influences. If you are the chief guest, get on with your meal. If you find that hard – and I can hardly write the advice, let alone take it – do your best.

Hands are a perfectly acceptable method of eating. In fact, in some of the classiest restaurants you won't get anything other than bread and your hands to eat with. I love it. In the particular restaurant I am thinking about, you also get a proper apron that ties round your neck and covers most of your clothing. Suits me!

Incidentally, I usually add 10 percent to the bill as the tip.

...AND DRINKING

A trickier subject, at least to western minds, is drink. While alcohol can be a difficult subject across cultures, it isn't in India. A good many Indians are teetotal, either because of religious teaching, cultural background, or personal wishes. It is no different drinking with them than with teetotalers in any country.

In my experience, the majority of Indians do drink, and with the same range of excuses as we use in the West. Tonic water contains quinine, so it can be used to help stop malaria – and some people I know take the opportunity to avoid malaria to quite extreme lengths, especially if there's gin mixed with the tonic water.

It is rare for business lunches to include alcohol, although drinking is not particularly frowned on.

When you do have a drink, you will usually be served nuts, biscuits, and other savories, some of which, usually the ones that look the most innocuous, can take the roof off your mouth. I hope it goes without saying that you should avoid all of these savories like the plague. They are almost as bad as the plague.

Most of the stomach upsets that I have suffered over the years have been after absent-mindedly taking a nut or two. It's not that the nuts will be prepared any more unhygienically than in your own country or presented in any way that is not acceptable. The bacteria will simply not be what you are used to, and while you can cope with your own country's germs, those in other places need to be treated with respect.

I don't drink tap water in India or even clean my teeth with it, although hotels will assure you that the water is "perfectly potable." There have also been one or two health scares about bottled water over the years – about as many as there have been in Europe. These are usually reports of some sort of contamination. I drink the bottled water, clean my teeth in it, and it is fine. (Some extremists, cognizant of these scares, stick to tonic water with something appropriate in it, like gin, even for teeth cleaning.)

The biggest shock for me was tea, or *chai*. I love tea. I like coffee too, and over the years had taken on board the view that adding sugar to tea and coffee takes away its enjoyment, as all you can taste is the sugar. I think there's a similar argument about milk, but it never really convinced me, and a tea planter of my acquaintance has told me that milk does add to the flavor and experience of tea by forming a chemical bond. With this in mind, I was really looking forward to going to India and drinking the best tea in the world.

If you want that, avoid tea at business meetings. It will come as a very milky brown substance, so sweet that you wonder how such a small quantity of fluid can absorb so much sugar. A request for no sugar will have one of two results. You will usually get black tea without milk, but still with sugar. Alternatively, you will get tea with half the amount of sugar. It is a simple fact that tea has to have sugar in India.

In hotels you will fare better, but it won't be the experience I was anticipating. You know what I mean: a measured sip, a brief reverie, some sort of statement that the tea was grown on the north side of the hill in an obscure village in Assam and harvested moments before the dew was burned off by the morning sun. I've given up trying.

AN INTRODUCTION TO NAMES

Once you've negotiated your first meal, it's time to work out what to do about names. I doubt you'll ever be quite comfortable, both in regard to what you call people and what they call you, but there is always India's saving grace. The reassuring thought for any stranger is that India is such a varied and large place and so cosmopolitan in its own right that social faux pas are generally not held against an individual. In a country where there are as many variations as states, it is unlikely that anyone could observe all the various admonitions relevant to a particular place or circumstance, even if they were written down. More than likely no one will notice. If they do notice, they won't have much more of a clue than you whether what you have said is an affront to civilized society. If they do notice and they know you have violated some important taboo, they will be far too polite to tell you.

You can obviously upset people in India quite as easily as you can upset anyone in any country, but in general failures in etiquette will be viewed as innocence where they aren't ignorance. It is important to keep that in mind.

This is very different from how westerners view social failures. To a Brit, a foreigner of any kind is probably in need of a bit of discipline or stiffening up, and they obviously won't know the ropes. The result is a sort of embarrassed pity. Americans tend to regard foreigners as somehow deviating from the norm, which is located about five miles west of Boise, Idaho. Their general response is bewilderment. The Dutch see foreigners as a challenge – and that challenge is generally whether they can learn their language before it's time for another cup of coffee.

Among Indians there is a wonderful sense of foreigners being different and strange and obscure, but probably OK now that they've given up invading. This means, probably paradoxically, that Indians are never quite comfortable and relaxed.

Into this context come names. Names, or more properly how to use names, will cause a great deal of confusion in any culture. Even within western Europe the variations are amazing – to cross from the Netherlands into Germany, for example, is to cross an extraordinary linguistic and cultural divide. The Dutch cope with the problem as easily as they move from UK English to American English when they address a Brit or an American in the same meeting. The Germans, like the Brits, get in a terrible muddle, although from different ends of the spectrum, with the Brits pathologically unable to call anyone by a title or a family name, and the Germans equally unable to call anyone by a given name.

As India is a region in its own right, names and the use of names vary, but titles are employed far more than an American, a Brit, or even a German might expect. The root of the problem is that there is no pattern. I think the only safe message about names in India is that there is no way of being consistently right or even consistent.

The strangest convention I have come across is where single names are also used as complete identifiers. One business colleague of mine always introduces himself simply as Suresh. There can't be more than 50 million Sureshes in India, but he is just Suresh. (If you met him, you'd see why and probably agree, because he is unique and tremendous.)

Then there is the issue of whether to use the given name or the family name. The first trick is knowing which is the family name and which the given name. There is a general rule that the family name comes last, which won't necessarily help much.

To give you the right context, let's see the range of possibilities. Many Indians appear to have three names, some of which they use. Toward the north it is more likely, but not certain, that the first name you see on a business card will be a given name. Toward the south it is likely that the last name on the card will be a given name.

You won't know what to call anyone, because some groups or teams will use the given name and some will use the family name – and not interchangeably.

One of my colleagues in India is Bhupinder Rana. Bhupinder is his given name. We are on given-name terms. He is known to the group, and me of course, as Rana. Similarly, Ramu Venkatesh, with his given name second, is always known to us as Ramu. That is except for a new Indian colleague, who decided that as Venkatesh was his given name, he would call him Venkatesh, as that was more friendly. It took nearly two hours of one-to-one combat for me to sort that one out. You can imagine that if it took a foreigner to intervene, this was quite a deep wound.

As you go further south, or as people from further south come to you, you will notice an exponential increase in the number of syllables in any particular name. Six syllables tries a western brain no end, especially when they all appear to be made up of "s" and "th" mixed in fairly random order. As a result, I have absolutely no problem with the Indian habit of calling people by their initials. It is quite alarming to discover people being introduced to you as "PVC" or "TCP," but if it means you can address them reasonably informally, I welcome it.

The other Indian trait that causes more of a problem is how readily they alter their names so a westerner will be able to pronounce them. It is done, of course, out of an excruciating need to be polite. Sometimes you won't even know it has happened. I called one Indian colleague "Nick" for nearly 18 months before I learnt that his name is Nachiket. That doesn't seem difficult to pronounce and once I knew, I found myself unable to call him anything. (That might have been the Indian politeness rubbing off even on me.)

Indians expect westerners to have difficulty with their naming conventions, just as they do when they meet people from different states or regions in the country. It isn't considered rude to ask what to call someone. As I am incidentally fascinated by etymology, doing so keeps me amused for hours. I often ask for derivations and these can be as varied as in western countries. A great many are related to religion, and you can get very complicated names that break down quite simply, even if you remain baffled. Narayan Gopalikrishnan, for example, is the name of a colleague with both given name and family name related to Krishna, a major Hindu god.

If you find it difficult to know what to call an Indian, they in turn have extraordinary difficulty with western names. This is where the title business comes to the fore.

Because India is so hierarchical, you will often get a "Mr." or "Miss" added to your given name, if you can persuade the person you are working with to call you by your given name at all. In moments of crisis – OK, when the customer was none too happy – I have occasionally become "Mr. Paul" and "Mr. Davies," both in the same sentence. (Just like in the West, the moment I became "Mr. Paul Davies" it was time to examine the room for means of escape.)

One answer should be to explain how you want to be called. I'm afraid that though this works one way round, from an Indian to you, it doesn't work all that well in reverse. If you make yourself too familiar, you may unwittingly be offending some sense of respect and politeness.

HIERARCHY

You will be part of the hierarchy in India, but it is incredibly easy not to recognize that obvious fact.

Without requiring anything like the Japanese sense of seniority and face and a tangible hierarchy, you do have to pay attention to the order of entering rooms and who shakes hands first. It won't be a black mark to get it wrong, especially to your hosts, but it will make your Indian colleagues uneasy.

Consider one minor example of how tricky the approach to the hierarchy is. I promoted the person who was looking after orders and disbursements. The first part of the job had been a sinecure for a long time before I arrived, so that might have accounted for some of his coolness about my suggestion of how to recognize his new status. I said I'd be very happy if he took over one of the cabins – cubicles – in our office. He just didn't know what to do with himself.

This was too much of an honor for him and I had put him in the awful predicament of having to work out how to ask me not to be so thoughtful. Even I could see his distress, and managed to water down the offer immediately. Once I had suggested that we give him a larger desk in his existing area, all was sweetness and light; he'd got the recognition without the presumption. Giving him his own office had completely disrupted his sense of what was proper in the office hierarchy.

So you are part of the hierarchy. Which part is probably the real question.

Indian society is fundamentally hierarchical. The hierarchy is based on the usual measures that are understood internationally. These include wealth, lineage, family connections, place of residence, educational institutions attended, seniority in business, job title, size of office, make of car, color of credit card, accent, and sometimes, if all else fails, academic qualifications. As with any particular society, only its members really know where anyone fits in the hierarchy.

There is one further qualification system in India. There is a caste system that you will be told no one pays any attention to any more. It's just that if you are an Indian the person you marry will inevitably come from your caste, and it is probably a good deal easier to do business with someone from the same caste – though that's an outdated idea that frankly doesn't mean anything nowadays. It's as well to ignore caste as an issue in day-to-day affairs, but keep it in the forefront of your mind because it may crop up at any time, even if you are being told that it is not important.

Your position in all this will be difficult to establish, both for you and for all the Indians in the group. It will be uncomfortable for everyone. You will be, however, indefinably important. This may show itself when you first arrive at an Indian company's office. I have had red marks put on my forehead, been given a sandalwood garland, and then, worst of all, had a Polaroid photograph taken. I was mortified.

Being India, the great aspect for me of this episode was not that it helped me understand my elevated and important position. It was the entirely genuine, but not malicious, amusement that it caused all and sundry. At least, I took it as not being malicious amusement.

THE FAMILY

In contrast to the western concept of the nuclear family of two adults and 2.4 children, an Indian may well have a "joint family," what sociologists call the extended family. As this isn't a sociologically determined book, I will confine my discussion to a few of the issues that might affect you or provide you with some insights.

On marriage, it is quite usual for the son to remain at home and his new wife to join him, living there as part of the family. Never mind the concept, as a son, of still living in the family home, I guess many new wives in the West might have difficulty living with their mothers-in-law, and many mothers-in-law might have similar difficulties adjusting to living with their new daughters-in-law. It's a very different perspective, although I do know that the same strains occur in India as would in the West.

More specific to my focus here is the rather inexact meaning of a number of further relationships in the extended family. Let me first consider the concept of "my cousin." When I first heard this expression, which occurs frequently, I put its prevalence down to both the existence of the extended family as an essential item of Indian life, and a rather broad and inexact western feeling that there must be lots of brothers and sisters in the average Indian family, all of whom have just as many children themselves.

That was obviously the reason why so many Indians could call on their cousins in a crisis. Everyone I met had a cousin or two ideally placed in a helpful position to facilitate something, whether it was getting that license renewal that had been dragging for months or being able to speak to the chief minister at a moment's notice.

Being a cousin is, in fact, a singularly inexact relationship. I have actually been introduced in India to a cousin who *was* a cousin – that is, the child of a sibling of a parent, which conforms to my more limited concept of what the word means. Other than that, every other cousin in India has in fact been related to the person telling me about them, but usually by the most tenuous of links.

I now ask most times "my cousin" is mentioned what the relationship is, because I'm fascinated by the amount of contact and keeping up that must go on. In contrast, I know that I only ever meet my own few cousins at funerals.

There is a general feeling in the West that every individual is related to every other person born in the country by being something like a sixth cousin. (When you work it out, it would probably be hard not to be.) There's also that game beloved of team-building exercises, where you work out that by only using five or six intermediary steps you can get to virtually anyone in the world. "Cousin" in India is only a formal recognition of this sort of attitude.

On several occasions I have been told that a particular cousin was exactly the right person to ensure that a transaction would take place at the desired time. It turned out that the so-called cousins had never actually met or had any sort of physical contact, even on the phone, and were only vaguely aware of each other's existence, except being called to mind at a moment of stress.

If that value of the word "cousin" is understood, there is an extension of family relationships that is much more all-embracing and even vaguer. This wider set of relationships is generally summed up as "my brother-in-law." This is a bit like being a cousin but is an inexhaustible extension, since when someone doesn't have a suitably placed cousin that he or she has never met, there's always a brother-in-law to step into the breach. I've not seen this extended into "my sister-in-law," but I'm sure it's only a matter of time.

SEXUAL EQUALITY

When it comes to relations between the sexes, I am generally puzzled, like any British man. Even so, India seems a much more straightforward place than other people report it, and I get confused by some of the books I've read about gender issues in India. I have come to the conclusion that the very western feel of ease and non-sexism I've experienced must be primarily among business people. I haven't enough experience of anything else, but I don't recognize the stereotypes I have seen referred to of women in second place. In business at least, you can forget any distinction between what you would expect at home and what you will experience in India. Western female colleagues have confirmed that it is no better and no worse than at home.

Certainly, the women I have dealt with in business are as individual as the men and just as likely to be dominant or subservient. There is no extra formality if a woman is involved in a group of men or the other way round. You can take a pinch of salt here and wonder whether I would have noticed.

In general, mixed meetings are no different from such meetings in the West – but I don't find single-sex business meetings any different from mixed meetings either, so perhaps I'm not sensitive enough. Of course, I only know about male single-sex meetings.

Even the convention of arranged marriages among middle-class Indians seems to be an example of sexual equality, since both sets of families are determined to achieve the best result for their children. Both arranged marriages and marriages for love exist, but the former is more likely.

There is a pleasing conundrum about arranged marriages that I have shared with my Indian colleagues. There are fewer divorces as a percentage of marriages in India than in the West. This is taken as evidence that arranged marriages are more successful than marriages for love. On the other hand, in India divorce is much more of a social disaster for all parties. I can't help feeling that that attitude is more significant than how the contract was entered into.

RELIGION AND RELIGIOUS OBSERVANCE

Religion and religious observance, as you might imagine, provide key insights into India. There is also a major sea change going on in Indian society, which is provoking a great deal of discomfort.

Mahatma Gandhi celebrated the fact that every Indian village had three, four, or five religions living side by side, if not in harmony then in indifference. The constitution of India enshrines the secular nature of the country. The ruling party, the BJP, head of a shifting coalition of up to 28 parties, is a Hindu party. There are religious tensions in various states, including communal violence. The wheel is still turning, but there are strong undercurrents that may affect your attempts to do business.

The usual advice – to be circumspect – is the best.

In relation particularly to Hinduism, it is often explained as not being one religion, more of a cultural understanding across a region, taking different forms and shapes. I don't understand it, but I do appreciate that the patience of Indian people is partly imbued by Hinduism. You will not have religion thrown at you, but any interest you show will be treated sympathetically. My questions have always been seen as proper to ask and I have learnt a great deal.

There is one Hindu god that I have a special affection for, Ganesh. He is the elephant-headed god, usually with a wheel behind his head and an encouragingly ample stomach. He can be extraordinarily relevant in business – among other things he is the god of new beginnings, and I have seen him invoked in an almost subconscious way. You might even catch sight of one of those present at a meeting stroking a statue of Ganesh as they walk past.

7
GETTING AROUND

The drive from the airport to your hotel was an introduction to cars and driving. As you set off for your first day in India, you need to understand about taxis. Taxis and taxi drivers are a subject in their own right in most countries, and India is no exception.

TAXIS, TAXI DRIVERS, AND PRIVATE HIRE

As in New York or Dallas, your taxi driver will probably only have a hazy knowledge of English. In India, that hazy knowledge can usually be supplemented by writing down the address you want. (I never found that much value in the US.) You can also use what is known in India as your hand phone or cell, phone your potential customer or supplier, and ask them to speak to the taxi driver.

Rather differently from any US taxi driver, your Indian driver will speak at least one common language with the people you are going to see, either a local language, such as Marathi in Mumbai, or Hindi. This doesn't guarantee you will get where you want to go, but it helps.

The most basic taxis are the three-wheeler cockroaches I mentioned before. These have covered roofs, but are open at the sides, noisy, smelly, not as uncomfortable as they look – they couldn't be – and very, very cheap. If you anticipate using cockroaches, don't accept 50 rupee notes when you exchange your currency, get them broken down into tens. I have used them, to the evident pleasure of the cockroach driver, but it isn't the type of vehicle you need on your way to a meeting, unless you favor a windswept, natural look. They are in any case banned from the more prestigious parts of the metros, like downtown Mumbai.

Then there are the exceedingly old black and yellow taxis. I think they are manufactured to look terribly old. In Delhi these are Austin Cambridges or, the same car badged differently, Morris Oxfords, still made, I think, under license and called Ambassadors. (The UK Austin Cambridge on which the Ambassador is based was not even the last model made. That was discontinued in the 1960s, but the one that flourished before 1958 is the basis of the Ambassador.) In Mumbai, the taxis are based on an ancient Fiat design.

Whatever the model, the taxis are noisy and smelly, and even more uncomfortable than they look, which is also pretty hard. They are astonishingly slow, especially the most common diesel ones. In an out-and-out drag with a bullock cart they will win, but not necessarily if it is uphill. You will feel every bump – the roads have a good few – and you'll feel it on your head, as you hit the roof with it. (Shock absorbers seem to be looked on as a good idea whose time will come.) The cars are well adapted to Indian driving conditions, however, and they do keep going regardless of the weather. In the monsoon, which usually lasts from early June to at least late September, I have seen a torrential stream running down a hill more or less stopping everything else in its tracks. My taxi made a stately progress of two or three miles an hour straight through it all.

Some of these taxis do have air conditioning, which adds a little to the fare. These are known as Cool Cabs and are worth having most of the year round. At least that is the case in Mumbai. One January in Delhi – where it can go below freezing and it had – when I was suffering from a very heavy cold, I was told to insist on having a Cool Cab. The argument was that if it had air conditioning, it was bound to have a heater. I wasn't sure of the logic at the time, but immediately I got out of the icy Delhi air I found myself in the icier air in the cab. My cold rapidly got worse.

These black and yellow cabs are the ones with taxi meters. They look vaguely like water hydrants in the US, and stick up outside the car, on the left of the hood. They turn over the numbers extraordinarily slowly, in a relaxed mechanical style that I find quite mesmerizing. There must be a preservation order of some kind on them, because the fares they show are hopelessly out of date. It is not at all unusual to have a fare showing, say, INR8 after 20 minutes or so. I am told by various Mumbaiites and Delhiites that there is a multiplier to be applied in order to arrive at the right fare, but I don't think anyone has ever written it down and it doesn't appear to be for foreigners' ears. The nearest I got was: "Oh, it's about five times what it shows."

I don't think it's anywhere near that simple. You have to find out what the fare is in a different way. If you're starting at a hotel, the answer is to ask for the printed fare table from the army of dispatchers outside the front door.

If you're returning to your hotel from somewhere else, you can ask your hosts at whatever meeting you are attending what the fare should be. If they are Indian, they will give what sounds like an impossibly low figure. This is, of course, what they would expect to pay and it *is* impossibly low. In India there are usually two fares or rates: one for Indians and one for foreigners. This applies as much to tourist attractions as to taxi fares. In my experience of taxi fares, if you double the Indian figure you will have the full fare including the tip. Taking such a taxi for a full day works out at a little over $20.

Although the inside of a black and yellow taxi looks none too clean, you won't get your clothes all that dirty as long as you are careful getting in and out. On the other hand, don't use the trunk for your briefcase. Many of these receptacles look as though someone has struck oil in them at some stage, and you might be surprised how far a little engine oil can go when being transferred from your briefcase to your clothes.

For less than $30 per day, plus overtime, you can rent a car and driver from the hotel. You won't need to dry clean your clothes after using it – but where is the challenge in that?

If you have got a driver all day, he will wait for you and probably sleep while waiting. The immediate lapse into sleep isn't surprising, as some of the drivers work 24-hour shifts with 12 hours off in between. I try not to think about what their reactions will be like at the end of several of those continuous days.

I always give the driver some idea of how long I will be. Not that I know – and you won't either – but it seems politer. More importantly, unless you specifically suggest to your driver that he has time to take a meal, he probably won't, as he will be concerned to be available as soon as you need him. I have also had occasions when a driver didn't have enough money to buy anything to eat until he got his fare at the end of the day. Fortunately, the first time this happened the driver eventually told me. Since then I always try to be sensitive to this possibility and I haven't known this to be abused.

Finding your car after a meeting will seem a major issue. The driver probably won't have a cellphone; if he does, he won't answer it. There are some straightforward facts that will help reestablish contact. The first is that all cars are known by the last four digits of the registration plate. If you have reserved a car the night before, you may be told that number to give to the dispatchers outside the hotel. They will use a loudspeaker system to call the car from what seems like the bowels of the earth. Secondly, the driver will, despite being asleep, somehow sense that you need him and appear.

I've never actually lost my car and driver for more than five or ten minutes – though even five minutes can seem a long time in such circumstances. It's worth remembering the four-digit registration number and taking a look at all the cars littering the sidewalk. I did once find my car using that method.

WALKING IN INDIA

Sidewalks are not there for anything as mundane as walking, of course. You can have your teeth done, get your hair cut, buy any number of miscellaneous items, have a shower as the monsoon comes off the roof of a nearby building or shanty, live there in various degrees of comfort, or just pile up any rubbish you happen to have around. If none of these activities and their kind is required, then you can park your car, motorbike, taxi, or cockroach there.

Walking on a sidewalk is an absolute no-no. If you manage to find an open section, not occupied by a commercial venture or the remains of an oil rig, you will break your leg falling down some ditch running across the path, at 90 degrees to the road itself.

Pedestrians walk on the road, preferably on the traffic side of any cars that are parked up to the curb. Any walking in groups is not done in Indian file. Two, three, or four abreast is the norm. A good deal of horn-blowing will be excited by this event, but no one takes any notice – not those banging on their horns, and certainly not those who are the subject of the noise.

Crossing the road on foot is quite difficult for a Brit, but for an American or German it is pure torture. It's not impossible, however, as it is on the beltway in Dallas where the pedestrian-crossing element of the traffic light cycle is about half a second long. (Like everyone else, I soon learned you had to take a cab to cross that road.)

For a true Mumbaiite, crossing the road is a supreme declaration of the value of human life. The logic goes something like this: I am a human being; all life is sacred; no one will kill me, much less the driver of a car; I can therefore walk without any form of care across any road, no matter how busy it is. Look at the cows wandering the streets: no one hits them, and I am a higher form of life than a cow.

It's amazing how sensible this logic is. It appears to me that because drivers know – you do just know – that the person ambling toward or away from you will step out in front of you to cross the road, a sixth sense works to ensure that you miss them. The sheer quality of the driving is such that whereas this would cause a major accident in London or New York, in India it's more or less expected, so nothing disastrous happens. This is the case even if the driver takes to the wrong side of the road to prevent mowing down the far-from-innocent pedestrian. Oncoming traffic seems to expect such a hazard and simply copes.

I've tried to cross roads in Mumbai like this, just not looking – partly because it is so dangerous if you look first. Looking seems to turn off the oncoming driver's sixth sense. It's as though they are baffled about what you are doing or intend to do.

I've found that I can't cross the road without looking, however. I've taken to going to pedestrian crossings or road junctions and waiting for signals. I've become as law abiding as an American or a German faced with jaywalking rules. But as we have seen, traffic signals aren't exactly regarded as the highest imperative. It's so dangerous that you wonder how there are any pedestrians in Mumbai still alive. And I wouldn't even attempt to cross a road in Delhi. I think the only completely safe answer is to take a taxi.

By the way, having a shower on the sidewalk in the afternoon monsoon rain wasn't an exaggeration. I think the shanty dwellers of India are some of the cleanest poor people in the world. Two seconds after the heavens open, at the point where most of the Arabian Gulf is being dumped on Mumbai, when even the taxis almost fail to negotiate upstream against the surging tidal wave, and the phrase "torrential rain" sounds like one of those terribly

English understatements, it's out with the Lifebuoy soap, nip under a friendly gushing corner of a shanty roof, and give it all you've got.

If you do any walking in India – and I still recommend that you attempt it, as it's a complete experience – you will be amazed at the number of people going in every direction at once, rather like the traffic. It's astonishingly orderly despite the chaotic feel. It's best, especially if you are a Brit with a keen sense of personal space, to abandon yourself to all forms of physical contact, brushing against, besides, and what feels like through the entire population of India.

In any case, physical contact isn't such a big deal to Indians. It's a part of life.

The trains are extraordinarily crowded – they make a London Underground or New York subway train in peak time look empty. Most of them don't appear to have windows, partly, I imagine, because this would deprive six or seven people at a time of a decent handhold.

You can see at least five people cheerfully occupying a cockroach or three-wheeled auto-rickshaw. In the same way that a cockroach can be made to slide through the smallest gap on the road, someone will get into the smallest gap inside them. The luggage is a whole other story.

Also in terms of physical contact, the most surprising sight for a westerner is to see two men walking down the street, holding hands. This won't be sexual – despite the *Kama Sutra* and other erotica, Indian society is very prudish in public – but just an expression of friendship. I haven't yet seen any business people walking along holding hands, you may be relieved to know.

Once you've walked the short distance from your car, or a longer distance between offices for a different meeting, you will encounter the greatest test of your tolerance of diminished personal space: the elevator.

ELEVATORS AND PERSONAL SPACE

I have often looked at those signs in elevators in the UK, Europe, and the US telling you the maximum number of people who can be safely accommodated and I've always been perplexed. There is obviously a fair margin for error, or for accommodating heavier than average people. On the other hand, if it says ten, I have looked around at the six or seven people crushed into the crowded elevator and wondered where on earth you would need such a sign.

It's in India – not that anyone would take any notice if it were pointed out. If the elevator says it has a safe limit of ten, you can more or less guarantee that in India it will take ten, at least, on a fairly regular basis. That's pretty close comfort and, as you can expect, all my concepts of personal space, tried to breaking point in a UK elevator, are worth nothing.

As in the UK, US, or Europe, no one talks in an elevator in India. I don't think this is entirely because it's astonishingly embarrassing. It simply takes all your concentration to be able to breathe, using both diaphragm and chest, in the crush. And you will be crushed up against men and women indiscriminately. There is nothing for it but, as the elevator gurgles and strains its way up – or, more worryingly, creaks downwards – to think about something more unpleasant. The matter to focus on for a Brit will be written on a metal plate inside. In nearly every elevator in India you will read: "In case of fire, do not use the elevator." While we all know what this is meant to imply, you can tell the Brits as they will be wondering what the chances are of causing a fire by merely taking a lift. Things don't always mean what they say in India.

While I am thinking about personal space, I ought to mention haircuts. Of course, I have only experienced a man's haircut.

Given my difficulties with invasion of personal space, you can understand that a haircut isn't something I generally look forward to. In India it goes further and becomes an act of violence. It is also somehow almost a religious act. I do know it was an experience that reduced me to talking incessantly about it after my first time.

I've had some good haircuts in India, in terms of what my hair looks like afterwards. That first time I had one, however – and not on a sidewalk but in a five-star hotel – I found the whole thing quite alarming. The cutting, to be fair, was fine. We even had one of those conversations that occurs in up-market hairdressing salons when your hair is being washed. You will recognize the occasions when the bored assistant says idly: "Are you going away anywhere nice this weekend?" My mischievous reply of "India" is usually accepted with the customary "That's nice" that applies to any answer, including Scunthorpe, San Diego, Bremerhaven, Melbourne, Biarritz, or the Moon.

Having negotiated this type of small talk, we were communicating quite well.

We were fast approaching that part of a man's haircut where there is a great deal of mumbling – where you are shown the back of your head with a mirror and in the nanosecond for which it is held up you get a good view of the hairdresser's nose hair, and you mumble some sort of remark in reply.

At this very point, a red-hot towel was produced from nowhere and wrapped completely round my head. It was done really adroitly, just like an executioner holding out his hand to the condemned person and flexing it so the victim is in a half nelson before he or she knows it.

As a Brit, I was caught between maintaining a very wobbly stiff upper lip and addressing the assailant in a haughty upper-class accent: "Unhand me, sir!" Silence was the better part of discretion.

Then the maniac began to beat me around, over, and what felt like through my head. At the end of a few minutes of this, I was released. His smile indicated that either he had enjoyed himself giving me a jolly good thrashing for all the indignities suffered by India under the Raj, or this was a particular specialty of Indian barbers.

It is, I am assured, the latter. Apparently, it is possible to say no. I just couldn't tell you when the most appropriate moment is and one certainly didn't occur as far as I could tell. I don't think an inappropriate moment occurred either. My head didn't feel much the worse for the experience after a day or two.

I have discussed this with a cross-section of Indians, all of whom find my version disconcerting. There is another way of telling the story, from the point of view of an Indian in a western hairdressing establishment, where – you'll never believe this – the barber won't even beat you up at the end.

Someone who was aware that I'm not awfully good at physical contact with strangers was a particular manager of mine, who felt that a massage in India would be good for my peace of mind. He arranged for us to have an ayurvedic massage at the same time. He hadn't actually had this kind of massage previously, it transpired later, otherwise I'm not sure even he would have done it.

It was an extraordinary experience. All clothing is removed, apart from underpants. My manager and I were positioned either side of what pretended to be a curtain down the middle of a room, with two tables, side by side, on either side of the curtain. The tables are like billiard tables with no pockets, and no baize, but a wooden lip all round. This, you soon learn, is to catch the oil. The table slopes away from where your head will be, to drain off the oil.

The two men attending to me tied a piece of string round my middle. Sign language ensued that suggested I remove my last piece of clothing. I did. A piece of hard toilet paper was produced and tucked into the string at the front. In what I can honestly say is a maneuver that few people outside a very intimate circle have ever attempted on me, the other end of the toilet paper was tucked between my legs, and a hand then took it up between my legs to wrap it through the string at my back. I may have whimpered a bit during this process, and I certainly caught my breath.

All hell was then beaten out of me for 45 minutes. During the first ten minutes I was repeatedly asked to relax. I suggested in no uncertain terms that being beaten up in a pool of warm oil by two strangers whose concept of personal space and what was private was severely limited was not likely to allow me to relax. Despite this full and precise explanation, we didn't seem to share any understanding, which might have been exacerbated by a language problem – but it did cause amusement to my manager just behind the curtain. In fact, he was so amused he got his thugs to stop and sat up – only to skid helplessly down the sloping table on his bottom and hit the wall.

My two maniacs produced what looked like an octopus, immersed that in hot oil, and proceeded to beat me with it. There was a sudden respite. All beating ceased and they started to rub the oil into my legs. I made some noises as they caressed my inner thighs. (I couldn't remember the last time anyone had done that.) "Pain?" they asked. "Tickles," I just about managed to say. More laughter behind the curtain.

By this time, the previously opaque toilet paper had become transparent, although as it was no longer attached to the string but floating off down the table, leaving me in some embarrassment, I don't think I cared. I'm not sure I just lay back, but I did do a lot of thinking about England.

Much later, my fellow victim confessed that he had never had such an experience before either. We had to rush off to a business meeting immediately afterwards, and we did our best to ignore the obvious distress of those we were meeting as they shook hands and smelt two oil slicks. It's not an event that either of us has repeated.

PLACE NAMES

As a final preparation for venturing out into the big open world of India, we ought to consider place names. Because the country has existed for so long and has been invaded and conquered so many times, place names are somewhat of a lottery. In recent years there's been quite a spate of places getting different names, roads getting a new identity, and railway stations somehow not being called Victoria any more.

Indian people get very muddled themselves about some of the pieces of this cultural quilt. There is no right answer, as it happens, to what you should call a place. All you can do is be prepared.

Most countries throwing off the yoke of imperial tyranny will move heaven and earth to change the place names back to what they were before the foreigners arrived. You can immediately see the Indian problem: which set of foreigners? The easy answer is to go back to before the Brits arrived. India as a whole has not seen the need for that sort of consistency.

Nevertheless, by changing the names of places, most countries will forge a fresh identity for the institutions of the new republic. They will usually do this as quickly as possible. Paint and sign manufacturers are one of the biggest beneficiaries of post-imperialism. India has followed this self-same pattern – but at its own pace and with its own sense of what is important.

There is a wonderful institution in Indian banking, now called the State Bank of India. I have dealt with that bank over many years and have genuinely admired some of its bankers as the best I have met anywhere in the world. I have also grown old waiting for the bank to make the odd decision.

It was in 1955 that the Imperial Bank of India changed its name to the State Bank of India at the behest of the Union government that owns it. In retrospect eight years seems a short time, but that is how long the Imperial Bank remained a visible symbol of Empire after 1947 when India achieved independence. There can have been no advantage to India, so nobody bothered. There are other examples of this pragmatic indifference.

The real focus here is on place names, where the speed of change has been remarkably slow. Some of the metros, the largest cities in India, have officially changed their names to one of the previous forms used before the Brits – and probably the Moguls – arrived. The only one that has really caught on is Chennai. It is very strange for anyone to use the imperial name, Madras; which is all the more confusing for Brits, who know Madras as a particularly hot curry. You will still hear Madras used occasionally in India, but if it is, the person concerned is trying very hard indeed to be polite and obviously feels uncomfortable.

The real acid test is Mumbai, the new – well, possibly one of the old – names for Bombay. My experience is that if I say Mumbai, any Indians will correct me and call it Bombay. If I say Bombay, there will be puzzled looks before someone interprets this impossibly difficult solecism as Mumbai. The answer is that no one, including the Indians, actually knows what the commercially advantageous form of the city name is.

Delhi is Delhi still, and New Delhi is just that, though for all the world it looks old and exactly like one of the biggest symbols of imperialism in the world.

India, bizarrely enough, remains India. Every Indian I have asked, after being puzzled that anyone should bother to ask what the country should be called, has eventually come to the conclusion that it is a good question, but not one that anyone has ever thought seriously about asking. In any case, I don't think Bharat will catch on now.

Out of all this confusion, I can state one thing with little certainty other than that I will be contradicted, although I know it is perfectly true. No one that I've met in India, including Bengalis and inhabitants of the place, can call Calcutta "Kolkata" with a straight face.

As for the new names for the international airports, I doubt many people will be able to tell you what they are. You certainly won't be able to repeat the names without seeing the words written down. You will hardly be able to repeat the names *with* the words written down.

OFF YOU GO

By now you may be as thoroughly confused as most Indians are by place names. The taxi journey you are facing can be a little daunting, so it's just as well to clutch at a few straws.

The meeting you are about to go to won't be the problem. After all the other cultural and social issues, you can almost relax. It will be conducted with the utmost politeness, will last twice as long as you expect, and will have started on time. Not the time you expected – but after all, any particular time is only a target.

Before we get to that meeting, then, some more timely preparation!

8
IST – Indian Stretchable Time

"There's only one word in Hindi that you'll need to know to understand this country," the chief executive of a major government-owned Indian corporation told me. "That word is *kal*." We were discussing how we needed to take forward our proposal to improve his business.

He had a most impressive, indeed enormous, office, book lined and decorated with an eclectic range of statues, carvings, and paintings. My potential customer's accent was naturally far more British and upper class than mine, betraying a long sojourn at British educational establishments.

It was my first trip to India and having picked my way through a decaying office block, with bits falling off every wall, the floor more like a ruin that was in the process of excavation than a serious walkway, I was probably betraying a lack of comprehension.

"You see, kal means something like the Spanish mañana, but it isn't anywhere near as specific," he continued. I now knew what to expect, as I've made the joke myself more than once: "Kal obviously isn't as pressing a term as mañana."

In fact, I was wrong. "Mañana is far more specific than kal," he said, "because mañana only means sometime in the future. Kal means yesterday as well as tomorrow. It really means something like 'not today' or 'not now.'" He added: "Any culture that doesn't need to know the difference between yesterday and tomorrow is clearly unique."

At the end of the meeting, I asked him when he wanted the proposal in. "Oh, kal," he replied. It was a delicious joke, made all the more acceptable because there wasn't a hint of a smile anywhere on his face.

My American colleague wrote him off as clearly unhinged.

Some time later that year, incidentally, the chief executive was arrested on corruption charges. I was extremely concerned. "No need to worry," a colleague said, "it's political. There's not a word of truth in it. He's innocent." Nine months later he was released and all charges were dropped. I mentioned this to the same colleague. "Oh," he said, "it's political. If he's been let off he must be guilty as hell." There's an important insight into India in that type of paradox.

I learnt a great deal from the meetings I had with that man. Nuggets that seemed to hold the key to India, however elusively, flowed from him all the time. I once asked him whether there was still any lingering resentment about the Raj, the period when India was part of the British Empire. He acted as though he was baffled. I assumed that I had transgressed some unwritten rule by introducing into the conversation something so horrible as to be unmentionable.

"Not sure what you mean," he began. "You were only here for 150 years. Whyever would we be bothered by something like that? Now the Moguls, they're a different kettle of fish. They were here for 450 years. There's still a lingering resentment of them. Of course, they only left 300 years ago."

The point about these illustrations is that they don't mean whatever you originally think they mean. If you can keep that in mind, especially when you are absolutely certain that you understand something in or about India, you will probably win through.

The right attitude is to comprehend that you won't understand but must simply grasp that the Indian approach is to encompass everything, and select whatever is needed at any one moment. The whole attitude to time is just like that. Time isn't an absolute in India: it's a moving target and once it's gone, it's always there. Indian S t r e t c h a b l e Time, the usual version of what IST stands for, is a brilliant encapsulation of so many attitudes and perspectives. However, it isn't mystical.

INDIAN STRETCHABLE TIME – THE FULL STORY

Indian Standard Time, IST, is exactly that: there is no daylight saving or summer time. It remains the same all the year round. As India is so large, it straddles two time zones. Having two separate times was clearly best avoided and the country adopted a compromise single time zone, which is half an hour later than it should be in the east and half an hour earlier than it should be in the west. During the European and American winter months, India is therefore 4.5 hours ahead of Europe, 5.5 hours ahead of the UK, and 10.5 hours ahead of Eastern Standard Time. During the summer months, it is 3.5, 4.5, and 9.5 hours ahead respectively.

That half hour is the very devil, and while it should present intelligent, literate, and numerate people with absolutely no issues, it in fact causes endless confusion.

Fixing the time of a telephone conference between India and the West, aside from the fact that it won't start at the time all have agreed on, is almost beyond the wit of humans to do. I've found you have to take a military approach. It's not quite necessary to synchronize watches, but you do have to agree what time it is in each individual place and then fix the time relative to that to have any chance of success. It can be cumbersome to say that the call will be in 25 hours from now, but it gives you a sporting chance, whereas 08.00 EST, 13.00 GMT, 14.00 European, and 18.30 IST, let alone it being kal, will simply not work.

There is a really good trick to let you know what the time is in GMT from IST, or from GMT to IST: look at your watch upside down and read it as though it is the right way up. So 13.55 GMT will show as 19.25 IST; 13.55 IST will show as 07.25 GMT. I often doubt that this is true, partly because I find working in a duodecimal system quite counterintuitive, but it appears to work.

I told one colleague about this and he got very excited. He thought about it and told me he would start wearing two watches, one upside down. I didn't have the heart to tell him that if he was going to those lengths, he could have one watch on IST and one on GMT.

In any case, I find it easier simply to make mistakes over the time, and not knowing the exact time causes me far less angst when I am in India.

All this accuracy with time is, however, a complete waste of the very thing you are attempting to pin down. Being on time in India is an art form – and one that does not imply arriving at the time previously fixed. Any appointed time is only a target.

Westerners find time and timekeeping in India almost beyond understanding at first. As a person who considers being late an absolute nightmare, it was really hard for me. It's not that the concept of being late doesn't exist in India, it merely means something else. It's as though someone says to you when you're inevitably late: "Well, at least you tried." In the West, that isn't enough and could be sarcasm. In India, it's a plain statement of fact.

My first few days in India were an agony of what I would have seen as late arrivals. The clue that I was worrying unnecessarily was when we arrived 20 minutes late – surprisingly early in Indian terms – to see a particular chief executive. He showed us into his office some 30 minutes after the meeting should have begun, with an apology for keeping us waiting. I didn't know how to take this. My Indian colleagues were also baffled that he should make such an apology, but decided that it was because he was dealing with a Brit.

The following story sounds apocryphal, but I have had sworn statements that it is true. A European couple living in India were invited to the reception of a particularly special society wedding. (I was invited as well, but the invitation only arrived the day before the wedding and I was in the UK at the time. I was told that this wasn't because I was an afterthought and it wasn't intended to be rude. I have come to realize that this was probably true, which is worth remembering if you are invited at short notice to such an event.)

Knowing that it was India, the European couple left it until 8.30pm to turn up for the 7.30pm invitation time. They waited an hour and finally decided that they'd got the wrong night. It was the general consensus when the reception started, some 90 minutes later than that, that the European couple must have got the wrong night or had been incredibly impatient. That this issue was discussed endlessly for so long revealed how absolutely baffling it was to the Indians, who couldn't quite work out whether it was a deliberate snub.

With all these cross-cultural misunderstandings, it's usually fascinating to see how each side reacts and how the logic appears unchallengeable from either perspective.

You will find, however, that the western sense of deadlines and absolutes will permeate your business relationship as normally as in every other contract. The only trouble for me is that it always seems as though my Indian colleagues and suppliers are putting on an act just for me.

One further remark: IST seems much more reasonable, even to a westerner, when you're in India. When you get back to your own country, you will find IST quite as baffling as anyone who hasn't been there.

As a foreigner you will probably be treated at least once to an interesting scene last thing at night, especially if you have had dinner with a number of people you are due to meet the following day. The first time it happened to me, I found it remarkable.

Very solemnly, the most senior person checked what time everyone would be able to start the meeting the following day. It was agreed, after some discussion, that 9.30am was exactly the right compromise. The leader checked with everyone individually that 9.30 was fine. He'd been to a good management school. One by one we all agreed that 9.30 was the best time we could imagine. "OK," he said, "let's make it 10 then."

The meeting started in any case at 11am, as you would expect after a brief sojourn in the subcontinent, but the point is that the whole performance was a polite, if desperate, measure to make the foreigners feel at home.

Almost the opposite experience was when we had set up a large meeting for 5pm. When the first guest arrived at 5.15, he was greeted by the Indian host, who added without any irony at all: "I knew who would be early." You can imagine the complete bewilderment this caused to a couple of our people who were new to India.

ARRANGING TIMES FOR MEETINGS

The major advantage I have found with IST is that it makes it possible to meet senior people at the drop of a hat.

I have taken the 8am flight from Mumbai to Delhi, arriving at 10, with no appointment booked with a main board director of a major undertaking, and have been in front of that same person within the hour. I have explained to various Indian colleagues how I used to have to give almost two months' notice to meet an equivalent person in a UK bank, and how this seemed quite reasonable to me. My Indian colleagues could always see through me. They knew that was just the sort of exaggeration I would make up for a laugh.

The corollary, however, is that any meeting arranged with much more than three hours' notice is likely to be canceled. It will be called postponed, but in reality it will be canceled. As a general rule, I would suggest that any meeting booked more than a week in advance will not take place – and it certainly won't take place at any time on the day it was previously arranged.

You may remember in Chapter 6 I stressed the need to take formal wear with you however casual the day's program might appear. The number of times I have been sitting in the back of a Mumbai taxi or car and received a call on my cellphone redirecting me to an urgent meeting with a deputy or full managing director is uncountable. (I could actually list sitting in the back of cars in Mumbai as one of my hobbies, because I spend more hours a year doing that than playing chess or even gardening.)

If you are in Sacramento or Frankfurt or Birmingham, this sort of rapid change in your daily agenda smacks of poor organization, and my head office criticized me on more than one occasion, but it is the remarkable reality of life as you bump over the potholes in Mumbai.

There is a marvelous word that appears to have little actual practical meaning in India, but sums much of this up: "preponed." You might initially think it is the opposite of postponed, and that's almost certainly its origin. It does have that feel about it, but I have been to a preponed meeting that started without embarrassment after the start time of the originally scheduled meeting. On the other hand, as the time difference was only about five minutes and you are beginning to appreciate what IST means, you can see the necessity for the concept even in such a circumstance.

My US multinational had a regional vice-president to whom I reported. His secretary and personal assistant in the UK was brilliant at arranging diaries and keeping several people's electronic diaries in sync. Because I was traveling very close to Afghanistan, or at least in that vague direction – East – our US masters and security chiefs insisted that Elaine kept a tight leash on me, knew where I was from hour to hour, and had my schedule updated as soon as it changed, just in case the marines had to come and rescue me.

I did my best to keep her up to date. She used to get irritated with me that there were so many changes. I could see her point and it was quite reasonable to have that view sitting in the UK. Latterly I think even she became inured to putting one word in the diary for each day: "India."

If a fixed time during a day is rather more vague than you might expect, some other time phrases threw me for a while and might need explanation, and will show you why a meeting fixed more than a few hours away is quite unlikely to happen. It was only on my third visit that I really worked out what "today," "tomorrow," "next week," and "two weeks" mean in an Indian lexicon within India.

Today means that there is an excellent chance of the event happening fairly soon, and certainly within 24 hours of the statement. It's the closest you will get to an approximation you can rely on.

Tomorrow means that while there is no guarantee, there is a strong determination for it to happen. There is no actual commitment to it happening within even the next 48 hours, but there is a shared realization that it ought to occur sometime.

Next week means that the event is obviously desirable, it is clearly difficult to refuse to contemplate it, but no commitment has been entered into. As far as I can understand it has few temporal connotations at all, but is a fairly warm endorsement of necessity.

Two weeks is a time period that is beyond the wit of man to encompass, stretching forward – and back – to a time unimaginable. You might as well dream of having tea without sugar or a whole day without a power interruption. It is that sort of fantastic concept.

Trying to map those understandings of time-related phrases onto a US corporation plodding steadily on with weekly outlooks, monthly forecasts, quarterly results, and the most sophisticated customer relationship management software that looks a year out is quite a challenge. Sorry: no challenge at all, it's just impossible. The only approach I eventually managed to take was to project a time scale onto what we were doing and add two quarters, half a year in European speak, to everything I had to report to the US. With the benefit of hindsight, I'd make that nine months.

There is a further twist to all this, however. In discussions with foreigners, Indians may not mean what the foreigner thinks they mean about time, but they don't necessarily have the Indian connotation either. The more you are accepted into Indian society and culture, the more likely it is that the Indian meanings will be the ones to trust.

You can appreciate how important it is to understand which of the two perspectives, Indian or western, is more applicable to the discussions. It won't be absolute, no matter how clued in to India you are or how aware the Indians are of western attitudes. It's not something you will ever be totally comfortable with, but it can be handled. After a while, you may even enjoy the uncertainty and indefiniteness. That's probably the time to think about that return ticket.

That's another point. In my first three years traveling to India I never once returned home on the flight I booked. That wasn't always because my return was delayed; I have returned home earlier than fixed, too. There are, of course, fixed-return air tickets at a cheaper rate than I was paying. I can't imagine what they are for.

I might as well give you another warning about return flights here. The majority of flights to the West leave in the early hours of the morning: 2.40am is quite popular for some reason. This may well be the Saturday morning flight, but you will be getting to the airport on Friday night. There is a tendency to call 2.40am on Saturday, not unreasonably, Friday night. But if you book a flight for Friday, you may arrive at the international airport to be told that your flight took off that morning.

Double check with the travel agent. Put it in writing. Insist.

It will still happen, and it did to me even with the international travel agency that was a subsidiary of a major international financial services company, which I had to use by company policy. By taking real documented care, you will at least have an audit trail – even if it shows, as it did once for me, that *you* have made the mistake.

Holidays – national and local, official and unofficial

National holidays flow on well within the spirit of kal and IST. With so many religions, it's almost impossible to visit India without getting caught up in a religious festival of some sort. They are usually not national holidays, as India is a secular republic. However, they can be general, nationwide, and observed locally in varying ways.

In my initial naivety, on my first visit to India and wanting to plan my year ahead, I asked for a list of public holidays. I received a remarkably limited list. Two of them sound suspiciously similar, but are separated by eight months. One is the National Day and the other is the Republic Day.

The list of holidays wasn't worth the paper it was written on. What with official, whatever that means, and unofficial holidays, religious and non-religious days, you will always be surprised by some holiday or another. Most Indians appear to be surprised by them too, as I rarely got any warning before a scheduled trip. On the first morning after arriving, I was usually asked why I had chosen this week as at least two days were holidays.

My first January in Mumbai, I chanced to be there during the Ambedkar festival. This is by no means official or religious or fully recognized. State institutions, like the State Bank or Air India, appear to carry on working.

Dr. Ambedkar was one of the authors, if not *the* author, of the Indian constitution. He had a particular concern for the untouchables and for equality of castes and was a remarkable man.

In his honor, a large part of Mumbai came to a halt. The crowds meant that we had to park about a mile from Nariman Point, where our meeting was to be held. I found it a remarkable experience to walk through a crowd of about one million – so the newspapers said, and I would have thought it was more – to get to a business meeting in our best clothes, on an extraordinarily hot, sunny day, when no one was apparently on holiday. Indeed, no one was officially on holiday. I liked it that the crowds didn't seem to mind us either, despite the fact that we stuck out like people who turned up at a party at the appointed time.

In addition to this informal collection of holidays, there are formal ones when the whole place does come to a halt. The hotels keep going, of course. They will usually provide some sort of celebration, like fireworks for Diwali, the festival of light.

The last time I was staying at a hotel during Diwali there was just such a display. Of course, no one was allowed outside where the fireworks were being set off. Promptly at 9.35pm, after an announced 7pm start time, the first rocket limped into the sky, and from the lounge on the fourth floor we had a brilliant view as it exploded rather prematurely. That was the last firework we saw, as all the other rockets and mortars screamed into the sky and disappeared immediately from our view, which was cut off by the top of the windows.

There are also strikes, or bandhs. Bandhs are unpredictable strikes that can be called for all sorts of reasons, generally without much warning. They can be violent affairs, and I would recommend you either stay in your hotel or in your office. I have only been caught up in one that was sprung on a city quite suddenly. It was sobering, but not without its lighter moments in what I saw. I never did get to the bottom of what it was about, but it wasn't industrial action about wages and conditions, at least not on the surface. I traveled through a large demonstration – naturally on the actual roadway through the middle of the people demonstrating – and got back to the hotel thinking that it had been peaceful and good-natured, only to learn that there were serious injuries as tempers had worsened later in the day.

On the other hand, you usually won't have any trouble walking around in the metros. I've never felt threatened, except by beggars at the Gateway to India in Mumbai, which was intimidating. My Indian colleagues tell me that women can also walk around without much fear of harassment, but one female colleague who came to India said she wasn't entirely comfortable walking around and wouldn't recommend it.

So, assuming that you have managed to arrange a day and time for your meeting, and that it is actually going to take place, the next chapter discusses what you can expect at the meeting itself.

9
MEETING DIFFERENCES

What we have discussed so far should have prepared you a little for your first meeting. Let's cover the parts of that meeting that will be familiar to an American, Belgian, or Brit:

❑ It will probably start.
❑ Time will elapse.
❑ You will end the meeting.

In those senses only, it is perfectly similar to a meeting in the US, the UK, Germany, France, or Belgium.

Not only will the time of the meeting have a rather quantum relationship with the appointed time, the times of the day at which meetings are held will probably take you aback. As you will already have read, breakfast meetings aren't all that common or popular in India. However, the rest of the day will be occupied with meetings in one way or another, even if they don't actually take place.

You can probably understand now why it is perfectly sensible to fix a meeting for midnight. You won't otherwise be able to guarantee that it will be possible for you to be at it. Since this gives an end time of about 2am, I can't recommend such an approach. I'm not a late-night person anyway. The only thing that keeps me going through such absurdities is the fact that it's only 9.30pm back in the UK.

There is, of course, no such thing as an average day. Nevertheless, the average day in India will be very long!

You mustn't expect the normal rhythm of western business meetings. Ever since I started attending or holding business meetings they have followed a distinct, allotted time that does vary a little by country. In the UK and in the parts of Europe where I've done business, that's an hour. In the US it's either just less than an hour, characterized as a progress meeting, or three hours, characterized as decision time. The first type of US meeting is pragmatically less than an hour, so that you can have back-to-back meetings throughout the day without time slipping away.

In most of these cases, western meetings start with a few minutes of light, phatic conversation. In the UK it's about the weather or the state of your lawn. In Italy opening remarks always sound to me like a violent disagreement. When questioned about the row later, it usually turns out to be something far more trivial and not an argument at all. In the US there is a similar period of polite conversation that is unfathomable to a Brit, but it normally revolves around sport, as in India.

In India among Indians or those who are counted as Indians, the subject is cricket. I can't say that nothing else has ever been discussed in my presence, but the answer is the subject is still cricket. Cricket discussions can start as you begin to shake hands – something that can involve shaking the same hand twice or more – and the discussion will carry on for quite some time. The time spent on these courtesies is rather longer than the equivalent in a US or European business meeting, which is true of most other elements of these get-togethers. As you start to sit down, which is a terribly uncomfortable ritual as usually no one knows where to sit and there is a great deal of waiting until someone else sits down, the cricket discussion continues. During the provision of tea or coffee, the talk is about cricket.

I usually get terribly muddled in all of this, and I actually understand the game. As one brought up on Geoffrey Boycott – an English batsman who was relentlessly determined, grinding away interminably for several days with perhaps 18 runs to show for it, but crucially not out – I can appreciate the finer elements of cricket.

The Indian cricket team, however, goes in for scoring runs, making spectacular catches, having a wicket keeper who looks all of 12 or 13 years old, and generally providing enjoyment. As with most things Indian, you can see the similarities with the concepts a Brit might know, but the differences are far more obvious. I've even known Americans and Europeans start to take an interest in cricket when watching India play.

If in the West it is unwise to discuss politics, religion, and sex, it is probably unwise to venture too deeply into the labyrinth that is Indian cricket. I have found that a few well-timed nods get me through the 10 or 15 minutes of small talk at the beginning of any meeting.

One reason for mentioning this is that if you are in a meeting and cricket is discussed at any length, it is a real indication that you are being accepted. Indian business people are too aware of American and European sensibilities and far too polite to impose such a discussion otherwise. The highest praise you can get from an Indian is to be told: "Great. You're thinking almost like an Indian."

I have listened carefully to and watched what is going on in Indian meetings and have decided that they are the opposite of meetings with Japanese people. In Japan, what goes unsaid is powerful. In India, unless something is said, repeatedly, often without any variation at all, it will not be seen as significant. If you are of the school based on "say what you are going to talk about, talk about it, say what you've talked about, and leave," you will still be astounded by the repetition.

Once the meeting itself starts, what do you need to know about the people around the table?

TRADERS FIRST AND LAST

The one real key to business life in India is to understand that Indians are above all else traders. Let me take a universal example to illustrate the mentality that you must come to terms with.

If you have ever bought a second-hand car from a garage, you will have the essential ingredients. When you bought the car, it is likely that all you were allowed to see were its amazing qualities, which were pointed out by the sales person in an extraordinarily positive picture of an ideal vehicle. Your own trade-in, by the time the same sales person had finished with it, resembled nothing more than a liability, crumbling into a pile of rust in front of your eyes. You should have been only too glad to part with it. You can then imagine how selectively different your own rust bucket will have become as the sales person points out what a treasure and investment it is to the next potential owner. All you have to do is transpose that to any interaction in India.

When *The Times of India* solemnly recalls on Independence Day that it is more than 50 years since India threw off the yoke of tyranny, bloodshed, and evil, that is just as true as the aphorism elegantly tossed in my direction that British rule was nothing of much moment. As with all traders, it depends on context and appropriateness.

If Brits look at India, they see a railway network that wouldn't have been there in that form without the British Empire. They see the Gothic buildings that masquerade as town or city halls, libraries, or museums. English road signs, English place names, monuments to British royalty, like the Gateway to India in Mumbai or the Victoria and Albert Memorial in Calcutta, and many other artefacts will proclaim a legacy of cultural improvement and cross-fertilization. Above all, there is the fact that *The Times of India* is printed in English, as are other important newspapers.

If Americans look at India, they see a muddle, where everything is left at the stage we all refer to as "that'll do for now." There will nevertheless be a sort of fellow feeling, possibly engendered by the fact that the US also threw off the yoke of tyranny held down on it by the Brits.

It is actually more likely that the fellow feeling will be stimulated by the fact that around ten of the hundred richest Californians are PIOs. PIOs are not to be confused with NRIs. PIOs are Persons of Indian Origin – that is, naturalized or second-generation citizens of a new country – whereas NRIs are non-resident Indians, who are still Indian citizens. By what might seem a mistaken logic, PIOs are currently very much more in favor with the Indian government and NRIs are less well regarded. It's actually not that daft: on the whole PIOs are much richer than NRIs.

When Indians look at India, the picture is quite different, even though it takes in all of the elements above. What they see is opportunity. Yes, there are the railways. Yes, there was the Amritsar massacre. And your point is?

If it helps the sale, then Indian railways owe their existence to the Brits. The Gateway to India, let alone India Gate in Delhi and the astonishing government buildings in New Delhi designed by Lutyens, are features and benefits that contribute to the greatness of India. After all, whatever the Gateway to India might have been built for, it was also the backdrop to that epochal moment when the last British troops marched out of India in 1947. Nevertheless, throwing off the yoke of Empire will be gladly shared with any American citizens. If it doesn't help the sale, however, it will be left unregarded.

This sounds cynical; it isn't. Indian business people are patriotic and very conscious of being part of a wonderful country, to a degree that matches any other nationality. It's just that you can take that for granted, as they mostly do.

Any conversation with an Indian is predicated on the idea that there is a deal to be had. More than lists of actions, proper minutes, shared understanding, and concepts of partnership, this is what a meeting with Indians is all about.

There are manufacturers in India. There are ascetics. There are religious people. There are politicians. There are all the variations in people that a billion souls can contain. Yet when all of this is taken into account, you can generally simply focus on what deal is to be done.

POLITENESS

There is a complication, however, that sits rather oddly with the idea of Indians as out-and-out traders.

The western concept of business people is that they are hard-nosed. Meetings might not descend into rudeness or bullying, though I have seen both, but westerners do cut to the point and use as many clichés as we can think of to describe being brutally frank.

Indians in general are the politest people you can imagine. Giving offense, even if it is unintended and provoked by the crassest behavior in the other party, is a crime against humanity, let alone the gods, God, and the future – and by extension, the past. I have received a sincere apology, falteringly delivered by someone who was apparently my superior, for an exchange of remarks that were to me about on the level of an observation about the weather. The person concerned had genuinely not slept worrying about it.

Indians are so polite that you must always be aware they will have extreme difficulty using the word "no," even when they might mean it. I'm not sure an Indian can even mean "no" without some threat to his or her sleeping patterns.

YES

Into this mixture comes the word "yes." That word is almost the most important linguistic introduction to Indian business life. In almost every business culture throughout the world "yes" means something different and the way it is used is very often significant. To an American, stereotyped or not, unless the yes is accompanied by whoops of joy and exclamations of excitement, as well as a rush of enthusiasm, preferably false, it means very little and certainly nothing positive. To a Brit, a yes that is not expressed quietly and with absolutely no enthusiasm at all means very little. Countless times I have seen Brits and Americans saying yes to each other in their own different ways, agreeing absolutely, and completely misunderstanding what the other means.

There is a rider to this. In more sophisticated, large multinational companies, the word yes, however embellished, has only one meaning, and that is completely negative. It means "over my dead body."

To a Japanese business person, the English word yes means only that he or she has been in the same meeting for the last two hours meticulously making notes and teasing out shades of meaning, and has formed an entirely different impression of what has been going on.

To an Indian business person, yes is the most awkward word in the dictionary – not least because of the Indian appreciation of irony. Irony is as full a part of Indian conversation as it is for a Brit. Because yes may have an ironic quality, all its other problems merely multiply. Just imagine taking every sentence in this chapter as ironic at the same time as appreciating its literal meaning, and then anticipate the effect on your sanity.

On top of this, India has a hierarchical society, as we have seen. Hierarchies depend on not giving offense. If you can't give offense up or down the hierarchy, you can't possibly say no to anything. "Yes" therefore has to stand for all sorts of words and can mean anything. It can be positive, negative, a contemplative pause, a way of fobbing off a young child – and worst of all, it cannot be interpreted by an outsider.

The answer is: don't take yes for an answer.

I have too often left the main meeting in India to create a small meeting with a subset of those involved – a favorite Indian approach – and found that we haven't yet even got to what I regard as the first stage, despite the main meeting having so far been characterized by what I took to be violent agreement, centered on the word yes.

My only method of achieving any sort of communication in such meetings focused on the Indian domestic market is to insist on being accompanied by at least one Indian. In addition, that person must have been convinced that I regard *not* upsetting me as extremely impolite and an offense against my esteemed position in life.

I still don't know what's going on in meetings, but I have learnt to say yes and for it not to be ironic or British or American. (I can't for the life of me give a Japanese yes.) After the meeting a gentle interrogation of no more than three or four hours usually results in me understanding from my Indian colleague the dynamics of what actually happened and what has been agreed.

The real advantage that you as a foreigner will have in any meetings like this is that when you say yes, all but the most internationally sophisticated Indians won't have a clue what you mean either. Even those NRIs or PIOs who do understand will only know that you probably mean something else.

OTHER LINGUISTIC TRAPS

There are all sorts of linguistic traps in taking Indian English, US English, and UK English as having common meanings for words. If you are used to the obvious problems between those who speak US English and those who speak UK English, you will already be on your guard and this need not detain us much here. However, as an example, the word "rascal" in the UK and the US generally applies to a child who has been naughty. In India, a rascal is a thoroughly bad piece of work that you wouldn't want to meet wandering around Mumbai of a night.

There are also some common usages that you might find odd. The main one I meet every day is dropping the definite article. It is far more normal for an Indian to say "I'll meet you at office" than "I'll meet you at *the* office." You will find that surprisingly offputting at first and then not notice it at all.

CORRUPTION

More directly important, there are a number of sensitive subjects that have to be faced, including bribery and corruption.

On one of my first trips to India I was discussing how to work with an Indian software company with its chairman. Suddenly he launched into:

"And you've no need to worry about bribing." I hadn't been. There's nothing like being told not to worry about something that is well below your consciousness! There was a pause in which I had long enough to wonder what he would say. He continued: "I'll take care of all that."

This brought me face to face with something I had been concerned about but very few people actually mention. Nevertheless, on the grounds that no government sets up a Corruption Vigilance Committee merely to give some relatives a job, I had known this was an issue that would raise itself at some point.

I have come to the conclusion that India probably has no more corruption, epitomized by bribery, than many countries. There are scandals, but there have been scandals in the UK and the US. There will always be individuals capable of villainy. Scandals are probably a good sign, as you can only have a scandal when the corruption is brought out into the open. The real difference comes in what people like to imagine are the gray areas.

Contributions to political parties – and, as often, individual politicians and their campaign funds – are one such gray area. It's difficult to judge as a foreigner how India measures up against western practice. The point is that you don't have to worry about these contributions at all, especially as they are more focused on the domestic market. These are internal affairs, strictly within Indian companies and rarely talked about or admitted. You merely have to know two things: that such contributions exist; and what your attitude toward them is.

The more difficult area for me is in the relatively small payments that undoubtedly change hands. Here I am talking about sums of about $2 or INR100 paid to ensure that a paper form moves from one desk to the next. I am told these payments are essential. I don't want to make comparisons with western practice, but I do know that with a $1 million development deal depending on a piece of imported hardware arriving at the appropriate office in Bangalore, it's very difficult to take a completely high moral stand.

Result: I believe that large-scale corruption is no more rife than in most comparable places although it is certainly present; contributing to political funds, presumably to gain influence, is widespread; and minor bribes to minor officials are part of the fabric of life.

I'm not suggesting that you turn a blind eye to such practices. I didn't, and I think I may have lost a deal or two because I wouldn't endorse them.

On the other hand, I was certainly successful without indulging in any bribery.

Indian companies will give you presents, by the way, and this is done openly and as part of the standard politeness. I have always found it difficult to accept, but I was told that not to do so would offend my guests. (You get into one of those paradoxes, where not accepting a present suggests that you think your hosts are trying to bribe you, and so they are offended at you for being so wrongly sensitive, because that is the last thing on their mind.) Some of the presents were exquisite, although in western terms not that expensive. I always attempted to declare them in writing to my own company and simply felt uncomfortable.

Looking at the opposite case, of you having to provide presents to companies you might meet, if you are like me you can just ignore it. Indian companies in general understand that it is not part of the cultural mix. (If they don't, I suggest that is a good indicator and a reason for qualifying them out of dealing with you.) Diaries and calendars at the western New Year are usually a very welcome token, especially to middle management and below.

If you have read my introduction to Indian Stretchable Time in Chapter 8, you will no doubt wonder what on earth the calendars are actually used for.

MANAGEMENT CONSULTANCIES

The use of an international management consultancy to back up figures, marketing strategies, and presentations is very common in India. You need to be aware of what it means.

In what follows, I am by no means suggesting that there is anything specifically underhand, illegal, illicit, or untoward in the use of management consultancies in India. It isn't that much different from elsewhere in the world. The motive in employing the consultancies is sometimes a little further removed from the immediate purpose than might seem appropriate, but the motive is usually more openly declared than might be expected too.

I will focus on one example. I had been developing a strategy to take call centers of the most basic kind to India, and was also interested in the technology and companies that might provide the service for me, or at least build the operation. I had a series of conversations with one particular Indian company and it was clear that they didn't know an awful lot about the subject. They were entering the market, however, and their lack of track record in that particular field was not necessarily a showstopper to me.

On my return to the UK, I was invited to meet the owner of the company at a hotel in London. He was accompanied by an Indian partner from one of the international management consultancies. We discussed everything, and the partner added not a word. I tried a few direct questions to him, but got non-committal replies. I took the attitude that I wasn't paying, so I wasn't going to get comments let alone answers, but that cynicism was misplaced.

After the meeting, I had a drink with the company owner. I pointed out the lack of contribution from the management consultancy partner. I said that he appeared to know less than I did about call centers; at least I had been involved with one.

I got a smile. In some confusion, I asked him point blank what value the management consultant was adding. He gave me a bigger smile.

It turned out that the fees for the management consultancy were part of the marketing communications budget. The owner was well aware that this consultant, not to say the whole management consultancy, had nothing to offer technically, operationally, or managerially. Its value to the owner was in being able to say to western companies who were thinking of putting their call centers offshore that the strategic planning for the Indian company was in the hands of this international management consultancy.

It was a comfort food or security blanket for western companies. Rather expensive, but no doubt cheaper than other forms of public relations. It was also not as expensive as employing the US end of the consultancy.

INDIVIDUAL INSECURITY

There is another sensitive issue that I should mention. Needless to say, I've checked this with a good cross-section of my Indian friends, colleagues, and acquaintances. They have agreed that what I'm going to describe is still a real issue. It has changed even in the years I have been dealing with India, but it is a cross-current of which you should be aware.

Quite rightly, Indians are extraordinarily proud of what they have achieved economically over the last 20 years. They are justly proud of having the largest democracy in the world. The Indian diaspora is one of the most successful globally. India's reputation is at the highest level in many fields, not least mathematics, and is growing in sectors such as pharmaceuticals.

Nevertheless, there is still sometimes a sense of insecurity when dealing with the West. I need to give you a scale to judge it by. It's not at the level I encountered in South Wales some 20 years ago, which went like this.

"Who lives in Blaencwm?" I asked, genuinely interested in the residents of this small village at the top of the Rhondda valley, previously a coal-mining area.

"What's wrong with that?" came the defensive reply.

Yet you may find there is some bristling or a downcast face at something you have innocently said that appears to disparage something about India or an individual. I still make the same type of mistake from time to time, because in India I am in an environment full of dynamism, excitement, confidence, and activity and I get lulled into a false misunderstanding of some deep feelings.

While individual confidence among Indians in India is rising perceptibly as the years go by, there is a fragility underlying some of it that is revealed in such sensitive moments. And the absolute need to be polite will make it very difficult for you to see it unless you are aware it might be there.

UNDERSTANDING EACH OTHER

India could not be the successful business country it is without there being the possibility of mutual comprehension and appreciation. I've rather concentrated on the pitfalls, on the basis that few people need help with the easier aspects of life. I don't think too many books are written on how to breathe, for instance.

I am, however, most conscious of something I've left out of all these warnings, intimations of doom and gloom, and horrors of far-too-sweet tea.

Not surprisingly for a Brit, with our penchant for deferred gratification, what I've omitted is enjoyment. To Americans and many Europeans, enjoyment is a relatively simple concept. You may have noticed that Brits are not all that good at enjoying themselves, but in India even a Brit can find enjoyment.

Westerners may tear their hair out over time in India. A meeting will drag on as they slowly turn into an air-conditioned ice block stuck in a foetal position, slumped for good in one of the pervasive low-slung metal-framed sofas. It'll be midnight before you know it – and even more alarmingly 7.30am very quickly after that. You will, however, find enough humanity and fun and laughter, and unexpected treats in words and attitudes, to make you sing.

The following anecdote still tickles me. We were in the back of a taxi in Mumbai, going along a dual carriageway. As usual we were looking for the offices we had been due at some 30 minutes before. Finding specific offices in an Indian city isn't a science – it's an art. Since it is an art, everyone can have an opinion and all opinions are of equal value. Nevertheless, despite severe disagreements, I've usually eventually found myself in the right place.

My Indian companion spotted the target office entrance on the other side of the dual carriageway barrier, which was too high to cross in the car. The same person immediately spotted up ahead a "No U Turn" sign. "Great," he said, "there's the place we can turn round." Only in India would the highway authority be so thoughtful as to place a No U Turn sign at the gap in the central reservation in order to show where it was possible to turn round!

By the way, when I explained why this made me laugh so much, my Indian colleague could see my point, but wasn't sure why I was making so much of it.

ENDING THE MEETING

Back to your meeting. In the West I'm a dab hand at managing meetings. However, I've tried in India and have come to the conclusion that Indian business meetings cannot be steered by non-Indians. After an hour in which I would have wrapped up, summarized, allocated actions, identified the date for next meeting some two months ahead, said goodbye, and generally completed the whole matter in my head, we will in contrast be heading very gently for some sort of agreement about what we are to disagree about. I'm making no suggestion at all that this is better or worse, just that it is always a trial for me.

A decent meeting takes about 30 minutes from the moment you know it's really finishing to the point where you are outside the office block. If you think I exaggerate, time it!

A real Indian meeting starts to conclude and wind down with a series of agreed actions. (Pay no attention. These are agreed at the meeting. Even if they are written down at the time or subsequently, these actions will be the subject of reinterpretation. There is a logic about this, but not one that I can generally appreciate if I am not in the subcontinent.)

Standing up will take place during this process. So will sitting down again, but not until you have probably shaken hands with most people and things in the room – even Ganesh if he's relatively near. More standing up will follow, and you will eventually leave the room together with your host or hosts. They will generally accompany you to the elevator. All this time the business of the meeting will still be going on.

When the elevator arrives, shake hands. As you all enter the elevator, including your hosts, the conversation will probably continue. Usually the final shaking of hands to conclude the meeting will take place in the elevator, as your host or hosts will stay on board to return to the dizzy heights. I have, it must be said, shaken hands finally again for the last time actually outside the office block, but only once.

At this point the content and substance of the meeting will be pretty clear to you. They will, however, bear little relation to what has really happened.

Sitting in the UK, I can feel my frustration rising. In Delhi or Chennai, I can almost enjoy these experiences because they are so far removed from my normal life and expectations.

You may nevertheless see why, although I'm not a big drinker at all, even I take keeping malaria at bay with a stiff gin and tonic so seriously once I get back to the hotel in the early evening, ready for the next shift of meetings.

MAKING IT WORK IN INDIA

The cultural understanding I hope you have gained from these chapters will provide you with a richer perspective on what the country and its people have to offer, as well as giving you more confidence to gain business advantage in working with India. Part III explores specifically how you can make the most of the opportunities for your own business.

Part III

What's Right for You

10
Making the Right Decision

You have reached the conclusion that offshoring may well be beneficial to your business, and you have decided that India is a country worth investigating to find the best supplier for your needs. What do you do now?

First, you will need to create a business plan. This is a document that includes much more information than you might think strictly necessary and addresses the assumptions you are making in your proposal to go offshore. What is discussed here won't be the full plan that is accepted by the board on a nod after it's been through all the bureaucratic checks and balances. This is the real document that you need to prepare to establish the necessity of moving processes offshore, thereby convincing skeptics and removing political fiefdoms from positions of influence. You need to show that you are developing a sound new direction for the company.

It is vital that it is a business plan and not simply a financial projection or an anticipated profit and loss account. It must deal with all of the issues and expose the apparently softer areas, like increased customer satisfaction, as well as the hard reality of a projected cash flow. The financial projection is absolutely necessary, but the business plan is more important.

There is a wide range of formats for such a document. An example of the headings that can be used appears below. This is not meant to inhibit your approach, but to suggest areas that will need to be included. The most significant of these areas are discussed in more detail in this chapter.

❑ Business plan objective
❑ Management summary
❑ Background
❑ Existing issues
❑ Assumptions

❏ Proposal and recommendations
❏ Measures and financial projections
❏ Actions
❏ Additional information as appendices.

The most important heading, other than the proposal and the financial projection, is that dealing with assumptions. This aspect of the plan is properly open to review by other people. They may not have enough specialist knowledge of the items covered elsewhere to add meaningfully to the debate about them, but they should be able to challenge the assumptions you are making and test their validity. If you get those right, the proposal will win through.

This chapter is written from the perspective of the person who has to create or at least sponsor the business plan. It is equally useful from the point of view of people who have to review such a plan, because it outlines the various elements, such as hidden costs, that you should be looking for. If you know what the producer of the plan is trying to achieve, you can often understand more clearly how the various elements in the plan are being created and where the likely holes are, for the benefit of both your company and the person producing the plan.

Assumptions

It is relatively easy to make it appear financially beneficial to take your business to India, because of the cost savings you can achieve. However, offshoring only, or even primarily, for cost savings is the wrong perspective. The real focus is where you try to create value around other business benefits.

All the cultural quirks already described, such as objectives not quite being what a western mind might want and IST not being an exact science, point to the fact that doing business with India will challenge your own assumptions about how agile and flexible you are. In India there is always another way of doing something. A cousin or a brother-in-law will turn up at the right moment, ready to save the day. Putting that into the business plan as an assumption in a way that will escape the beady eye of some cynic paid to dismiss all innovation will tax your ingenuity.

This kind of flexibility is built into working with you by Indian companies and it can get your business through the most difficult scrapes. This adds to the earlier emphasis on understanding one another's intentions. If you are automatically on the same page because you have worked hard to ensure that you are, flexibility is a strength. If you don't really understand each other, it's a basis for calamity. Putting a value on that and accounting for it as a risk in a business plan is well nigh impossible. On the other hand, if you are reviewing such a plan, look to see how it is dealt with.

You might be able to include this sort of assumption by stating that India is a country wrestling with overregulation, deregulation, and liberalization and because of that people have become adept at finding new and constructive ways of doing business so that petty restrictions can be bypassed.

Similarly, incorporating assumptions, no matter how justified, on the value that higher-quality work might bring, the advantages that arise from being able to reconfigure what you are doing quickly, the benefit of enhanced customer service from a more involved work force, and the improvement that Indian business can bring is not going to be that straightforward. The hard-headed, not to say bone-headed, people in head office will merely discount anything of this kind as too soft to measure. The skeptics will enjoy the opportunity of exposing your woolly thinking. The uninterested will treat your plan with indifference.

It is nevertheless worth the struggle of getting these factors into any plan, not least because the real message about outsourcing work to India is not contained in the undoubted cost savings.

Measurements

You need to have measured everything you are currently doing in order to get a baseline against which you can measure your progress. You will be surprised how much additional cost this will involve, if only because you will probably have some sort of confidence that such measures already exist. They may well exist in some form. However, they are likely to be out of date, and they measure what used to be the case even when they have been updated. You may find that the existing measures are therefore largely irrelevant.

You will need a range of measures in which you have confidence. Spend some time considering what is relevant and then ask yourself what you might need to know in a few months' time, what the relevance of any soft measures such as employee satisfaction might be, and even how granular the measures need to be.

It's not a bad idea to start with the perceptions of your current employees. These soft measures will help you immensely later on. Once a department realizes that it is – to put it emotionally but probably accurately – under threat, you will have a mass of reactions and responses. How you deal with those will affect not only that department, but almost the whole of your company and very many of the employees. Measure that perception initially and you will be grateful later.

A particularly important measure at this stage is how satisfied your employees are with the current working patterns, work load, processes, rewards, and opportunities. It is probably tempting to rely on any existing employee opinion survey, but this is unlikely to give you the baseline you need.

For example, you need to consider processes in terms of productivity: number of events or cases handled by each employee against time, mistakes, reworking, value added, responsiveness of the department to flux in work pressures, management overhead. Then you should move on to customer satisfaction, whether the customer is an end user or an internal user of the service. None of the other measures can tell you much without that last correlation.

You will need the current cost base addressed from many angles, probably some different from the ones you use now. This base data should already be readily accessible, but experience suggests that it will be inadequate. These costs will need to include the usual suspects like wages, information technology, premises, telecommunications, and management costs, but should also attempt to look at regulatory and other such costs. The latter will not diminish when you go offshore, but they may suddenly appear to be new costs at some stage in any offshore project.

In addition, you will need to include the cost of measurement as a separate item throughout the project. How you do so and where you include it is a personal decision, but one that needs to be taken.

Financial projection

Producing a convincing and relatively accurate financial projection is not the difficult part at this stage. Of the various financial projections for offshoring to India that I have produced over the last few years, only one, not skewed by other factors, failed to show cost savings of well over 30 percent.

That exception had some special factors. First of all, it showed initial costs based on using fairly basic skills that were among the lowest paid in the UK. Some of the Indian replacements, at the same skill level, were to be deployed on site in the UK, at least initially. The percentage loading that employing Indians in lower-paid jobs in the West creates is enormous – subsistence and board will cost at least as much as the salary. Then there are the air fares. Even so, the plan was adopted as it was a project for which we just couldn't get the necessary skills, so the business case didn't turn on cost.

Despite all the hidden costs you can possibly imagine, you will be hard pressed not to show a substantial return in your financial projection. It will frankly be compelling even if you take worst-case figures throughout.

Capital costs for buildings and equipment in India are generally on a par with your domestic costs. Utility costs are marginally below western costs or equal to them, although you will have to allow for telecommunication costs that are probably some 20 percent higher in the end. Wage and other people-related costs are usually between 50 and 60 percent cheaper. In general, the longer out you project your financial plan, the better the overall prospects will be. Even so, and even with start-up costs, you should be able to show a return on investment within 12–18 months.

What you may not be able to take account of in these figures is the increased productivity you will achieve, which is why the supporting text and examples will be so important. Depending on many factors, including how many shifts you use, you will probably achieve at least a 50 percent increase in the use of the assets you are employing, and in some cases this can be doubled.

Start-up costs

The main issue for the financial projection at this point is how to deal with start-up costs. There is nothing untoward about them. These costs are simply what you would expect in the UK or the US or Belgium, although Indian costs will generally be lower. You will have to allow for money to lease or buy premises, with the appropriate back-up power supplies and other contingency equipment, build the internal office environment, install communication links, equip offices with the appropriate technology, probably import a fair amount of equipment, recruit the right people, train them, test them, create the management structure, gain all the necessary permissions from the national and state governments, ensure that all taxes are paid to the right people on the due date, contract buses to get people to the site, especially if the hours to be worked aren't part of the IST working day, create canteens, and generally do everything you would expect whether it was Dallas or Delhi.

Building the internal office environment, by the way, is just that. When my company equipped new offices in Mumbai from scratch, there wasn't a single piece of flat-pack furniture or any modular desk units used, and the whole office was built by carpenters from original materials. How the foreman organized it all is a mystery because there were masses of people involved, all of whom seemed to get in each other's way, and yet the whole place was ready in less than six weeks, beginning with a bare concrete shell.

The start-up costs can be worked into your contract any way you like, just the same as at home. They can be a fixed cost up front or whenever, or built into the contract price for the services. The problem is that even though the scale of costs is not what you would pay in the West, they will seem relatively large. That will provoke endless and disproportionate internal debate.

This debate can lead to insisting on doing it all yourself. The initial argument will come from someone who knows a realtor based in the West that has offices in India. This agent could take care of finding and securing the premises, and after that it would simply be a matter of putting someone in India to oversee the whole interlocking range of contractors. Think of the money that will save.

The clue to the difficulty comes in the use of the word "simply." Even cousins and brothers-in-law are hard-pressed to execute all these functions in the right order in India.

You will need to quantify as many of the start-up costs as you can, and create both a profit and loss account and a cash-flow projection. The moment the project becomes cash positive is clearly the first milestone and will be encouragingly close to the start of the project, even in a worst-case spreadsheet.

Hidden costs

Any business plan makes allowance for costs such as travel. Offshoring to India will require higher investment in these costs, so much so that travel is sometimes a hidden cost, as underestimates frequently dog such projections. There are other hidden costs too.

You have to make quite an allowance for travel and subsistence costs for western business people going to India. There are some legitimate tricks that will repay good organization in terms of airline fares, because they are an expensive element in any projection concerning India. (The planes are usually full, too, which must make them reasonably profitable routes for the airlines.) If you are making two return trips to India within a reasonable space of time, for example, book the middle two flights in India. Business-class tickets bought in India can be about half the price of the same tickets bought in London, New York, or Frankfurt on the same carrier.

Despite this saving on international routes, internal air flights for westerners are also relatively expensive. There are different fares for Indians or those living in India.

You should cost a business week in India at a minimum of $7,000 including business-class travel there and back, and this does not include any opportunity cost, which may be almost impossible to account for. You won't need that many separate business weeks in India to skew the costs part of your business plan. Not many business plans are realistic about the cost or the frequency of such trips.

If you decide on having people in India during set-up, there are some further issues and an insight or two that might be useful. Rental on property in Mumbai is relatively cheap. The cost of actually having a residence – the Indian word – in Mumbai is not cheap at all, however. Real estate prices are some of the highest in the world.

The key to this paradox is tax. Rental income is taxed very highly. Rents are therefore low. On the other hand, a prudent landlord in Mumbai wants to know that the property will be looked after. A huge, in fact enormous, deposit is therefore required and this is available interest free to the landlord, who can deposit it in an interest-bearing account to their own benefit. This counts as tax avoidance in India.

The Indian Treasury and the whole tax regime for foreigners are pretty cute. There is a range of indirect taxes that may eventually amuse you with its comprehensiveness. One favorite is the luxury tax. It is difficult to be sure whether it is a tax on luxury, or the sort of tax you can wallow luxuriously in if you are a tax collector. This tax is levied at 10 percent on all sorts of things in five-star hotels, including telephone calls. There is another 10 percent tax on most parts of your hotel bill if you are a foreigner. Foreigners, of course, pay higher hotel rates anyway. Nevertheless, there is in all this taxation an extraordinary failure to capitalize on an obvious opportunity for a tax official. Where the luxury tax is levied, it doesn't add 10 percent on the tax already levied; it is merely 10 percent on the principal.

Other in-country costs are broadly what you would expect when traveling in the US or Europe. If you gain in one area, you will certainly lose somewhere else.

Apparently hidden costs at the western end of the equation are much more significant. There will be redundancy or redeployment and retraining costs to consider. One business plan, which had made allowance for these issues to some extent, could have fallen apart at this point. These projected costs multiplied alarmingly but only, as it turned out, because the finance director didn't want anything to do with taking work offshore and kept insisting on adding more and more costs. That is a warning of what can happen in an extreme example, but is put this graphically to ensure that such costs are properly taken into account and not forgotten.

A second element of cost that may appear to be hidden is how much capability you leave in your domestic operations. This might more properly be considered part of the contingency and business continuity elements of the project, but you will need to consider it here, particularly if you are reviewing a business plan. There are many reasons for leaving a stub of capability, including maintaining control, having a better and continuing insight into what is happening in your processes, a sense of insurance as part of an exit strategy, and some elements of security.

The reasons are sometimes valid, but in general you should probably leave some ability to restore your capability. It is prudent to consider this question and make some allowance at least.

This area is related to whether you have a sourcing strategy, rather than merely an outsourcing strategy. This is not a trivial matter and requires great thought. The one word of advice is not to accept any formulaic guidelines.

There will be another cost that you should account for in this area, which is the cost when you announce to your existing work force that you are outsourcing work to India. You will obviously lose productivity and commitment unless you take targeted steps to account for this. That precautionary cost will be less than the cost of mitigating actions.

One method is to pay completion bonuses to your existing staff. As a guideline when assessing what these might be, some significant sums have been paid – even as much as an extra quarter's salary for satisfactory completion of the handover, with interim bonuses of a month's salary during the process. You may not want to go to these lengths, but there will be costs here that might not be obvious. These costs will be greater than if you were outsourcing in your own country, because if you are putting processes offshore it is unlikely that staff will be transferred to the outsourcing company, so your redundancy costs will be higher.

Another area of hidden costs will be your supplier's lack of domain experience. The Indian staff will learn quickly and the issue will disappear fast, however It won't have too great an impact on your financial projections, but you must consider all the ways in which this lack of domain skill will affect your costs.

The Indian business model relies on a slick recruitment process, with a personal and corporate network supporting a whole approach to identifying just the right people and ensuring that they are in place to fulfill your requirements. This works really well in the areas that Indian companies are most comfortable with, which is now extending into call centers and other areas of business process outsourcing.

It isn't scientific, there are few guidelines, and in areas where there are complex processes to be taken on there is evidence that Indian companies are not knowledgeable enough about what type of person to recruit for any particular domain. How costs build up here is not yet entirely transparent, because it isn't widely talked about. However, it is clear that the wrong profile of person for any particular role will have an impact on performance, and that will have an effect on your financial projection.

You should be proactive with your supplier and provide more help with such profiles than you might expect. Again, this might be an additional and hidden cost for you.

Training in general will be an obvious line in your costs, but you will probably not uncover the full range of hidden costs you will face. My advice here is to err quite heavily on the side of caution based on the sensible estimate you first come up with. Some organizations, such as the World Bank, suggest that almost 50 percent of implementation costs will have to be spent on training in one way or another. The Bank's concomitant advice is not to try to drive out every rupee of cost from the implementation process, which might account for what seems to me a high proportion.

Do note one characteristic of some western companies taking work offshore that builds cost into the process alarmingly. The selection of just the right supplier can reach extraordinary lengths. In one case, desk work had identified 220 Indian companies that could be asked to supply information about their capabilities. This was whittled down to 22 companies over a number of stages, and then, after another major process, to two. Those two companies were deliberately kept running in parallel as long as possible. You may think that this kind of information would not necessarily be publicized, but it was presented at a public conference with some pride.

It was obvious that initially not a soul trusted anything the Indians could do. Perhaps unsurprisingly, the other burden of the conference presentation was amazement at the Indians' high standards, the quality of the premises and the back-up systems for when there were power failures, and everything else that forms part of the standard Indian supplier's pitch.

The cost of this process was immense and didn't seem to command a line in the breakdown of costs. And all of it occurred after the initial process had identified India as the country most suited for offshoring. It won't surprise you that this was an exhaustive process too. Much as you would expect from such a risk-averse company, it was in total agreement about going to India to check things out and understand how India works. It may reassure you that, having been through all of this, complete with endless, equally painstaking site visits, the main message was that the process had been thoroughly successful and taking business processes offshore was a highly recommended step.

If your company has this type of mindset, do make allowances in the business plan for heavy costs for a pilot and slow ramp-up until everything is proved to work. At the same time, consider carefully the section on pilots below.

Reliable commentators who have taken work offshore will usually suggest that you allow 24 months for the project to be working as effectively as you envisage at the start of the process. This time frame can be beaten – it may take

only 18 months, and you will have a good working system within 6 months –
but keep those two years in your mind when you are doing the planning.

Another hidden cost that you may find surprising is how much effort will
have to be put into internal politics and squaring off every single person who
can object.

Finally, especially in projects where your own company is in charge on
whatever basis, you will need to allow for unforeseen delays. These may occur
in any area, even obtaining any of the tens of permissions you will need. It is
appropriate to try to account for these costs. It may be, of course, that the 40
percent margin a contracted supplier would be putting into the bill more than
covers this type of cost if you are doing it all yourself.

Social costs and development benefits

Do look at the social consequences of your potential activity and get that into
the business plan as part of your assumptions. In the category of social costs I
would count any political backlash or public relations criticism that you
might experience if you are perceived as exporting jobs and people's
livelihoods.

Making an overt attempt to deal with these issues should not be a nugatory
gesture. If it is merely putting a plaster on a gaping wound, it will be worse than
doing nothing. The migration of services to low-cost countries, just like the
migration of manufacturing that began some 25 years ago, is going to cause
social pressures and there will be consequences that will affect quite a few people in the West directly, and most citizens of the West indirectly.

This is a serious subject that I will return to in Chapter 16 in more detail. It
is not all bad news. There are some positive aspects you can bring out, but if
you are creating a business plan in this context it is as well to take a gloomy
view at first. These costs are almost impossible to quantify, but that doesn't
negate their existence.

There is a double-edged sword here, as in most business developments
enabled by IT. Undoubtedly it is a force for good in the world to bring development, work, and some prosperity to India. In turn, that will make India a more
engaged member of the world economy, capable of buying more goods and
services from the rest of the world, including the West. On the other hand, the

immediate difficulties created for western economies could be challenging enough to undermine the very businesses that are benefiting initially.

There are answers to these questions that stand up to intense scrutiny. The business plans you create nevertheless have to identify all the hidden costs, including these social costs. They may be difficult to make palpable – but that's why people who create business plans are paid so well.

Return on investment

Standard business plans for western companies aren't all that good at showing benefits against time, except in the crudest way, partly because no one usually believes any such figures.

Nevertheless, do devote some effort to considering this aspect of your business plan's financial projections and your assumptions, and more than is usually necessary, as it is a major advantage of offshoring in India. Relatively simple charts showing return on investment may be enough, but you also need other measures, such as when the project becomes cash positive, in order to bring out the real quality of what you will achieve. Even using a straightforward Indian supplier, with an acknowledged 40 percent margin, then inflating every cost you can and recognizing the hidden costs, you will be in the cash-positive part of the project quickly and the return on investment will be positive in probably much less than a year.

Cost avoidance

The concept of cost avoidance is going to be difficult to show in any financial projection, and it will be greeted with cynical acceptance if it is appreciated at all, but it is an element of taking work offshore that anyone with experience points to as a potential further benefit. It is a real opportunity of the type that most business planners will see perhaps once in a career.

To take an example, when moving a large number of analysts offshore the World Bank cut its costs by at least 50 percent, judging by public announcements. This was a major step and a real competitive gain. In addition, quality and productivity went up, with more insights being generated into the underlying nature of the work itself and the data that was being considered.

The board member who sponsored this transfer, Fayezul H. Choudhury, had been quite confident that merely replacing his previous staff – who had become accustomed to a work pattern that was engaging enough but not exciting any more, and so had grown into the jobs and didn't find them a challenge – with new staff, who had to be trained and were the subject of intense management scrutiny, would have been beneficial wherever he had placed the work. In India, however, he now had younger, more highly qualified staff who were motivated by what they saw as a superb, life-enhancing opportunity.

The matter that caused Choudhury the most pleasure, nevertheless, was the way in which the immediate benefits of outsourcing the entire department were realized fairly quickly, and those advantages continued to grow for the almost two years it took to establish a settled and properly functioning operation. They then revealed unexpected benefits.

Those centered on what he considers is cost avoidance, and I am using his term.[1] He had taken the view that he would not reduce costs to the absolute minimum in the outsourcing program, because the cost reduction he was able to achieve was more than sufficient. He was taking some $6 million out of the bottom-line cost, which was a useful enough amount. As a result, he perceived that he could undertake some further activities that he had long known were highly desirable, but hadn't been able to get the headcount or the budget to do.

The Bank is now able to carry out work for a much reduced cost that would have required a further 75 percent increase in the original budget onshore, and since that work is generating further income, Choudhury sees this as a major advantage. He transferred the work of 60 people from head office but employed 100 people offshore. He also retained more staff at head office than were strictly necessary merely to transfer the work. The extra work this department is now able to do is what he terms cost avoidance.

Choudhury was able to move rapidly from mere processing to higher-value services, such as data mining and more specific analytics, and create an in-house process reengineering group. This group could look with fresh insight into how processes were addressed and carried out, and were able to put in place much better ways of accomplishing the jobs that needed to be done.

Claims based on this type of experience will get a cynical response within your organization if you try to capture them in your business plan. You will need to find a way of expressing them subtly but persuasively. You may find, for example, that offshoring is a way of increasing headcount so that your business can address new opportunities while reducing the cost base. That sort of opportunity does not happen often in the career of most senior managers.

The issues of contingency, disaster recovery, and business continuity, discussed below, might be viewed in this light. While the danger is that you may remove too many cost benefits if you go too far in this direction, cost avoidance is a powerful tool to be aware of.

Contingency, disaster recovery, and business continuity

These three issues are different, but can be seen as aspects of the same insurance policy since the remedies are at least overlapping in most cases. The cycle for most companies starts when there has been some form of disaster, such as a power failure or even a terrorist attack, and day-to-day operations have to be restored as soon as possible.

Offshoring can provide an opportunity to consider these issues in more detail and perhaps more dispassionately. Going offshore usually triggers even more concentration on the questions that need to be answered, as the risks seem that much more highly delineated. This is a benefit to most businesses, but it usually causes problems for the business plan.

The immediate benefits are that you are creating a second site and probably retaining some vestiges of the original capability in your domestic operations. Whether this cost, perhaps best seen as incremental, will be shown in your business plan for offshoring your operations is a good question. It is not possible to give an answer appropriate to your particular requirements here because of the variables involved, but it is worth considering the fact that while you are potentially saving costs, prudent cover for contingency, disaster recovery, and business continuity is nevertheless required.

Taking into account contingency costs for matters going wrong and working out how you would recover from a disaster and maintain the continuity of your business are all prudent actions. Including them in your business plan will thus be seen as a responsible way of meeting possible objections to going offshore. The downside is that you are complicating matters. There is a justified aversion to considering too many issues at once and offshoring is usually enough of an issue for most business decision makers. It depends to some extent whether you can suggest that accounting for all three problems is a further benefit of going offshore or whether it is seen as extraneous.

My own business plans have always taken these issues into account.

The pilot

You may be forced into undertaking a pilot of your offshoring program. Most business planners are inured to the problems of pilots, which are usually disproportionately expensive, so they tell you little about the real costs and are generally an excuse for rather poorer planning than would take place if you were operating for real from day one. In most examples of offshoring, pilots are for those who don't or won't understand the benefits. If a project manager wants a pilot for an existing process, don't trust your project manager.

You will have gone through an enormous amount of assessment and due diligence before you get to the point where a pilot is at all appropriate. If it's a business process you are already carrying out in the US or the UK, you know that the process works. If you are worried about data links or telephone circuits, you can test them. If you have concerns about how the process to be taken offshore will link into your existing processes, by all means run the two processes in total isolation in your home territory, but this should be happening already in any case. If you are concerned that in the hands of Indians the whole process will come unstuck through cross-cultural misunderstandings, ask to see a reference site.

That's not an argument against starting slowly and ramping up, which is reasonably prudent. Yet you may be surprised how quickly you can outsource even a complicated business process to India. Taking a rather complex financial services administration process offshore was planned to happen over six months, a time frame in which there was a fair amount of contingency. It didn't need a pilot and it became fully effective more quickly than that.

Your final plan

One of the pleasures of working on projects for India is that the evolution of any particular business plan is full of surprises. Finding the right way of dealing with them is difficult, but never less than a pleasure. You will find odd quirks of costs and cost control that can be dealt with by taking a different approach, or, like the cost avoidance above, be faced with the pleasant task of using something really beneficial without facing much of a challenge.

The business plan will usually go through several iterations before it metamorphoses into the document that will be submitted to the board. Sometimes this can be tedious. In the case of business plans focused on offshoring to India, however, there are always enough opportunities to keep the process alive and challenging. The benefit is that if you take all these factors into account, the final business plan will actually make business sense as well as gaining approval.

11
Due Diligence and Avoiding Risks

After you have identified what you want to do and probably with which company, and have some idea of the business plan and the benefits to be achieved, it is as well to understand how to approach due diligence and the elimination of risk. It may seem premature this way round, but it is always helpful to know as much as possible before serious negotiations start.

Recognizing rogues

There are as many rogues in India as there are anywhere else in the world. If people are straightforward and honest, the difficulties of doing business across cultures can be resolved out of a genuine endeavor to do the best for each other. If the people you are intending to do business with are actually rascals, in the Indian sense of being thoroughly bad, you have two challenges. The first is to detect that they are not well-intentioned and it is certainly more difficult to determine that when you try to do so across cultures. The second is to deal with that discovery.

The charm and politeness, the relaxed approach to time and to life, and the general good humor that are intrinsic parts of life in India are all much more tricky for a westerner to read or see through when they're ill-intentioned. I doubt anyone needs advice to be on your guard or not to trust to instinct when all your instincts are at sea. On the other hand, you may find yourself mis-interpreting behavior that is simply different from what you would expect.

A good, neutral illustration of this might have occurred to you if you have already dealt with an Indian sales person. Most Indian sales people in the West have a completely different approach from the kind you have been used to. They haven't adopted anything new at all, and that is the problem. Too often they will have had little training in appropriate western soft skills such as listening and discussion. You may find them aggressive and pushy and almost impossible to deal with, particularly in the UK where such an approach is rarely welcomed. Even in the US, where it is not bad manners to have enthusiasm and show it, the Indian sales method does jar.

Indian sales people will explain forcefully what they have to offer and go into some detail. Almost whatever your response, they may well repeat what they have already said, until you feel yourself reeling under a barrage of words. Whether you are British, German, French, or American, you will find this overpowering. In one extreme case, even the emphatic statement "I'm just not at all interested in what you have to offer" was apparently interpreted as a clear buying signal inviting a further torrent of much the same information.

Watching an Indian sales person selling in a very Indian style is good preparation for any negotiations. It would be easy enough to interpret this behavior – which merely reflects misunderstanding, or innocence, of cultural differences – as a sign that you have a rogue in front of you. The behavior pattern is not, however, any sort of reliable indicator. And it may be that working across cultures eliminates most chances of a reliable indicator.

The most effective rule is to take care when something you believe to be virtually impossible is still not seen as being a problem. This may not indicate that you are dealing with someone who is up to no good, but it does identify someone you are probably better off *not* dealing with. You may get to the point of asking such questions deliberately when you are uncertain. Be aware, nevertheless, that even this test may let you down on occasion in India, and if it does it will probably be because the person you are dealing with hadn't really understood what you were asking.

I have made other mistakes when trying to establish whether the person in front of me is straightforward. I was seeking to get something through Customs rather faster than the threatened ten days. I had been told by all my reliable sources that it was impossible to get this shortened to three days. I mentioned this to a new business acquaintance, for whom nothing so far had been a problem and who didn't seem quite as straightforward as he should be. Reducing the elapsed time to three days was not a problem either, it seemed.

I wrote him off as a rogue and someone to be extremely wary of. Then his *brother-in-law*, as it happened, actually came up trumps. On the other hand, the fact that his claim to be able to do something everyone else regarded as impossible was well-founded did not mean that he was at all easy to deal with.

Be more on your guard than you would be with someone in your domestic market, but not unduly suspicious. The same advice is equally valid for Indian companies trying to assess whether to work with western ones.

There are more formal checks that you can make to back this up, as we will see later, but these are never a substitute for your own assessment.

Indian civil law

There is one fatal trap that you must avoid, the best metaphor for which is superglue.

Books such as *Bleak House* by Charles Dickens portray English civil law as slow enough to make a glacier seem fast, and as destructive as that same glacier, usually to the appellants. Matters do not appear to have improved over time. Worse, however, is Indian civil law, which was modeled on the English system. It has all the flexibility and user-friendliness of a land mine, threatening to blow up should you or anyone close to it look like moving.

It is far from unknown for even relatively simple matters, such as dissolving a partnership when both partners have already agreed terms, to drag on for more than ten years. The slightest hint of a dispute over one element of the agreement to dissolve the partnership and it can become virtually impossible to achieve. There are good examples of people having their health almost ruined by the stress this can create.

It is absolutely vital that any contract you draw up to work with an Indian company is under *your* local law. Even so this may not help you that much, because if you are examining the entrails of a contract and are prepared to go to law, you really must be *in extremis*. Recourse to any form of court is a bad last resort, but how bad should depend on the qualities of your national legal system, with which at least you will be familiar. There is a better chance at home that whatever else happens or fails to happen, you won't be looking at a gorgon and suffering the consequences.

This may sound alarmist and you will no doubt find any number of people who have had nothing but speedy resolution of every issue under Indian law. That is not the general experience, however, and you will also be able to meet people who talk about the life-changing experience the Indian legal system can be. Notice that I said life-changing – not life-enhancing.

If you do elect to have the contract under your domestic legal system, you will find that your courts will uphold your choice of legal jurisdiction, provided this is not against some other principle, such as public policy.[1] Of course, local mandatory laws probably still apply and Indian courts may well accept jurisdiction. On the other hand, your domestic court judgments are generally enforceable in India.

Lawyer Angus Finnegan also gives further advice, including the idea that a Request for Information (RFI) or Invitation to Tender (ITT) should be specifically excluded from any contractual agreement, and that you should include a copy of the draft contract in any RFI or ITT for the potential supplier or partner to comment on it. In any case, you will need a transfer agreement, a services agreement, and the contract.

You must take full legal advice, in addition to the comments in this outline.

The Indian Administrative Service

In similar vein, dealings with the Indian Administrative Service (IAS), the successor to the Indian Civil Service formed during the Raj, will show the same qualities of perfection. IST, already a thing of beauty and a joy forever – or, at least, a joy for rather longer than you might expect – becomes a palpable object in the hands of the lower ranks of the IAS.

In contrast, you may well be surprised at the levels of activity you can witness in an IAS office. People will be moving around, some purposefully. Papers will be moved from desk to desk and huge bundles moved from office to office. There will be queues of people to address every officer worth addressing. These levels of activity seem largely to produce heat and very little light.

This is ultimately unfair to the IAS and there are significant exceptions. Particularly in Delhi, there have been important changes in approach, attitude, and even style. There are a number of people, some who have been brought in from the private sector to act as catalysts and others who are career members of the IAS, who show the finest qualities of administration and dynamism. You will be impressed by their professionalism and their determination to do the best for India. They may well help you significantly, because they will recognize the value you are bringing to the country.

There is a slow but important change happening in the IAS, certainly stimulated by the deregulation that is occurring in India and perhaps reinforced by its membership of the World Trade Organization. Whereas before you might have got the Indian equivalent of a shrug of the shoulders – a gesture that uses most of the body, all of the face, and both hands – now, once you reach a reasonable level in the IAS, you will get action.

India is a country where knowing the right people is almost essential and having access to the right level of officials is important. While it is perfectly possible to work around the issues without that sort of influence, it is still a good deal easier if you know where to go and whom to see.

The contract

One of the astonishing paradoxes of Indian life centers on the status of the contract with your supplier or partner. Any Indian business person you speak to will reiterate the adage that the contract isn't important. This usually sounds to westerners very much like the truism that if you have to refer to the contract after you've started working together, you haven't got a business relationship that is worth enough to justify continuing.

It isn't quite that. It's more a reference to the sheer difficulty of enforcing a contract in India. This shows the importance of the issues and approaches that I stressed in earlier chapters, such as understanding each other's intentions and making sure that the other person is trying to understand yours. In short, you have to know whether you trust the other person and that their word is their bond. That isn't any different from dealing with any other country or even your own, but in India it is much more important to understand what is happening and why.

The contract with your Indian supplier, even if taken under your domestic jurisdiction, will be viewed in the light of their experience or knowledge of enforcing a contract under Indian civil law. On that basis, you may well feel that a contract that will not be much use in a crisis is relatively easy to dispose of. The paradox lies in the amount of time and attention the contract may consume.

If it is any comfort, the contract process is much worse if you are creating a contract in the Indian market to sell something or provide a service in India. Every clause will be scrutinized down to the last word. In those cases I have tried everything short of locking the lawyers from both sides in a room and throwing away the key. I bow to no one in my pedantry over the use of commas. Actually, I bowed to no one in my pedantry over the use of commas until I met the full might of an Indian lawyer. Most of the Indian lawyers I have met are brilliant, but they have taken to a new level the concept of adding value by questioning everything.

Any contract under Indian law will be on stamped paper. This dignifies the process no end. These contracts are almost works of art – as is figuring out the amount of stamp duty, where opinion seems to count for more than facts. Nevertheless, the additional, say, INR120 for dated stamped paper will be a minimal extra expense. Securing the actual bits of paper on the right date is another matter!

The case presented here is the worst and it may be that your contractual negotiations are just as complex as normal, but not at the level that can happen with Indian companies. It will be probably be more akin to the usual stasis you expect in western corporate life when everything is agreed and simply waiting for the lawyers' imprimatur.

You do need, however, to be prepared for a process that is completely out of proportion to the efficacy of the outcome. The rationale appears to be that this relentless process will drive out your mutual understanding and create a shared view of what the project is in fact about and how it will be brought to fruition.

The agreement

It is best to focus on the actual agreement that you have reached, which you should formalize as soon as you have a solid basis from which to proceed. That's the key.

You may also now see why all my criteria about choosing a company to work with are focused on management quality and alignment with western business practice. If agreed actions are merely holding arrangements until the other side works out whether it wants to do something or not, and time scales are nothing but targets that it may endeavor to meet, you won't have much of an agreement in western terms.

If you have any form of written agreement with your supplier outside of the actual contract, treat it seriously. That is your mutual lifeline. You will be surprised how seriously it is taken, and for good reason.

This is a suitable point to stress the relative importance of such written documents in India. No matter how seriously you may take written and signed documents in your home country, treat them with more respect in India. While the wording can be subtle, it will be precise and you need to consider the actual words carefully.

As a small indication of one difference between Indian and UK law or even custom and practice, a letter from a potential customer in India that mentions an agreed price is more than an expression of interest. There are different opinions in India, as you would expect, on the exact meaning to be attached to such a letter. These opinions range from stating that such a letter with a price agreed in it is a contractual obligation that can be taken as an order, through to a more careful lawyer who demurred from accepting such an extension, but still agreed that the letter was highly significant.

Exit strategy and risk analysis

Any contract or agreement must have an exit strategy for both sides. This equivalent of a prenuptial agreement is essential. It is valuable in its own right, but its first benefit occurs when you are discussing it. Curiously enough, if you can understand in detail what will trigger a need for an exit from the contract for your potential supplier or partner, you will have a much better understanding of the approach and intentions they are bringing to the proposed project.

In many cases, being forced to consider in detail what will trigger a need for your exit will offer two advantages. In the first place, you will understand, at a time when there is little emotion, much better how you can extricate yourself. Secondly, it will also make overt something you may not have put into words or even consciously thought about: your hopes, concerns, and worries over the proposed project. This may sound straightforward, but being faced with sorting out exit strategies and what would trigger one has been an eye-opener for many people.

Whatever other benefits there are, you will need a documented exit strategy and a documented basis for any exit in the contract.

Finally, you will need a full and well-analyzed understanding of your risks and liabilities. This is no different from any contract in your domestic market, but there is a higher premium on this offshore, not least because internal critics will use this effectively if you have relegated the issues to an afterthought. It is a truism that liabilities are considered last, but this should not mean that they are never considered early enough.

Account management

Account management is always important, but it is even more important in the context of dealing across cultures. As a secondary benefit, the degree of understanding of account management that the Indian company has can help you assess whether that company truly understands your needs and approach.

What is at issue here is not the quantity or even quality of account management activity, or whether, for example, you should be managed as an account on an exclusive basis by one person. You will be able to judge what the appropriate level of attention is to your needs. It is vital, however, that you do see a sensible structure for managing you and your business as an account, and that you are comfortable with the person or people assigned to this role. The importance placed on this function, its reporting structure, and the level of person in the role or roles will tell you far more about the company you will be working with than any number of polite conversations where nothing is an issue.

The escalation process – for example, what will trigger high management involvement – is another vital indicator of how the Indian supplier is approaching the deal. Account management and escalation should be tightly linked; if they are seen to be, this is a cause for some confidence.

Apply the normal frames of reference. If the main person managing you and your business is an out-and-out sales person, you will know whether that is appropriate and will be able to understand the motivation behind the appointment. You will be able to judge the person's seniority and will also know whether the additional cost of being account managed in your domestic market is appropriate or not.

This is not to say that account management will necessarily be a problem or an issue. The concepts are generally well understood. Use it as a checking mechanism – as part of your informal due diligence and a way of testing whether you have used the criteria for selecting a supplier or partner properly.

You can also use the proposed reports to you on performance and the frequency of any suggested review meetings as part of your due diligence. This approach won't differ much from dealing with any supplier in your own country, but it's as well to be reminded.

Company accounts

As another part of your due diligence, you will need to verify the Indian company's accounts. These have to be lodged with the relevant authorities every year. The complex process of getting the accounts verified, signed off by the auditors, and agreed by the board is quite a nightmare, because it is taken seriously. That is a cause of reassurance for you.

The process is taken so seriously in fact that in one instance, as the deadline approached for me to get on the plane to Delhi clutching the documents, there was a fully fledged discussion on whether the auditors would sign off the accounts if the board hadn't agreed them or whether the board would agree them if they weren't signed off by the auditors. Logic and facts didn't come into it. The only answer in the few seconds before the flight closed was to agree with everyone and inform all sides that everyone had already signed.

The accounts will mean as much or as little as accounts normally do, but you do need to look at and analyze them. They will give you at the very least the usual snapshot of what the finance director thought wouldn't raise any unpleasant questions or start any investigations. They will be full enough to satisfy someone that an earnest attempt to file accounts has been made. In fact, accounts in India will comply as much as any other country's accounts with what is covered by the phrase – shorn of its grandiose capital letters – generally accepted accounting principles.

As usual, it is watching, talking, and walking around that will give you the best insight into a company. In the same way that any statements about attrition rates will be immediately shown up by well-timed questions, you will gain a great deal of insight from these apparently innocent activities. A few questions to people who work for the company at various levels will probably tell you more than the accounts, but still take the accounts as seriously as the Indian company does.

You will be focused on specifics when you read them, and yet apparently unrelated or only marginally related matters will tell you how to judge the veracity of what you have in front of you. If you have an insight into the quality of the facilities and staff, the real nature of the management, especially the operational management, the way that training is regarded, and the general approach to issues, you will be able to judge whether the accounts look reasonable.

Regulation

Offshoring does not mean that you lose your obligations to domestic and international regulators. The Financial Services Authority in the UK, for example, is very clear on this: "It is absolutely vital that outsourcing does not involve loss of control over the quality and performance of the function."[2]

This remark fairly reflects the regulatory principle: "A firm must take reasonable care to organise and control its affairs responsibly and effectively, with adequate risk management systems."[3]

The same approach is adopted internationally by most regulators and in different business segments. The FSA is quoted because financial services companies, and particularly insurers, have been in the vanguard of moving offshore, so the regulator is more directly and immediately involved. It is key for you to maintain compliance with your industry regulators even when the processes are offshore, and you will also have to have in place processes to guarantee compliance, where possible.

Due diligence needs to cover this aspect, even though it isn't at first sight related to the potential supplier or partner. At second sight, it becomes obvious this must feature in your discussions and is part of the basis of taking work offshore.

Public and employee relations

Another part of the due diligence and risk management process is how you deal with the enormous public and social interest that offshoring is rightly starting to generate. There have already been examples of public relations disasters where companies have announced they are moving hundreds of jobs offshore and then faced a barrage of protest from employees, unions, politicians, citizens, and the media.

You will be faced with a number of conflicting demands and picking your way through the minefield is not recommended unless you have a strategy for dealing with the issues. In Chapter 16 there is more detailed consideration of many of the issues and how to address them responsibly. What is important here is to understand the necessity for careful analysis.

Any unions you have to deal with will make what seems a thoroughly proper request: that you should be open about your planning from the earliest stage and that consultation is the key to successful implementation of your project. You can judge whether that request is actually reasonable and whether you can respond positively in the light of the commercial factors that are driving your decisions and the effects that early disclosure might have on the productivity of your existing work force. Nevertheless, you will have to consult your unions if you are in a unionized environment and you must have a plan for when you do that, with careful reasoning for whatever your decisions are. The same goes for consulting your existing employees, whether unionized or not.

You will need to consider how you are going to deal with any other interested parties in what is becoming an increasingly high-profile business move. Even if you are handling all the issues in the responsible ways I outline in Chapter 16, you may still face attack as people's livelihoods are being threatened. You may be able to stress the positive effect your move will have on poor people in India and the world economy, but whatever your approach you will need a sustainable argument. One UK company, Prudential, which announced its intention to move hundreds of jobs offshore more or less as a fait accompli, was pilloried relentlessly and suffered enormous damage to its brand. More recently another UK insurer, Aviva, which owns Norwich Union, met the same response.

Your own team

You may already have a good idea of the type and number of people you will require for your own team and some may already be working with you. You need to establish your own team initially on paper, so you can start to build the cost picture, but soon it will also have to exist in practice so you can plan properly.

Every organization will approach the question of who should be in this team differently, and the numbers will differ depending on the way you are tackling the project. If you are merely seeking a supplier who will do everything in a completely outsourced model, the team will be considerably smaller than if your company is doing everything itself.

There is only one significant guideline that fits all types of projects in relation to the size and composition of your team. Always ask yourself three questions. These may be obvious, but they should be asked in a particular way and obviously answered honestly, especially the third one.

The first question is whether you do really need a particular role for the project. The question should be asked this way round and not as whether you could do *without* the role. The second question is focused on the particular person or people who will fill that role, and be especially hard with yourself if more than one person is apparently required. The final question is to ask why you have come to these particular conclusions. All too often the answer to the third question is that this is the way you always undertake such projects, or point to the risks involved and the requirement to cover every eventuality.

What you do need, especially for India, is a few good people, and the fewer the better. Not only it is a matter of the huge incremental cost of a further western person being involved in proportion to the cost of using Indian resources, but also the smaller the team is, the faster you will work. The reason this becomes so significant for an offshore project is that inevitably it will become important for every team member to go to India. This happens time and again and the logic appears to be overwhelming. Without that person making a visit, time will be lost, extra costs incurred, or risks lie unexposed, or perhaps all of these and even more. This may be true, but smaller teams require both fewer visits and less time spent in India.

There may be a correlation between the number of people who visit and the number of projects that succeed. When examining successful projects, however, the size of the team does not seem to be a major factor, except in the start-up costs.

Look at the project or program team in terms of the roles required. Some individuals will cover more than one role, so the following does not indicate the size of the team, only the areas of expertise that need to be covered, even if not all have to be covered full time.

You will need program direction or project management skills, depending on the size of the undertaking. Business planning is an essential element. You will also require a specialist in human resources and another in internal accounting. Depending on how you approach the project, you will need varying degrees of technical expertise, especially in information technology and communications, which are usually separate disciplines at this architectural level. You will require a particular set of training skills, focused in two areas: training trainers, and the ability to design training programs rather than to give them. You will need support from procurement, but the type of input that supports and does not control.

It is usually essential to include a middle manager from the department or departments that are affected, as these people understand the processes. While this isn't counterintuitive because it makes sense as soon as it is mentioned, any number of companies don't get to this point at all and tend to work with the most senior manager of the department, or, in extreme cases, the technical or senior business support departments.

You will, of course, need a project office manager and other areas of support. However, these roles, with one further person as part of the team, cover many of the essentials.

Before I address that one last role, it is worth reinforcing the idea of a few good people from another angle altogether. Anything to do with offshoring is extraordinarily sensitive. Keeping the team small will help you control how information about the project is handled, how it is released, and whether it is leaked. You needn't be unnecessarily secretive, but rumor, external interest, and internal political gossip will be significant factors in any sizeable project. Commercial advantage and competitive threats are interwoven and you will have to consider all aspects of the information flow.

For this reason, and for reasons of knowledge, contacts, and a disinterested approach, many consultancies will suggest that it is vital to have outside help in key areas, particularly in the cross-cultural aspects. Although there may well be self-interest here, it is an issue that needs to be considered. It isn't possible to make a blanket statement, because only you will know whether your own team can encompass the subjects concerned.

More importantly, run the project or program off-site. There are disadvantages in doing this, especially in terms of communication and ready access to corporate knowledge, but these drawbacks pale against the massive advantages of running the team off-site from your normal offices.

The advantages of being off-site arise from the ability to focus totally on the project, without outside distractions, especially where one of the team members is required just to fix something on an hourly basis, and from the greater ability to maintain project security.

The final area to be considered picks up that last member of the team, the business sponsor. Without doubt this has to be a board-level role if the project has any size or potential significance at all. However, it can't be simply another job tacked on to a board member's existing range of responsibilities, like a sort of hobby.

I have seen two different disasters in this respect. In the first, the business sponsor was only a direct report to a board member, which just didn't work. There was a perceived gap between the strategic thrust of the whole project and the level of involvement, and while this was not the only effect, it was significant. There was a level of indirection that defeated the team. In the second, the project was merely added to the apparently most appropriate board member's agenda. When we are talking about taking six months to implement a major change, across continents, the person has to be more responsive than this situation allowed.

To be successful, not least against a potentially awkward internal political structure, the project requires ready access to and support from the board. The difference that board-level sponsorship makes is extraordinary. Things move faster, especially if the board sponsor, at the request of the program manager, can drop everything and visit India.

Be prepared

Any discussion of due diligence and risk management will inevitably give the impression that it's far too difficult and that there are many issues lying in wait to trap you. This chapter may make you wary, but it should not discourage.

You will gain huge competitive advantage from an offshoring project through cost reduction, improved quality, and even a new infusion of thought and effort into your company. All the issues outlined here are real and serious, but they are only different by degree from the issues you face in any project or program.

Being prepared for the worst is often the key to success.

12
Negotiations and the Art of Haggling

I t is a good idea to anticipate an art form in India and Indian business life – the style of negotiations – before you get involved in them in earnest. You will already have seen some indications about the use of language in previous chapters. Now we've also got to contend with body language, attitudes, outlooks, formality and informality, and different cultural expectations.

Negotiations in India are very different from what you might be used to, although you mustn't, of course, throw away everything else you might have learned in a negotiating course or gleaned from experience.

In this chapter I introduce negotiations with Indian companies from quite an extreme viewpoint. What is covered here is my experience of dealing with Indian companies in India engaged in negotiations over a project concerned with the Indian domestic market. The negotiation style you will encounter will be different from this in degree, but not in style. Showing you the underlying approach may give you a better understanding of what is going on in the minds of those opposite you. In the psychological warfare that the best negotiations can become, this extreme perspective should be extremely helpful. Judge what follows by whether this helps explain certain attitudes and perspectives that may prove puzzling in the heat of the moment.

What you will actually participate in will be a hybrid affair, somewhere between your own national approach and the Indian approach. It won't be like a negotiation between Indian companies, which as a foreigner you couldn't do unaided, any more than an Indian could successfully negotiate a contract between two companies from the same western country. Such events are tough and are culturally specific. If you are ever in that situation, you must have your own local national to interpret. Even then, you will need to be sensitive enough to understand the signals. Nevertheless, by getting a flavor of what a negotiation is like between Indian companies, you will be better prepared for what may seem an odd experience.

While this chapter is some preparation for negotiations with an Indian company, you still need to deal with the added ingredient of unpredictability. You will probably find that your Indian supplier or partner has been through the mill of negotiations with western companies. Their style of negotiation will usually be a hybrid of western and Indian approaches. That can make life exciting, not least because there is no homogeneous negotiation style across the West and you can never know whether your opposite number has previously dealt with Americans, Germans, or Britons. It can also prove intriguing or alarming, depending on your equanimity at the time, as you may unexpectedly encounter silence when all the preparation has focused on repetition.

It is also true that the elusive negotiations that lead to a win–win contract will be very much possible. An initial contract will be seen by your Indian opposite number as a starting point from which to build a long-term relationship, out of which the true value will emerge for both sides. At various stages in the negotiations this will seem far from the truth. It will nevertheless be a firm objective for the Indian company. With that in mind, don't relax, but do investigate how you can reach that type of contract.

You will find that asking the skilled negotiator opposite how whatever is being proposed is supportive of a win win contract will be extremely useful. That is not a ploy – in this case – but a way of assessing how the negotiations are being approached.

If you haven't met any Indian sales people in your domestic market and looked at how they deal with you, it is a good idea from the moment you arrive in India to watch the various interactions, and to take the view, sometimes encouraged by professional trainers dealing with negotiation skills, that every interchange is some form of negotiation.

Body language

For a westerner the immediate problem in face-to-face negotiations in India is body language. There is sometimes nothing for it but to close your eyes, sometimes literally as well as metaphorically, as much as possible. Otherwise, every fiber in your being will cry out that what you are seeing is at variance with what you are hearing. The conflict this may create in your brain can be amazing and must have something to do with the primacy of vision in our sense and perception of the world. Even after years of dealing with the contradiction between what is said and what you can see, and even knowing that there isn't really a contradiction, you may find it hard to deal with it rationally.

It is well known that Indians roll their heads when listening to other people. It definitely isn't a shake of the head, because it is a rolling action. As a westerner, however, you are likely to experience it as the persistent and insidious image of someone shaking their head at what you are saying.

In its purest terms this head movement, which is sometimes referred to as the Mumbai roll, is a very much more visible example of what television people call "the noddies." The noddies are the sequences recorded *after* an interview, where the interviewer is filmed alone but looking intense and nodding as if following a complex argument from another person. These sequences are cut into the filmed report at what are considered appropriate moments.

Considered in this way, the Indian head movement is an extension of being polite and is not intended to give offense. It is both highly visible and, within its own perspective, absolutely correct, and is a way of showing that every word is being appreciated. The trouble is that it gives westerners the wrong signals, even when you know inside and out what is happening.

I have been making presentations and having discussions with Indians for years and I am comparatively used to seeing a whole room of people with rolling heads demonstrating that they are listening intently, but to me apparently registering disagreement. I am used to it, but remain entirely uncomfortable. As I watch, my left upper brain tells me that this is logically absolutely fine. My right upper brain finds it artistically stimulating. My lower brain – both left and right – says "Run!"

When the lower brain kicks in and recognizes danger, you are in trouble.

Not surprisingly, the opposite perspective also applies. Even highly westernized Indians find immobile heads unnerving and have the nagging feeling that the audience has either gone to sleep or is merely ignoring the speaker.

You can draw attention to the issue if it gets really difficult and use some form of humor to help you cope, perhaps drawing your Indian colleagues' attention to the fact that when you keep your head still, it doesn't mean you have lost the plot.

While the head movement is much the most visible example of different and offputting body language, hand movements are if anything even more different. In any discussion you will see people's hands being used very expressively and quite elegantly. You won't necessarily need to understand these hand movements, but there is a particular flick of the hand or hands that westerners find both ingratiating and difficult to deal with. The hand will start cupped with the palm upwards and toward the speaker. After what looks like a dismissive flick, the fingers point away and up, with the back of the hand toward the speaker. The nearest equivalent in the West is a gesture that pushes someone away and out of your mind, although that movement is very much stronger and ruder in execution. This Indian flick has a sort of completeness about it, and implies that something can be done with no real nonsense or too much concern. It isn't dismissive, in fact, but instead rather positive.

You simply have to be aware of a different body language lexicon. Naturally for your part you will be giving wrong or different signals, but because of Indians' greater familiarity with western gestures and body language, this will probably not be as important.

International negotiation styles

In addition to the different style in non-verbal communication, there is a completely different approach to negotiation from the standard UK, US, or European models, which are themselves different from one another.

In the following cases, the description concentrates on what passes for the opening gambit or gambits in the final negotiation session as a way of distinguishing the different styles. Once that stage is over, much like a game of chess when the opening is past, the variations are too many to countenance. The object here is to identify differences at a relatively simple level to put the Indian approach into context. You will see – at least if you ever try to sell a service or product to Indians in India – that the phrase "final negotiation session" is also as inexact a term as you could find.

Inevitably, the descriptions of negotiation styles in different countries that follow will seem, and might even be, exaggerated for effect. Because that might undermine their value, they were checked for sense with a number of people who all, no matter what nationality, began by asserting that what you are about to read is inaccurate and different from their experiences. During the discussions that followed those dismissals, however, there was more and more recognition of the validity of the overall message, and people who initially rejected these caricatures even supplied anecdotes to support them.

It is also perhaps worth saying what we all know to be true, that negotiation skills are extremely personal, and that negotiation style is therefore as much an exhibition of personal as national characteristics.

In continental Europe there are as many variations between countries as you would expect. There is usually a common theme, nevertheless. The final session of serious negotiations only begins once everyone on all sides has agreed, outside the negotiation meeting, almost exactly what is going to be signed. The actual final negotiation meeting is nonetheless intense hard work and normally detailed, teasing out all sorts of meanings and issues. The whole process is built around what the word "teleological" was created for. We all know what the answers are, but unless we ask the questions, we'll never get there.

This closed result is unlike the Indian approach in almost every way, although you do have to know exactly what your sticking point is before you get this far in India.

In America, the objective seems to be to get negotiations over as soon as possible, but with one serious side issue. That issue is flexibility. It is paramount to come out of any negotiation having displayed flexibility. Most, if not all, negotiations with Americans appear to start with some avowal along the lines that the approach to the negotiating table is based on flexibility. Unless at least one protagonist starts by saying "I'm prepared to be very flexible," it's likely that however successful the negotiations are, they will leave a sour taste in the mouth. Of course, the frequency of the remark is often in inverse proportion to the flexibility of the eventual outcome.

This insistence on flexibility and drawing specific attention to it would be inexplicable in India, as it would immediately suggest, quite correctly, that the negotiations would not be flexible. All Indian negotiations are characterized by flexibility, which is perhaps why they appear to be so rigid and follow such a well-defined path. If that sounds as though it is merely a rhetorical flourish, that would be to underestimate the rigidity of the form of negotiations in India and the flexibility that will be displayed during the process.

In the UK, negotiations are possibly the strangest in the world, because they appear to involve no negotiation at all, at least to start with. I have sat in absolute silence in UK negotiations for what seems longer than anywhere else or in any other context. The climax of the initial stance arrives at the point where, having made what is often claimed to be the last, or the best and final, offer fairly early in the process, nothing more must be said. There must be no fidgeting, no staring out of the window, humming, or doodling. Silence.

Not until someone breaks do the discussions proper begin, but with a clear understanding of where the balance of power lies depending on who gave in first. This is in many ways the complete opposite of the Indian approach.

Indian business people will tell you that despite the insistence on flexibility, which is off-putting, the people they can deal with most effectively – which is quite openly defined as achieving the most appropriate deal for both sides – are Americans. The directness of approach that Americans naturally employ is more akin to an Indian style. Continental Europeans, despite any language difficulties, are the next easiest for Indian business people. The British and the Indians, despite their long association and their shared understandings, generally find it more difficult to negotiate together.

This is not meant to establish a pecking order of rightness, but to give some sort of indication about the scale of difficulty you may face.

Negotiations in India

In negotiations in India, the whole point initially is to show that you are firm in what you have said and that you really mean it. Under no circumstances must you show any weakness or willingness to compromise. Just remember that showing flexibility at this stage is anathema. This must be a reaction to the fact that the final contract position with an Indian company can move a good deal from the initial position.

A final negotiation meeting is therefore a trial of strength, similar to those you may be aware of in the West, but with some variations. You will probably find that this is physically a trial, since not only are there likely to be considerable numbers of people on both sides, but it will take hours to get through even the initial positioning.

The form is quite rigid. Imagine you are the supplier. You will be invited to state your offer, which you should do in some detail, preferably adding some extensive reasons why you have established this position. The potential customers will demonstrate their politeness by rolling their heads all through this performance and then, because you have prepared yourself to take rolling heads as a positive sign, they will surprise you by rejecting outright what you have offered, usually on the grounds that it is so far different from what they are expecting that it is almost inconceivable a supplier could make such an offer. This will be said with such misery and resentment that nearly all heads will remain immobile. They will give detailed reasons to support their rejection of your offer. With due firmness, you as supplier must then repeat, preferably word for word, the original statement of the offer. The potential customers' response will be their initial response repeated word for word.

Then all parties must repeat their positions in turn until all are thoroughly bewildered.

At various points this exchange of offer and refusal will be broken by one of the few acceptable interruptions, which is a request by one side to be able to confer in private. On the return to the original negotiations, it is important for the person whose turn it is to speak to start by saying "I must repeat..." and then to do exactly that. I have been in negotiations that have taken this form for more than five hours.

Of course, in such marathons there is one further acceptable interruption, other than the usual breaks for food and comfort. It is permissible to invite a third party to come in and explain what is wrong with either the offer or the refusal to consider it. Whoever is invited to do this is normally introduced as an independent third party who can give an objective view. In no case will you find that the independent third party will ever prejudice his or her objective and disinterested position by giving other than exactly the same view as the side that invited the objective view in the first place.

In really extreme cases of this negotiation performance, there will be no result, despite the hours that will have been invested in it. However, this is usually caused by a mistake: someone, possibly a foreigner, getting impatient and not understanding the rhythm of the meeting.

On one occasion, at what seemed like a really final moment after a good few hours, I lost the thread, snapped shut my time manager – I know how to act decisively – and hustled our entire team out of the meeting room, down in the elevator, and out into the hot sun before anyone realized what was going on and stopped me.

Outside, I faced a baffled team – and they were my own side. Apparently the potential customer team sat in the room for another hour or so waiting for us to return. The sensible thing to do in this circumstance is to conjure up some way of saving face and return, but I'm afraid we went back to our office. Both sides did genuinely laugh about it afterwards, at my expense.

The trick is not to lose patience, but to keep on going relentlessly. A negotiation like this will terminate. It may seem impossible, but a signed contract will be the result, although the lawyers will get involved and weeks may pass. However, what tips the repetition over into agreement is still a mystery.

Be persistent. Perhaps more in keeping with the continental European model of negotiation, there will be some areas that are undisclosed but accepted, a sort of subtext. There is no easy way of dealing with this, but awareness of their existence may help you recognize such elements when they occur.

The best and final offer in an Indian negotiation may well be comprehended in a different way. For example, there can be a mutually understood and equally unspoken formula for determining what the relationship between that best and final offer and the contract price will be.

In one negotiation I was involved in, it eventually turned out that in general that difference was 8 percent. This figure came out explicitly because the other side became so exasperated with me. I hadn't moved from our sealed bid, which had apparently been accepted. By accepted, I mean that we had been chosen as the vendor. In situations like this, however, the price is still not anywhere near fixed, even though the vendor has been chosen on the basis of the lowest price in a sealed bid.

By the way, if 8 percent seems very precise it is, as it represents the average between the sealed tender and the usual eventual price.

This form of negotiation won't be exactly what you will be dealing with, but there may be some fixed figure that your Indian company will be aiming for. That would explain some of the persistence and repetition.

Given what I have said here, if you are the potential customer rather than the supplier, at the start of your final negotiation your potential Indian supplier may be a little fazed by your failure to invite the Indian company to state a final price with copious reasons, and even more bewildered by your inability to carry on rejecting this with heartfelt reasons.

You could always open the negotiations with just such an invitation. Of course, if you do so, you may find that the representatives of the Indian company will be even more perplexed by you doing so, as they know westerners don't bargain in this way. It is best to expect that the negotiations will most likely be a hybrid of both systems.

Whatever the state of mind of your potential supplier, he or she will be a tough and generally wily adversary. You may have worked with some great negotiators in your time, and you may claim that you are not that bad yourself. You will still find that dealing and negotiating with Indians will leave you with the greatest admiration for the way such events – and you can see them as almost theatrical experiences – are conducted, and how Indians really do aim to achieve that elusive win–win result. There is something deeply impressive about the use of attrition that other forms of opening negotiations can't match. While you may not enjoy the experience, it will be a challenge and will teach you a great deal.

The main message is that Negotiation 101 isn't going to help a great deal in the opening, if protracted, stages of final negotiations, although you'll obviously need all that hard-won, traditional insight into negotiation that training and experience can give. Without a doubt, know what your walk-away point is. Make trial closes. Offer incentives that actually give little or nothing away but create a better environment. Create avenues where your customer or supplier can claim the moral high ground.

By all means employ every weapon in the negotiator's handbook. In the end you will be so weary, you will probably settle at any price.

Market testing

One subject that you may want to raise during the negotiation is the question of market testing, or combating some nervousness that the deal you have struck today will not be that competitive later. You will know the right moment to do it in the negotiation process, and there won't be a good, right moment once your contract is signed.

This concern plagues some companies more than others, it is not an exclusive worry about offshore work, and it really does depend directly on your relationship with your supplier. It is worth considering in the Indian context because, with the commoditization of some services, prices are falling, margins for Indian suppliers are being eroded, and over time you may find that you are paying rather more than you might elsewhere.

For a different reason, some companies who have entered the market suggest that you should conduct your final negotiations with two Indian companies. While this shows how much respect you have for the ability of Indian companies to strike a deal that is favorable to themselves, and it does help remove some of your cultural difficulties, the cost of doing so will be high.

It is not a real answer. The network between Indian companies will render the tactic rather ineffective. Although there is very little evidence of any formal cartel arrangements, Indian companies have very good market intelligence. They will know with whom you are still negotiating even if you try to keep it quiet. Remember that there will be a cousin, or at the very least a brother-in-law, somewhere in the mixture.

There is also what appears to be good intelligence circulating about the value of any particular deal and what current market rates are. There won't be price fixing as far as it is possible to determine because it is not needed – and this is guaranteed to some extent by the competitive nature that Indians bring to business. It is probably better to tap into this market intelligence and you will find that in many cases your chosen potential supplier will be reasonably happy to help you understand where the price points are. At the price negotiation stage, you will be able to gather some interesting pointers at the very least and this makes playing two suppliers off against each other rather nugatory.

Nevertheless, in a market where there are potentially declining prices, it is a reasonable idea – on the basis that you will continue to work with your current supplier – to build in some, probably more formal, market-testing mechanisms for later in the life of the contract. You will know what sort of process you will feel comfortable with, and you do need to get to that level of detail in these initial discussions. It may alarm your supplier, but an alarm at this stage is a good deal easier to deal with than a confrontation later.

It can be a positive step and statement for your supplier. After all, while you are testing the pricing, you are really making a commitment to carry on working with that particular supplier. Of course, you may end up in a different discussion if pricing actually moves the other way.

Recognizing when you have a deal

You may sometimes have difficulty appreciating the moment that you actually have a deal, partly because the negotiations are so protracted, partly because of the cultural barriers. Even negotiations in your home country with your chosen Indian supplier can get confusing, though the extremes of behavior may not be there.

What follows is not an infallible signal, but if something like it happens it means you've reached agreement – despite the fact that no one has yet shaken hands, stood up, sat down, shaken hands again, or nodded or rolled their head.

At the end of a particular session – it will scarcely be the first, unless you are very lucky – your protagonist may offer some rather abstract musings. This isn't whimsy, but a declaration of sorts. In my case, I was asked whether I understood what neem and jaggery were. This seemed like a difficult question in the middle of repetition and persistence. Neem is a particularly bitter plant; jaggery is extraordinarily sweet. We had had the neem, apparently, now we could enjoy the jaggery.

There was the signal. We were now relaxed. The story confirmed that we were. We had a deal and although there were still some loose ends, the basis had been laid down.

The agreement

Few Indian companies see the first contract as the main aim. In almost every case, there is a much larger prize of a continuing and expanding relationship with you, and that encourages a commitment to a fair and satisfactory arrangement for all sides. This obviously cannot be totally relied on, but it is worth remembering as the fundamental perspective.

In return, it is worth considering whether you want to wring the last possible paise out of the contract. If you begin to be aware that there is a striving for a mutually beneficial commercial arrangement, that could be worth a great deal to you over the years.

Remember, too, that negotiations with an Indian company will first and foremost be focused on arriving at a written agreement, and that although the contract itself is on the agenda and important, it is not what both sides should probably be focused on.

Western negotiations can end with a general, airy sense that the lawyers will sort out the rough bits. There is no such feeling in India. The agreement you reach will be the basis of your relationship – warts and all. There will be differences, obviously, in the negotiation process if a contract is negotiated under your domestic jurisdiction between a western and an Indian company, but the same spirit will underlie the approach.

13
The Right Result

So, you have selected a supplier, developed a business plan, reached an agreement, and got the contract signed. Now you need to focus on implementation. This is the moment when the allocated months in the business plan that originally seemed entirely adequate – if not rather generous – for setting up and delivering the service now seem an impossibly short time, especially if you recall the long list of tasks that would be dealt with on your behalf that your Indian supplier or partner presented to you. The predicted elapsed time might be as short as six months before the first output occurs from any of your business processes. While this is entirely feasible, it is challenging.

It is as well to keep explaining to your company that it will probably in fact be 18 months before the whole center is producing effectively and starting to deliver the additional benefits you anticipated when creating the business plan.

This exact moment, the point where you begin to take the first steps outlined in the business plan, will determine whether you will be as successful as you can be, reducing costs to a minimum, improving the quality of service, and providing a warm glow of satisfaction on all sides, or whether you will merely be reasonably successful. That isn't much different from the start of any new project, and the usual imperatives apply.

It is worth remembering that being comparatively successful against what your company was doing before the project started is only a poor result. The objective is to be comparatively successful against the achievements of the best projects in India. Unless your preparations for the start of the project or program have encompassed more than the business plan, you will already be fighting a rearguard action and you will be lucky to achieve success.

You will need to develop, preferably with any chosen supplier, a standard project plan, identifying the usual critical paths and the ideal sequence of activities. Much of the content will be directly derived from the business plan, but it will need to be supplemented with additional information.

How you record and analyze your experience in this project will determine your longer-term relationship with India. Your Indian partner or supplier will be looking to the longer-term relationship – from this point on, so should you.

The payback will come over the longer term and that is directly in your interests. In the same way that the supplier who can deliver the best solution technically may not be your best supplier for some of the reasons covered earlier, the most efficient delivery of the first project may not be in your best interests over the longer term. In short, don't cut every corner.

This will underline the importance of understanding the hidden costs in your initial business plan. During the first implementation phase you will have to draw on the money you have brought out into the open that may have initially been hidden costs.

In this chapter there are various recommendations for how to plan and monitor activities, and how they should be reported. In addition, I have always found it valuable to keep notes that record both issues as they arise and lessons to be learnt. Of course, these can become electronic concrete, filed away and never consulted. For that reason I never make my notes a narrative and I use PowerPoint, on the basis that unless something can be encapsulated in a few words in a bullet point it will never see the light of day again. If you hold a project review, it is instructive to present what you have recorded.

You can't entirely eliminate the extra difficulties of working across cultures, no matter how experienced you are. You should, however, have had enough preparation to be able to deal with any surprises in a determined and focused way, having accepted that what you can expect is the unexpected.

The normal ramifications of any project, wherever it occurs in the world, will still have to be dealt with. The ways of working that govern your company won't change just because you are working in the subcontinent. The sensitivities and range of interests that will come to the fore because it is an offshore project will, however, heighten some of the more emotional elements and certainly aggravate any existing internal political tensions.

Internal expectations

Throughout the progress of your offshoring activity, from the initial germ of an idea to the start of implementation, you will encounter all sorts of internal expectations. Some may be negative, expecting that the project must fail. Some will be too optimistic, and there will be disappointment when matters don't proceed as easily and quickly as some hopes might have suggested.

Whatever those internal expectations are on day one of the implementation, they will probably be unreasonable. The way of dealing with people who expect disaster is to encourage them at a low level. At the same time, you won't need advice to seek to discourage the optimists.

The real difficulties center on those people who have developed, or have had developed for them, impossible expectations. These can range from those intimately involved who let their imaginations and caution run away with them to those who have stood on the sidelines but have little information.

The first advice is to have in place the controls on information that are advocated in Chapter 11. This is quite straightforward in practice, especially if you have taken my other advice to run the project off-site. It is, however, not a complete answer.

You also need to ensure that you start setting – or resetting once the process has started – the internal expectations you want. At first this will be to a relatively small audience, because this project will be so commercially and competitively sensitive that it should not be known outside those you intend to be informed. Nevertheless, it is vital to get your message across. Although it is often counterintuitive to begin the implementation of a project with a focus on what is essentially internal politics, if you don't you will suffer.

Concentrate on when it will be possible to see change and benefits.

You will need to ensure that your audience understands that they will not see any changes, let alone improvements, for at least six months. The measurements you took before the project started and continue to take throughout are vital in creating and reinforcing appropriate expectations. The main point of these measures is not to dispel any soft, hazy glow of nostalgia for what used to be, but they may help do that too.

Micro-stepping

The essential paradox at the heart of most of the advice in this chapter is encapsulated in the fact that you are building the foundations for the long term but in order to do so must focus on the short term and the project plan. One answer is a micro-stepping approach, a technique that has some currency in India.

A micro-stepping plan should try to identify every single distinct action and expose it to close observation. It is like a highly granular traffic light system and should allow you to look at the data, consider what has been achieved and what should have been achieved, and indicate where the areas of stress are. The objective is not to have a management report, but a continually updated plan that you can monitor at a glance. It may seem surprising, but a micro-stepping plan eliminates many tendencies toward micro-management, precisely because you have the information available.

The best format for such a document is down to personal preference. The one I use is a spreadsheet, with a different sheet for each month. The extreme left-hand column contains the higher-level tasks, and the immediate column to the right of that is a list of what has to happen to deliver each task, broken down into separately described events within the overall work item. The key here is the level to which this column descends. The acid test in my experience is that the minimum is what can be accomplished in a day, as opposed to less than a day. The days of the relevant month head the columns to the right. For every day a task has an activity an x is put in the day column, and a different color x is substituted when the activity is completed.

This doesn't do away with Gantt charts and flow charts and project plans of the most beautiful design, but it does provide you with an instant view of what is happening, what was supposed to happen, and what did in fact happen. That view is assimilable without too much of a struggle. That's my second objective.

The main advantage of using such a plan, however, is to see how well the relationship with the supplier or partner is working. The document should be produced by that supplier. The best time to get it produced is before you sign the contract, preferably at as early a stage as practical. First, it will be a higher priority for the supplier at that point. Secondly, it will tell you a great deal about the company you propose to work with.

As a review tool and a shared repository of where the program is at any one moment, a micro-stepping plan is first class. There is enough detail for you to spot any fudges, but not so much detail that keeping it up to date becomes like an examination revision timetable, where you spend so much time updating it that there's no time for revision.

Don't manage – monitor

The other advantage of micro-stepping is that it will force you into the most appropriate role when offshoring. Your tendency will be to manage what is going on. The much more successful attitude is to *monitor* what is going on. Any ideas of managing need to be curbed. If you are using an Indian company or companies, they will not need you to manage them, but you, for your own peace of mind, will need to monitor them.

There are other reasons. Management in this context does its best to eliminate invention and new approaches, because it focuses on compliance with a given set of rules. It removes any real incentive for your supplier to think outside the box. Monitoring does the opposite. It shows that you are concerned and involved, but it also shows that you are seeking to work in partnership or at least alongside your supplier.

Monitoring should be backed up with a number of reinforcements.

You will need to put your own member of staff into the project, offshore. The trick here is to insist that the supplier or partner pays for this person, on the understanding that when you both agree the role has become superfluous, he or she will be removed from the offshore site and the supplier will gain by not having to pay his or her costs.

This idea needs a slight refinement. It is not a person but a role that the supplier should be paying for. In many ways it is good to rotate the person doing the role among different members of staff. One indirect benefit is that you will be exposing more members of your staff to Indian approaches, Indian quality, and the enthusiasm that Indians bring to their work. The more direct benefit is that different people will examine different aspects of the process and you won't have any danger of the person becoming accustomed to what is going on. The indirect benefits for the Indian supplier are that they will have more immediate contact with the customer and be able to look at what goes on through fresh eyes. Indeed, the exact person you put into the role will probably have less effect than the fact that someone is there.

Just because your supplier is paying for a member of your staff doesn't eliminate the benefit of having other people able to go to the offshore site. Monitoring is a way of life, not a single process. Other members of your team can be useful offshore, and probably with the same indirect benefit identified above: they will be exposed to Indian enthusiasm.

Reporting framework

A good part of what has to happen, despite the project plan and the microstepping document, won't actually be visible to you. The fact that you can't see it happening doesn't necessarily mean that progress isn't being made, but out of sight should not mean out of mind. As part of your monitoring activity, from the very start you will need to have an agreed program of reporting and reports. This is a scale issue. If you're simply trying out a couple of programmers, it won't matter too much. Once your project gets to be more than that, you'll need a good, solid framework.

You might consider sundowner reports. This is a variation report, whether from an agreed date or an agreed deliverable, or merely a variation in a minor matter. The quality approach Six Sigma is behind this concept. It is also what it says. Every day, at close of play Indian time – which to be frank may well coincide with the end of your office day despite the time difference – an updated report should arrive covering every activity on the project plan. This is not a vast textual exercise. Repeating "no progress" against an item every day may be all that is needed. While it isn't exciting, it is essential to know where you are.

Sundowners do keep everyone on their toes, as long as *you* read them. That is another reason you want them to be succinct. It also underlines the fact that the role of the business sponsor may be part time but is continual.

If you like this idea, the sundowner has to be agreed on day 1 – the day after you sign the contract, not the first day of implementation. Unless you insist on it from that moment, you will find it extraordinarily difficult to instate later, as it is not second nature to project teams of any nationality.

Such a bureaucratic measure will generate objections, especially to providing daily reports at the beginning of a major project when there is precious little to report. This objection is easily dealt with: you're asking for an electronic document to be updated and sent and the time taken will be minimal, once the information is available. If the protest moves on to saying that getting the information on a daily basis is tough, the person you are dealing with isn't up to the job.

Again, avoid moving from monitoring to managing. If there is a variation, establish what will be done either to assimilate or eliminate it. Don't manage it.

You will obviously need different reports for different time scales, for various milestones, for your internal meetings, and for reporting back, but you will find that the basis outlined above tends to make such reports merely a development of the information you already have.

Account manager

By insisting on these apparently short-term demands immediately, you are of course laying the foundation for the long term. You will be learning as early as is really practical whether you are going to be able to make the relationship work as you need it to.

You will remember that out of apparent chaos, Indians are able to create order at the very last minute. It happens too many times for it to be an accident, and it is a supreme achievement. On the other hand, just as you would regard a golfer who was particularly adept at getting out of the rough with some doubt as this would betray a remarkable amount of time practicing the skill, you may prefer to know about this Indian business expertise only *in extremis.*

You can be utterly confident that when required, everything and everyone will pull together. If a situation can be retrieved it will be. Of course, it is better not to get into that position in the first place. This good advice is sanctimonious without some indication of how to achieve that.

In addition to reports from the project team, keep in touch with your Indian company's sales person, or, if you have one, your Indian company's account manager. Let's use account manager here to cover both eventualities.

You will remember the advice to examine how the Indian supplier will manage you and your business as an account. When you move beyond the sales stage, you will discover another important result of account management.

For the supplier, the main reason may well be – probably should be – that it is looking to extend the contractual relationship with you. By keeping in close contact, the account manager should be sufficiently aware to understand where your initial project could fit into a larger picture.

For you, the immediate interest is different, though over time you will find you have the same need. If you, or more probably the program manager, have a formal review with your account manager every week, month, or at an appropriate interval, you will learn far more than if you merely interact with the project team. This is almost arbitrage – at the very least the minor differences between the two versions of what is being achieved will give you insights into where the project is.

This approach is beneficial onshore, but offshore it is doubly valuable. You might think both you and the account manager will be just as remote from the project team and privy to the same information. Nevertheless, the different personal contacts the account manager has with India and the project team, and the different imperatives under which they are operating, will result in quite different perspectives from yours. Of course the account manager is a sales person, with all that implies, but you will know how to interpret any gloss.

Any disparity, however slight, between the different sets of reports will be invaluable. Incidentally, if there are no disparities, that is rather more suspicious.

No surprises

Bad news doesn't improve by keeping; in fact it goes off even more. The main issue here is the extreme reluctance of any Indian to be anything but polite, and this may include trying to disguise a slipping delivery date for as long as possible. Make it clear early on that this is unacceptable. Insist on a lack of surprises as one of the key measures of the project. This may cause some astonishment and you may get all sorts of reassurance. It is still worth documenting.

You will no doubt have made some mistakes in the specification and be asking for elements in the project that prove more difficult in practice than anticipated. Your own project manager will have covered that sort of eventuality in his or her contingency planning. Your supplier will have bent over backwards to ensure that every problem was removed, but there will still be snags. There has never been a project that was perfectly specified, nor one that didn't cause friction between customer and supplier. You can deal with the problems, no matter how serious they are, if you have notice of them and if both sides have confidence in each other.

Defining what the measure of no surprises will be is difficult, but opposite numbers sitting down and working it out will make it more real, more understood, and will make a difference to a potentially huge cultural issue. In the West there is a reluctance to come clean about difficulties early enough. Indian politeness exacerbates this intensely.

Structural difficulties

You've had an introduction to the paralysis that may result from a brush with Indian civil law, and you've seen that the Indian Administrative Service can be a challenge. One branch of the latter is Customs and Excise, which is considered here as an illustration of how to deal with Indian officialdom, as well as how to know if your supplier is as aware as you need it to be.

The best comparison to Customs and Excise is the Indian Post Office, which is astonishingly reliable. You can trust that your letter or parcel will get through, almost no matter which part of India you are sending it to. There is an esprit de corps among Post Office employees that is a lesson to many service companies, and you will occasionally see generous tributes to employees who have gone through fire, flood, earthquake, and the monsoon to ensure that the post reached its destination. But what is not of the essence for the Indian Post Office is time.

The adventure with Customs is similar. You can guarantee that whatever is shipped to India will come out the other side of the customs procedures. Exactly when your goods will appear is sometimes not too much in focus, however. Your supplier can make a difference, and as much as two weeks can be lopped off the raw delivery date and the actual delivery that can be achieved. That can be important. If you need a certain piece of hardware to be with your supplier in India, it will be doubly significant.

This is actually, although usually tacitly, recognized by the Indian government. Whatever you do, faced with such structural difficulties, don't accept that anything is impossible. Experience with Customs and Excise is a paradigm of all structural difficulties in India. When you run into any difficulties, you can remember that the government doesn't want them to exist any more than you do. There's always a way through.

This isn't working

You must be prepared to say that the project or the relationship isn't working if you find that is the case. It's curious, but Indian politeness may rub off on you or at least on your project team, and it becomes difficult to draw attention to something going wrong, even if you know it is. There may even be a reluctance to report back to you or the project director. This may sound absurd, but it does happen.

You need confidence that your team will take the initiative. Often enough, especially because of the cultural issues, there will be more of a communication gap than anything else, but the possibility of this occurring still needs to be discussed.

Staying on track

There are various stages in a project where enthusiasm gives way to depression, followed by the slow climb to reality, and then the mundane delivery. As with any project, it is possible to predict these stages. Having done so, you need to take action and have in place ways of dealing with the descent into low morale.

One key piece of advice earlier was to baseline your existing processes and implementation. You will need evidence of progress to keep the project team working effectively and the continuing measurement process should help. It will be worth the extra cost, although people may mutter that you are pulling the plant up to examine its roots far too frequently to let it grow.

You may also find benefit management processes such as those that Cranfield University in the UK has created will help maintain fixity of purpose, especially in the team. There will inevitably be moments, as there are in any project, when you wonder what on earth possessed you to get involved. At that point a few guidelines and useful processes help enormously.

14
Creating Further Advantage

Achieving competitive edge or, in the case of IT outsourcing, regaining competitive parity through significant cost reductions has been the initial objective in moving most work to India. Making that first step, if you are working at any scale at all, will present difficult challenges. Achieving success is not guaranteed, but unlike conventional outsourcing projects within the domestic market, visible cost advantages should give you some comfort. With such structural success inherent if not built in, you may be tempted to rest on any laurels that happen to be hanging around when you do achieve those cost savings. If you do so, you will eliminate most of the longer-term advantages of working with India.

Your first deal with India should be seen as the starting point for adding a whole new dimension to your business, not merely as an end in itself. It is easy to lose sight of this perspective, as the cost savings and benefits leap out at you, or, more likely, as the pressing issues with your first project take your mind off anything but the here and now.

You have seen how important it is to baseline yourself against what is happening in other projects in India, and if possible in the rest of the world. For internal reasons you may only wish to compare yourself publicly against what your company was achieving before, but do remember that you are part of a monumental global change, taking service work from the West and transplanting it in the East. This revolution in how business is constructed and operates is so important for your own company, particularly at this precise moment, that you have to keep in mind why it is happening and view your results in that light.

It is not solely about making cost reductions, although that is not to belittle that result. It is about making the most *appropriate* cost reductions and, at the same time, achieving enormous gains in other ways for your business. The scale of the revolution, the speed with which it is happening, and its sustainability would probably be in doubt if immediate cost reductions alone were the only or even the eventual major benefits.

In this chapter, and to a limited extent in the next, the other drivers are considered. If you merely achieve cost savings you will have benefited, but you will not have grasped the real extra value that is being created in fracturing how processes are handled in modern companies.

Reexamining what is core

When you are fully immersed in a project, it will be extraordinarily difficult to take a broader perspective on what is happening. The first injunction here is to be aware of that wider view again, and to stimulate some internal discussion on how to achieve better results, both from your first foray into India and then during your longer-term relationship with Indian business.

You need to go back to first principles so that you can have a firm basis for moving forward. There are a number of stages.

The first part of looking at a wider view should encompass the context of your existing contract. As soon as you are confident of the service and relationship with your supplier, or your own management capability if you have now taken over a facility that has been built for you, you need to go back to your own business and examine it closely. It will be intellectually difficult to focus there, but it will reap dividends. In the light of your experience, consider again the key question of what is core and non-core in your business.

When the analysis of what is core was first introduced in Chapter 2, it was emphasized that it has to be seen as a process. The history of outsourcing IT development and then business processes has shown that what is considered core will shrink over time. Translating that theoretical understanding into practical business sense is usually quite a problem, even for strategic thinkers. If you have just made a major investment on the basis of an analysis that you are being encouraged to challenge perhaps as little as 12 months later, you can see the difficulty this can cause.

The second offshore project for any company is usually bolder and more draconian in its concept of what is core, reducing it more significantly than most people find acceptable at first sight. The logic, and the reason why this boldness will be adopted despite the discomfort, is that this will be seen as circumventing the process you are caught up in. Knowing that in another 12 months, on the basis of experience so far, you will inevitably have to go back and reanalyze your assumptions about what is core means that most people come to think they might as well make that intellectual leap now.

With this body of knowledge it might seem possible to short-circuit the initial, less radical analysis, and make a much bigger move the first time. For many right reasons, such as risk aversion and the need to move in assimilable steps, this is not generally possible for the first project. It makes a more rigorous step in your second project more essential, however.

Changing what you do as well

Less apparently challenging but equally valuable is to reexamine what you are doing once you have taken the business process offshore. We have seen that the advice is to outsource your processes as they are. It may be that they are inefficient or ineffective, but you have survived with them thus far. You can now examine them with the benefit of new eyes and unfamiliarity. In the close examination of what you do, you may also find you have further insights into what is core, so this is not a completely different step from the previous one.

In the six months after the start of a particular call center service offshore, two business analyses were carried out. If this sounds coordinated that's misleading, but it was fortuitous.

Alongside a separate focus on reducing what was considered core so that it could also be taken offshore, another reevaluation started with what the output of the call center process was meant to be. The company was incidentally pleased with the new service and believed it had taken an enormous step. The call center provided a straightforward service, answering simple, factual questions from potential customers. It gave out timetable information and fielded complaints of various kinds.

The previous measure had been the number of calls taken, with some softer measures, such as whether the potential customer thought the information was relevant and then helpful. In discussions with the Indian company providing the outsourced service, it was realized that this particular quantitative measure was probably wrong in terms of the business results required. The real measure had to focus on whether potential customers became *actual* customers, and then to decide whether the way the call center handled the queries could make a difference, for example by being friendlier and more encouraging.

The idea was raised that making use of the call center more engaging and less off-putting could change the impact the company made. If the information could be presented or given out in such a way that it encouraged customers to think well of the onshore company, it might well influence take-up of its services.

Interestingly enough, the initial concern with the appropriateness of the measures employed became less important. It was realized that creating a reliable and valid correlation between a more customer-friendly call center and greater take-up of the company's services was probably too difficult to achieve quickly. That didn't stop the thought process and the reexamination of the way the call center functioned, however.

The first major change the company and its Indian supplier made to address the accessibility of its service was simple. The automatic voice response system, the disembodied voice that invites callers to select a menu item by pressing a number key, was replaced by human intervention. By removing the system some cost was added back into the operation, but nowhere near as much as if it had been contemplated in the West.

Most people are familiar with the sheer mind-numbing imbecility of the slow dance through such options, wondering which is closest to the choice you really want. You are always worried you will have forgotten what the options are. If you do manage to choose the wrong one, you can end up in the endless circles of Dante's inferno.

The cost of deciding to have a direct response was higher than the self-screening automatic system because a few more agents had to be employed, but the improvement in customer satisfaction – or, rather, lower customer frustration – at a comparatively marginal cost was an overwhelming benefit. The soft measures showed this, because people were phoned back and questioned about their experience.

The hard measures of whether more people in fact became customers were designed in parallel, but were difficult to check for accuracy against a wealth of other factors that probably influenced decisions about buying. In a brave move, it was agreed that even without the hard measures, the improvement in the call center's output justified the extra cost.

Further incremental steps were taken to change the apparent output of the call center, using soft measures to confirm the results where hard measures were problematic. By conducting this reexamination, a further real benefit was realized. The separate requestioning of what was core was reinforced by what had happened in considering the outputs of the call center. It was possible to think about the core in a more incremental and less intellectually challenging way, because how the call center now operated changed how the company thought about its activities.

The capability that had been left onshore was initially seen as a whole order of magnitude different from what had been outsourced and therefore beyond question part of the core of the company. What had been so far untouched centered on selling and ticketing. It was seen originally as real customer interaction and too close to revenue generation in the business.

A dual analysis now reexamined the existing, apparent core. The first related to what the output of the simple information call handling was meant to be. The second looked at the cost savings that had been achieved in the outsourced service and the changes in image that had been possible. By degrees, once the questioning started, it became more and more impossible to justify the initial idea of what was core. It was decided that core in this case really could apply only to the onshore design of the services and products, marketing, and the company's public relations activities.

The element that apparently tipped the analytical balance was achieved by calling direct sales and ticketing "fulfillment," because that seemed to reduce its importance. The real difference, as opposed to this cosmetic element, was in first of all examining what the call center output should be, and then following through a logic that showed how intertwined information and sales actually were for the company.

Instead of following this kind of natural, evolutionary process, which was successful enough but not so much planned as stumbled into, you should take an active role in reexamining all the assumptions that underpinned your initial decisions, as soon as you begin to feel comfortable with the new service provision. It is deceptively easy not to, especially when you have a success on your hands. However, you too may have had experience of watching a business person who grew revenues and profits by 20 percent year on year over three years being lionized for this performance within his or her own company, while he or she had in fact managed to shrink the company's market share as the market was growing at 30 percent.

Your benchmarking is against other companies going offshore.

I stress once again that the dangers of being self-satisfied are higher if you are outsourcing to India, especially for your first contract, because the opportunities to succeed are so high and it will be difficult not to make enormous strides.

Staff quality

It is probably difficult to grasp the opportunity that a different standard of staff can offer you in India. When you look at the quality of potential recruits, you may initially not realize the considerable difference in those you have the opportunity of working with. Higher educational standards and different perspectives may not seem that significant when you are thinking about people being engaged as call center agents. You will in all likelihood change that view once you have begun to work with such people in India.

Western call center staff don't tend to be graduates. They are also comparatively not well paid, nor in a job with status and expectations. In India, in contrast, they are.

Whatever you assume about your business and the business model you adopt once you have made that strategic move offshore, factor in a reassessment of your processes and their outputs in the light of having a different kind of staff working for you. With a more highly educated work force you have the opportunity to rethink what you are doing from the ground up. Examining just one constant of business planning will illustrate that a step change in your business and operational model may well be possible.

The late twentieth century produced a multitude of research that pinpointed the comparatively low cost of selling an existing customer a further service compared with the massive costs of gaining an entirely new customer. It is possible to think of the 1990s as the decade that discovered cross-selling as a management goal. Huge efforts were devoted to establishing what the current ratio of products per customer was, creating a business plan that would, say, add an average of half a service or product to every customer, and then implementing a sales campaign to achieve it. While the frequency of revisiting the goal, and changing the campaign to achieve it, always suggested that the actual results were less than encouraging, that doesn't mean that the objective was wrong or inappropriate, only that the means of gaining it were suspect.

Many cross-selling initiatives foundered not least because the staff who were retrained to do cross-selling couldn't then do their proper jobs. In many cases this was not their fault, since they were driven by inappropriate priorities and incentives.

You may have had the experience of standing in a queue in your bank branch waiting for the teller to finish dealing with the customer in front of you so you could pay in a check, only to discover that the teller had launched into a discussion about whether the person had adequate life insurance. You could put the failure to cross-sell down to the crudity of the training or the inappropriateness of the moment. You could question whether staff were able to recognize the appropriate moment for a sales engagement. You could legitimately ask whether it was a staff problem or whether management objectives were seriously at fault. In any number of cases, such activities have soured the relationship between customer and bank.

The value of the concept is not altered by such an example. If it is reduced to the simple nostrum that selling an additional product or service to an existing customer has to be more cost-effective, it is indisputable most of the time. Nevertheless, it is not a simple matter to translate the concept into reality, otherwise it would have been achieved ten years ago.

With the different kind of staff who are going to be in your employ in India, coupled with the significant opportunity to change the way you are dealing with potential customers and a reduced cost base that should give you more freedom to try out new approaches, cross-selling should once more be on the agenda. While the way to address the concept will be different in each business environment, this may be one of the key developments that going offshore enables.

You will also be able to pilot such a new business initiative offshore with far less risk. By doing so you will not be flying in the face of my strictures against pilots of your outsourcing activity mentioned earlier. In that case, you already had a process that worked to a satisfactory degree. The business pilot discussed here is for something new.

The second benefit from having a more highly educated work force, and one that is trained specifically in the process rather than having gained experience over a number of years, is the productivity and quality gains that are possible in India. Quality measures are more difficult to quantify unambiguously, but productivity gains are relatively easy to demonstrate.

In many cases, there will be a whole range of measures that show productivity has increased. Taken without quality assurance such gains are open to suspicion, but in most cases the experience is that quality measures will have improved.

In the example of removing the automatic voice response system, the number of additional agents was rather lower than first envisaged because the staff were able to deal with more calls than the equivalent onshore staff. In another instance, call handling times were reduced. Documents processed per employee were higher by an order of 7 to 10 percent. The quality measure, even if loosely defined, was at 95 percent, compared with the equivalent onshore of about 92 percent. The turnaround time, which was set at 24 hours in the service level agreement, was in practice about 15 hours. Whereas the service was costed using 235 full-time equivalents, in fact only 187 full-time equivalents were required.[1] Such examples are not rare.

Your new employees will also tackle different tasks, and it is not unusual to receive additional analysis of your data, giving you new insights into what is happening in your business. The value gain here is normally constrained by your own ability to cope with a different response to the job in hand. You will nevertheless be surprised at the ingenuity of the Indians working for you and the ways in which they can add value when you have confidence in them.

An Indian company that started a medical transcription service for a group of hospitals (mentioned in Chapter 3) was asked to move into more and more areas, including, crucially, customer billing. That was more complex than it sounds, because underneath the invoices the customer saw were the raw costs associated with medical events. One of the human intelligent agents in India handling customer billing noticed two aspects of the costs involved.

The first was that different hospitals had very different cost structures for what was apparently the same heart bypass operation. Secondly, different surgeons had different cost structures for what appeared to be the same operation.

There were many caveats here, not least that one hospital might have been dealing with more seriously ill patients and that there was no correlation between cost, effectiveness, and the outcomes under consideration. That is important. For most patients, and perhaps for the marketing departments of the hospitals concerned, surviving and then having a healthy life are rather more important than knowing that the surgeon involved is more efficient in cost terms.

Nevertheless, the raw cost information was presented to the client. Over six months all the information, gleaned from the data that had been supplied but never analyzed cost-effectively or in a timely manner, was used as a management tool, and resulted in significant improvements in individual approaches to such operations. The Indian company was asked to extend the analysis and a mutually successful further service was developed.

This type of added value will not happen in every contract, but there is enough circumstantial evidence that it is becoming common. There is another benefit, which is just as true for outsourcing in general. It may be that the right sourcing will give *you* an appropriate amount of time to devote to your core business and so come up with beneficial developments yourself.

This reanalysis and development of your processes should ideally wait until you are confident with your first initiative. It isn't inappropriate to start earlier, but all the evidence shows that doing so too early will make you more cautious. The objective here is to ensure that the next step you take is a bold one.

Sweating the assets

The costs of buildings and infrastructure in India are broadly the same as they would be in the West. You do have an opportunity, however, to a greater extent than seems possible in the West, to use your assets more effectively.

With the difference in time zones between India and the West, a process that requires an active response from your staff to customers, internal or external, will be working from afternoon Indian time through to early morning, depending whether you are on the West Coast of the United States or in mainland Europe. This means that at least one eight-hour shift is free for back-office processes that do not require direct contact.

Many service centers that were designed for single-shift operation are in due course utilized for two shifts and companies claim they can achieve an average utilization of between two and two-and-a-half times per day. Sweating your assets like this is obviously a major advantage, and it does reinforce the attractiveness of considering the second and subsequent projects as soon as you are comfortable.

The real output

Reexamining the nature of the outputs from your processes can be partly built into your business model by periodically having a formal review of any service level agreement (SLA) you have in place between the offshore service center and head office. Another opportunity for fine-tuning or improving process outputs can be achieved by having a similar review of those outputs.

SLAs are the easier issue to deal with. In the first instance you will, in all probability, be putting a known process offshore and you will have a good understanding of what you want out of the efforts your staff put into making it work. Nevertheless, it is still worth examining in some detail on a regular basis what the SLA is and whether it remains appropriate.

This moves beyond the usual issues with SLAs, which can be notorious for any manner of problems. In the worst examples the SLA is met in full and yet the end user does not get a service that is adequate, let alone of sufficient quality. It may seem that this is a problem for the supplier, but to have got into that position in the first place points to a more serious underlying issue, that one side or the other did not sufficiently understand what was required.

There are numerous examples where a service level agreement was being met or exceeded, but the customers, both internal and external, remained unhappy. Monitoring the service levels means questioning how valid they are as well as how reliably they are being carried out. Good business management is still required, whether it is in Pune or Hanover.

A formal review of an SLA inevitably starts with comparing performance measures against the SLA. That is always the simplest part. The focus during the formal periodic review should be on the appropriateness and applicability of the existing SLA.

The Indian value add

The most important value an Indian supplier or partner can add to your business often lies in unexpected areas. To appreciate that, you need to understand how to work with your supplier to gain the best results for both sides. One key benefit of working with Indian companies is the flexibility they can bring.

At one level this flexibility is readily understandable. Although no business model anywhere in the world can allow for processes, people, or resources to be turned on and off at will, you will find you can change what you or your supplier do, alter the focus of your processes, and apply more people to a particular bottleneck in your business operations in a much more demand-driven way in India than you can in the western business environment. Maintaining a close relationship with your Indian company, even if you are dealing with it merely as a supplier, can repay all sorts of dividends and provide added value for you.

Flexibility can also be less immediately quantifiable. Discussing with the Indian company what you need and brainstorming can offer numerous different and unexpected ways of tackling problems, from the immediate to the more deeply seated. In contrast to the advice that you must distrust an Indian company for which nothing is a problem, at some point you will inevitably discover that there is nearly always a way of making reality what has suddenly arisen as an idea.

The continuing role of your supplier will be important. Remember all the good qualities that Indian education and social patterns produce, and work with your supplier and that culture.

When you are waiting for an Indian business person to turn up, when you have some vital piece of equipment mired in Customs, or when head office is demanding to know the exact minute the new outsourced process will start, it can be difficult to see all the positive sides of working in India. Yet as soon as you allow your Indian supplier to work with you, immense benefits will flow.

The supplier will have very good insight into what is going on in your process, partly because they will be looking at it as a strange event, not one that has been there for ever. The Indian staff will also be motivated to deal with what you want in all sorts of different ways, partly because they won't have any folk memories of failures when attempting to do things differently.

All this is reasonably straightforward and you will develop a relationship that suits you both, bearing in mind that whatever form of contract you have arrived at, it is in both your interests for it to continue in the long term. In addition, there is an extension to this that you should monitor as part of the value of dealing with Indian business.

New directions

Keep a close eye on where your Indian company is heading, what new avenues it is looking at, and how it is changing in its structure and go-to-market stance. This is not to reinforce suspicion or to suggest that you have to be extra careful and wary. The reason is far more involving and interesting than that.

Indian business people are agile, subtle, and very clued in. If there is the slightest whiff of a trend that might prove advantageous, your Indian company will know about it – before you do. It may be that whatever the supplier is doing is quite distinct from your interests, but by following your supplier you are far more likely to stay ahead of the game than if you look at your western competitors or suppliers.

Indeed, when working with Indian companies and senior business people, one of the biggest challenges will be keeping up with the various initiatives produced. There is a downside to this, as you may feel there is a lack of focus on real issues and be bewildered by all the opportunities under consideration. I have experienced this and struggled with mindsets that have already moved on to something new while I am trying to create a definite form to the last concept. Nevertheless, it is always stimulating and you will learn a great deal.

While it is extraordinarily difficult to quantify the value in all of this, there is a value in just having the Indian and western perspectives rub against each other, causing sparks and fresh ideas.

You will also know when you are winning and understanding what is going on in India. It's when you ask an apparently innocuous question and get a smile of recognition back. That is a real signal – and you need to follow it up! You will have penetrated a bastion of shared understanding that usually exists only between Indian business people. Though you may not understand what it is you have stumbled on, you will discover something new that is worth exploring.

15
Breaking into the Indian Market

I n addition to the potential offered by offshoring to India, your company may want to investigate the opportunities of supplying its own goods and services to the Indian domestic market. That market is still tiny but is growing quickly, up to five times the US rate of growth. As outlined earlier, the World Bank is predicting that India will be the world's fourth largest economy before 2050. It would be a real mistake to miss the growing opportunities there. Your Indian supplier or partner could be a conduit to a market that will shortly become explosive.

As I stressed earlier in the book, no figures about India are reliable in themselves, but it is nevertheless important to understand certain facts about the Indian economy. It still has a foot in its past, providing commodities to the world market, and yet is surprisingly diverse.

Agricultural production is a high proportion of the economy, at over 25 percent. This figure would be higher if it were not for rich countries subsidizing their agricultural exports, depressing world prices, and reducing the value of India's agricultural products. That decline in agricultural commodity prices has really depressed India's gross domestic product.

Looking at countries' gross domestic product comparatively is usually the only way to comprehend it properly, but this is limited because you can only use the most up-to-date figures for the slowest country to report. The baseline here, on that basis, is the year 2000. All the figures in the next few paragraphs use the same criteria and source.[1]

In that year, the gross domestic product of the USA was about $10,082 trillion. France and Germany reached approximately $1,537 trillion and $2,189 trillion respectively. The UK got to $1,524 trillion. China had a gross domestic product of about $5,019 trillion. India was at $2,394 trillion. These last two figures, with China about double India's size, are continuing to diverge, as China's economy does appear to be growing at about twice the rate of India's.

The per capita figures show the real differences between the West and India and then China and India. Per capita income for the US, Germany, France, and the UK was $35,401, $26,538, $25,975, and $25,407 respectively. In China per capita income was $3,976 and in India it was only $2,358.

Therefore 1 percent growth in the US is substantially more in money terms than, say, 5 percent growth in India, but compound growth shifts the picture over a number of years.

However inaccurate the figures are, it is clear that India isn't yet a crock of gold. Its potential is the focus, and it must be stressed that the actual opportunities can only be addressed with patience and sanguinity.

IT and telecommunications

At a micro level, it is possible to give a snapshot of the sort of revenue opportunities India presents in its domestic market. Official Indian figures for the domestic IT market show that revenues reached about $6.5 billion during 2002–3, of which software and services accounted for around $2.8 billion. The ICT market during 2001–2 was worth $5.9 billion.

A subsidiary of a multinational IT and services company assessed the total market it could address in India, for hardware, software, and services, as worth about $400 million in 2002. Of that, only about 10 percent was economically addressable: the cost of sale was too high and the return was too low because the market is so price sensitive. Individual account directors in the UK had targets in the $50–100 million range. When the profitable total market space you can address is less than a single account would actually yield in the UK, you can see that India is not an obviously tempting domestic market.

The argument was therefore that the Indian domestic market wasn't worth addressing and in fact that was perfectly correct in the short term. From its small base, however, the overall market in India is growing third fastest in the world, as we saw in Chapter 1. The potential is huge and worth understanding. From this basis, you might be able to appreciate when is going to be the right time to begin taking the Indian domestic market seriously.

Of the more than one billion people in India, there are about 150 million English speakers. Although the correspondence with western society is scarcely exact, this number of people is usually referred to as the educated middle class and is probably the target market for an international company. The market itself, including fast-moving consumer goods, is growing at more than 6 percent, whereas the rest of the world is barely managing 1 percent.

In some market segments, investment to address this group of people is increasing very fast indeed. In IT and telecommunications spending is growing extremely rapidly, as liberalization and the need to compete with global companies entering the domestic market focus Indian minds on deficiencies in their own capabilities. The best estimate is that spending on IT in financial services, for example, is growing at 30 percent.

The State Bank of India is investing in new branch systems, mainframes, back-office systems, payments systems, and customer management systems – all at once in a major attempt to remain competitive. This was from a low base, as its spending on such infrastructure used to be severely limited. Its branch systems were just that: even where a branch had a system, it was stand-alone, and data was transferred at best by phone, probably by floppy disk or paper, and mostly not at all. As a result, the opportunities are vast – in size if not in profitability. The bank has nearly 10,000 branches. Equipping every branch with a telephone is quite a large undertaking, no matter how price sensitive the market is.

The size of any bank's total investment is not what it would be in the West, yet we are seeing a revolution in spending and, even more significantly, in attitudes toward investment. The largest insurance company in India, the biggest in the world by number of policy holders, had an IT budget in 2000 of some $29 million that it could spend externally. When people were cheap, it was more expensive to automate. Only a few years later, that perspective is dying. After all, you can't send a runner with a cleft stick and a message from Mumbai to Pune, let alone from Mumbai to Dallas, every day.

To give some more figures, government spending on IT systems is growing at 25 percent; investment in IT in transportation is growing at over 15 percent.

As far as telecommunications are concerned, commercial and government spending is growing at 25 percent. The number of phone lines is still running at about 1 percent of households, which are likely to be larger than western equivalents. Even now only about 10 percent of middle-class households have a landline. The proportion of cellular phones is larger that that, and that market is increasing enormously as any walk through Indian metros will show, even though India, unlike China, is committed to a huge investment in fixed lines. It is said to be installing more of a fiber-optic backbone than any other country.

If we move from business-to-business to end-user services and consumer and fast-moving goods, we see the same enormous growth patterns, from a low base. For instance, there were some six million credit cards in India in 2001, and they were owned by fewer than two million people. The current estimate is that card holder numbers have doubled since. You don't need a credit card unless you have the ability to buy and the propensity to do so, and the potential market for credit cards is huge.

Price sensitivity

You nevertheless have to deal with a level of price sensitivity that vividly demonstrates the elasticity of demand. Differences of less than INR1 – that is, about 2¢ in US or Europe and about 1.3p in the UK – can provoke an enormous change in consumption.

The best example is the cola wars. In India they are almost entirely focused on the price of a bottle of cola, as the advertising reveals. Taste? Glamorous associations? Celebrity endorsements? There are references to all of those, but price is number one, on every poster and in every television advertisement.

In 2003, Coca-Cola eventually implemented a strategy that enabled it to compete with Pepsi, the market leader, after it had bought the number two brand in India, Thumbs Up, and run it down. Its strategy had many ramifications, not least important logistical and market support measures such as providing fridge loans to village traders, but the most significant elements were reducing the size of the bottle from 300ml to 200ml and making the price INR5, about 10¢ in Europe and the US and 7p in the UK. This was effectively about half its previous price and approached impulse level. Coca-Cola claims Indian revenues of about $1 billion, but doesn't make much, if any, profit.

This price sensitivity is not only at the fast-moving consumer goods level but in business-to-business, and is enshrined for government-owned enterprises in sealed bids, decided apparently entirely on the lowest price. The government procurement process is overseen by the Corruption Vigilance Committee (CVC), which does have real teeth, even if one impression is that only the lowliest rascals get caught. It is quite usual to see board members move heaven and earth to meet the regulations that the CVC is there to oversee, and that is always reassuring to foreign businesses. There is an important anonymous route to the CVC, which people do use.

It is possible to win contracts without having the lowest price, on the basis of quality and fitness for purpose. I have done so, but I have also lost contracts on wafer-thin price differences. In either case it will be nail-bitingly close – and full of stress, for all sides. For the government organization it is particularly nerve-racking. If you can take a detached view, it is interesting to watch the question of whether it is possible to go for a higher-priced bid climb through the hierarchy.

Then there is taxation. The prices of imported, especially luxury, goods might lead you to think that prices are similar to those in the West, implying western margins. This is misleading. Most have high tariffs on them and then there are various sales taxes. The margins will have been cut to the slimmest possible – probably slimmer than you can contemplate at the moment.

India is also in the throes of introducing a value added tax (VAT) system, just like Europe. (Every time a product or service is sold on it attracts tax at a percentage of that sale price. A business buyer can reclaim the tax paid against the tax collected. When an end user actually pays, the end supplier can reclaim the tax already paid, and remits the balance to the relevant tax authority.) The introduction of VAT is designed to regularize sales taxes across the country, but it may not do that – and that is one reason suggested for the failure to introduce VAT effectively. Being India, the implementation date in various states has come and gone with no noticeable difference – and no VAT.

The message should be clear: don't expect to make much money in the Indian domestic market, at least for a few years. You can, however, build a market position now and neither the cost of entry nor your investment risk will be huge, especially if you consider the methods suggested here.

Being number one

One school of marketing and business development suggests that only number one in any mature market, as long as it has at least 30 percent market share, makes money. Number two and possibly number three in that market break even, and everyone else probably loses money.

If you could become number one in your market segment in India, in contrast, it might not guarantee a profit, but it would be a good platform for the future. Becoming number one in such a rapidly growing market, with political stability, a recognized judicial system, and a free press, looks an attractive prospect. Market domination means that you will be well placed once the market grows. Then, if you look at the multiplier effect from the sheer number of people who could be your customers, there is reason to consider India's domestic market properly because it, in turn, might reduce your unit costs.

The scale of the opportunities

In the complete opposite of a medieval executioner who had to hang, draw, and quarter victims, in that order, and ensure they were kept alive to suffer all the way through, my object here has been to suppress too much enthusiasm for the current Indian domestic market, while keeping you interested in it.

Nevertheless, having suppressed any nascent excitement, here is a flavor of the reasons why even now you should start to understand what India might have to offer. Some of the major projects that are being seriously considered in India are quite extraordinary. The sheer volume of needs creates its own logic and immensity.

A national identity card program is proposed. As yet there is no social security, national insurance number, or identity card in India. There are thought to be more than one billion Indians who need such a card. At even $10 a card – complete with infrastructure – you are talking about huge revenues. What is more, there is a national security issue – in fact a whole series of national security issues – that are driving the need for an identity card, whether it is the dispute over Kashmir and Jammu, infiltration from Bangladesh, Tamil insurgency, Naxilite terrorists in Andhra Pradesh, or organized crime. When national security is at stake, governments tend to spend the money.

The Home Ministry and the Indian consultancy that advised it knew it was ridiculous to contemplate creating a billion identity cards at one go. It certainly couldn't be done quickly. The suggestion was therefore to address three-quarters of the population, and to take three years to do it.

This was still plainly nonsensical. Assigning 700,000 cards a day, every day of the year for three years sounds daunting, even if you had first compiled the database, yet this is the scale of the task. It was proposed that fingerprints would be used, that each fingerprint file would be about 10Kb, and that 700,000 such files would be created every day. By the end of day one, the last file would have to be checked for a negative match against 699,999 other files. After 10 days, the last file would have to be checked against nearly 7 million files, as would every one of that day's 700,000 files; at the end of year one, it would have to be checked for a negative match against 250,000,000 files. The significance of the negative match is that each file has to be checked against each existing file – because you can only come up with a positive match if there is a duplicate. There shouldn't be too many duplicates, unless the whole system is corrupt. Every file therefore has to be checked against every existing file.

Even the figure of 750 million records and identity cards also presupposes that no one will die, no one will be born, and no one will change their name in the proposed three years. The scale of this national identity project dwarfs anything else in the world. The current largest project involves only some 70 million people and will take more than seven years.

The project will go ahead for security reasons, nevertheless, probably on a state-by-state basis. Providing any services or products for it will generate a continuing flow of work, if not huge profits, for many, many years.

As another indication of scale in India, an opportunity was presented to me following a delightful exchange with the chief secretary of one of the state governments. He started by flattering me and said I obviously knew a great deal about outsourcing, so would I like to consider taking on the administration of the state government? With a sinking feeling that I was being drawn into one of those quagmires that marketing and management training never quite prepares you for, I asked him how many people he was thinking of transferring.

It was difficult to give an exact figure. He thought, however, that I should budget for 1,300,000 people. I thanked him for the opportunity. "Oh, there is one further point before you take this on. We want to keep about 100 back."

Why was this? "They're the ones who are any good," he said. "We'll hang on to those."

It is seriously worth considering the scale of investment that will be made in Indian infrastructure. New roads are being built, new manufacturing capacity is being created, energy supply is being tackled with new urgency and control, and education is being targeted as one of the nation's priorities in a way that has not been possible before. The cycle of investment is going upwards and there will be huge demand created throughout the economy.

Finally, there are two longer-term suggestions. You might like to consider a further benefit for your own company out of investing in the Indian domestic market, if you are in the business-to-business sector. By having a presence in the Indian market, using Indian resources to deliver projects domestically, you will be able to create a resource pool, trained in your company's goods and services, that you in turn could use offshore. What better way to train a project-focused group of people than in live projects?

Secondly, because the Indian economy and services infrastructure is having to change, it may be worth having discussions with appropriate Indian decision makers focused on their domestic market and offer to help create their strategies in India. By doing so, and ensuring that new Indian processes are similar to western methods, you will be able to suggest that transferring business processes offshore will be that much easier.

In both cases, doing so was advantageous to me and represented a win–win strategy.

Reciprocity

Reciprocity is a deceptively attractive business idea that is usually far too difficult to make work. My experience is instructive, partly because it will show you why it could be different if you address the Indian domestic market with a narrow definition of reciprocity.

After a few years' serious engagement with reciprocal trading as a concept in the West, I have decided that it is actually not possible. I was looking at cases where, if the company I represented bought from another company, that company would agree to buy from my company.

There are legal challenges to such an arrangement, especially if there is any hint of a cartel, but the real killer is the lack of flexibility. I found it a little like signaling in a game of bridge. When you signal in bridge yourself, it is absolutely reasonable and obvious. When your partner signals, however, it's almost impossible to tell that a signal has been given, let alone to interpret it.

At least, that's how the post-hand arguments work out.

Similarly, reciprocal deals make perfect sense when you benefit from them and it is obvious why they are valuable. However, when they cause you to lose competitive advantage or flexibility, they are unacceptable and not recognizable as falling within the definition of reciprocity.

My advice is to steer clear. Reciprocal trading of this broad type is not going to work, especially in a multicultural environment.

A narrower concept can work, nevertheless, and the term reciprocity is still useful, as it develops from the relationship between you and the Indian company. The focus is not on a quid pro quo but on working together because you already have an effective relationship.

While the cost of entry to the Indian market won't be high in cash terms, the licensing and permit hurdles to overcome can be daunting and you will need local insights and relationships.

I have set up a company in India for a British organization. Without the inside track that my local knowledge gave me, it would have been a non-starter. In fact, the organization had received a pretty flat rejection by the Reserve Bank of India before I intervened.

You need that inside knowledge even to contemplate entering the Indian domestic market, so who do you know who can help? Your Indian supplier or partner.

It can start with discussions about how to take your wares into India. Since your supplier or partner is already in an export framework and has the local knowledge you need, the chances are reasonably high that there is something worth exploring. It goes beyond that, too, even if not immediately, because India is a clearing house for much of southeast Asia.

Your suggestion may initially meet with bewilderment. Your supplier will be aware that there is a lack of revenue opportunity in India. He or she will know about the price sensitivity, the cultural issues, and the real bone of contention, the fiscal advantages enjoyed from export revenues. Helping a western company enter the Indian market will provide absolutely no fiscal advantages and look like a long bet with some daunting opportunity costs.

There is a winning card in your hand, however, that will turn the conversation into a genuine exchange of ideas. Not only are Indian business people flexible, they also have a real, though often submerged, belief that India's domestic market will be important and that they will soon have to consider addressing it seriously themselves. Such a proposition will therefore get under their guard in two ways – it's a novel and exciting possibility and, more importantly, it's a huge potential market that they know best how to address.

This is a business discussion that will have value, even if it doesn't lead immediately to results, as you will have placed the issue on the agenda. In most cases your Indian supplier or partner will come back to you with suggestions after having thought it through in great detail.

16
Corporate Social Responsibility

Over the last ten years estimates suggest that some 10 million jobs have been taken offshore from the US alone, to various locations. A good proportion of these have been in manufacturing, but as services jobs are taken offshore in increasing numbers in the next few years, this number may be dwarfed. Losing professional jobs is going to be more high profile than losing manufacturing jobs, as professionals usually know better how to create political waves.

We are already beginning to see the first signs of resistance, with some US states contemplating legislation banning offshoring for government work. The appearance of websites such as www.stopoffshoreoutsourcing.com points to a growing sense of unease. There has been some effective lobbying in the UK – low key as yet, but nevertheless serious – about the migration of services jobs. As mentioned earlier, Prudential Insurance of the UK had a public relations disaster when it revealed it was going to outsource thousands of call center jobs to India. Under intense pressure, it gave a commitment that it would not enforce any compulsory redundancies in its call centers until at least 2005. And prompted by the fact that by the end of 2004 Norwich Union, a UK insurance company that is part of the Aviva Group, will have nearly 4,000 jobs being carried out in India, the UK finance-sector union Amicus is asking for a European Parliamentary inquiry into the impact of offshoring on the European economy. Amicus is also suggesting that final-year students should not accept jobs with companies that are taking jobs offshore. More positively, another union, Unifi, has gained the concession from Barclays bank that staff made redundant by jobs going offshore will be given doubled notice periods.

There have been reports of other European countries being alarmed and France has shown the first signs of intransigence. The EU has started to use phrases like "socially intelligent" to describe the approach it requires if work goes offshore, *immediate* economic grounds are also necessary, and companies should not close *profitable* operations. Many conferences on offshore projects incorporate discussions about a backlash in response to jobs moving offshore.

Nevertheless, we need to get these points into perspective. There are other initiatives that are more forward looking, such as requiring a proportion of any savings to be spent on retraining. I have also engaged in a number of conversations with trade unions and other relevant organizations to understand their perceptions, judge their levels of awareness, and see what the likely response is. There are serious concerns, and it is entirely appropriate to start thinking through the repercussions and issues in a logical way. The starting point is an ill-defined but important concept: corporate social responsibility.

Corporate social responsibility (CSR) usually implies some sort of continuing commitment and investment in the underdeveloped or low-cost country. While this is not at all wrong, it needs to be broadened. However, even companies that enshrine some form of corporate social responsibility in their ethical statements are sometimes astonishingly reluctant to grapple seriously with such ideas, opportunities, and issues. Before bringing the argument closer to home, we should start with global concerns.

There are two concepts absolutely at the heart of corporate social responsibility, whether it is aimed at India or your domestic market, and these will inform this chapter. The first is sustainability, and in a corporate context this has many meanings. The most important is that the social investment of whatever kind, whether it is time, materials, money, or effort, has to be able to continue when the current business sponsor moves on, is moved on, retires, or the company ceases its investment.

The second is that it must be demand led. However well meant it is, too often CSR investment is triggered solely by what the potential donor company has to offer, regardless of need or demand. Government ministers in developing countries will readily identify projects where an inappropriate investment has actually cost the recipient country more than any benefit it might have derived. All of us need to be aware of such unforeseen outcomes and take steps to ensure that we don't reproduce them.

There is another issue related to social responsibility, exemplified by call center agents adopting western names. It may be that the unease or perhaps disquiet that this concept causes is well based, although the motivation appears not to have been demeaning. On the positive side, it shows an engagement with business requirements that is typically Indian. As you will have seen with place names, there is rather less concern in India with erasing any signs of the imperial past than might be expected and certainly there is an ability to embrace the demands of western commerce without getting too concerned about what might be less significant details.

The concern must be, however, that this does not actually make a good statement about the West and western commercial attitudes. Particularly when most western countries have second- and third-generation nationals whose families came from the subcontinent and have names that are perfectly well accepted, it appears to be culturally insensitive to persist with what must have seemed a reasonable idea at the start.

Raising this concern has been met with furrowed brows in India, of course, and a sense that it is not that important. Once it is raised, however, it does provoke a debate. The immediate questions are usually concerned with accent neutralization, and whether this is an example of the same issue. The answer to that is much easier and probably straightforward. There will be accents in your own country that you find difficult to understand. Ensuring ease of communication is not a cultural issue in that same way, and whether English is of a regional variety or not there is no correct accent, only accents that are readily understood across the world.

There is another element that this concern with disguising cultural identity introduces and it is going to be very important, although it isn't yet a major public issue. It is whether or not to identify where your support or processes are located. If one of the arguments in this book is that it probably does not matter where your processes are carried out, it may seem a paradox to consider this now. The answer is that technologically and operationally it may not matter to you where your processes are carried out. Commercial considerations may be different. It may well be worth thinking whether this has other ramifications, particularly in the public relations arena in the short term, but in other ways over a longer period.

If an Indian back-office services center is likely to be more customer friendly and gain higher results in quality assessments, there will come a time when knowing that your work is carried out in India will be a positive recommendation. At the moment it is almost certainly a matter of indifference or a negative factor to most western end users or customers, which is why this argument docs not appear earlier in this book. Soon it may be a real differentiator and you may wish to consider when it will become a message with value for you.

Such cultural matters and perceptions are changing all the time. Our sensitivities are also changing. It is perhaps inappropriate to try to predict other examples, but the purpose of raising such a point is more to show you that it is necessary to examine your assumptions on a regular basis. It is not at all fanciful to foresee "Processed in Noida" as a tag that has real value, and who knows what else related to India might add value to your brand.

Any company board looking seriously at offshoring in India has some obligation to look at being part of the development of the country. It doesn't need to be a major business driver for you, but it is something you should be aware of. If nothing else, the most cynical mind will be able to see that higher prosperity will be good for political stability in India, which in turn is good for global stability and international commerce, and this can help justify any decision to take work there. Such work will have a positive effect on India's development and help increase its prosperity.

So your investment in India, in even a small offshore project, can be a force for good. Even if your company goes no further and does not look at other aspects of corporate social responsibility, it will have made a difference.

Your local economy

Let's look at the other half of this coin, where charity perhaps should begin, and see why moving services jobs offshore is going to cause much more political concern at home. Moving IT jobs in application development and projects offshore did not cause too many political ripples, partly because the numbers of jobs involved were relatively small. With call centers of 2,000 people being moved offshore, however, there have been enormous repercussions and national as well as local debates.

Much of the concern has often been rather sensationally driven when you consider that many of the call centers are being moved with no forced redundancies, merely relying on natural wastage. In western call centers there have commonly been staff attrition rates of over 40 percent. There are also some examples of generous terms to leave a call center that is being transferred overseas. Nevertheless, that doesn't disguise the very real issues when call centers are relocated from economically unsuccessful areas.

When more highly paid and more highly skilled jobs from companies' back offices are moved offshore, the issues will be much more stark. Taking 80 professional and well-paid jobs out of any local economy will affect many more than simply those people and their immediate families. Local traders will feel the difference, as will local shops. When those jobs are relatively highly skilled – in, say, back-office life insurance claims processing, where there is hardly any natural wastage and few jobs in the same line to be picked up – the outcry can be enormous. The disastrous effects on people's lives are also real.

There is no doubt that many individuals are going to suffer in this change. To ignore the corporate social responsibility that goes with employing people and not dealing with the issues properly may damage your reputation and even your brand.

There are some mitigating factors, if you and your company can take a different perspective. Alongside the advantages presented by offshoring, there is an enormous opportunity to look at what else you can do with your existing work force. You will not, of course, save costs if your Indian operation is merely an incremental cost, but the opportunity is different from that. Instead of saving, say, 40 percent, you might budget to save 30 percent and use part of your existing work force to develop new revenue streams or create internal capabilities that will support other areas of your business more effectively.

I have had two chances to do this type of reanalysis. In the first case I finally had to admit that it was difficult to do much. The structure of the company was too inflexible to make the type of progress I needed. In the second case, where I had the opportunity to experiment at little marginal cost, analyzing what else an existing highly skilled work force could do to add value, there were worthwhile avenues to explore and a small experiment was created. I was also, at the very least, deferring redundancy costs and possibly avoiding them.

Offshoring will change the relationships between the departments in your business in many subtle and some profound ways. Your company will inevitably become less coherent, less cohesive, and probably less sure of its identity. At the same time, it will become more focused, because what it actually deals with within the strict confines of the company is less in quantity but more important in terms of value to you. It should become more responsive, as it is dealing with less information but analyzing it in more detail, so that trends and changes should be more visible. The internal network of knowledge will change. You may have worked for a company that actually functioned by knowing the right person who understood either where the skeletons were buried or how a certain process could be made to function. That type of company has to change in this new corporate environment.

The incentives for thinking in this way are strong. You may not avoid redundancy costs because your experiment may fail, but even a chance of doing so in a positive way must be worthwhile. You will be increasing your costs, obviously, because you will be paying for the offshore project and keeping on some of the current staff. Yet when else would you have the chance to actively develop a new way of doing or supporting business?

There has also been a slightly different focus on this same understanding, presenting the cost savings of going offshore as a general incentive to greater investment in your home market. Even McKinsey's has addressed the issue. The work seems to be speculative with little in the way of hard facts behind it, but it is clearly an idea that will need to be explored in more detail. Cost savings generated by going offshore represent a major competitive gain to your country and could trigger both new investment and greater prosperity.

The wider perspective

It is important to have local concern for the people you employ both at home and in India, but it needs to be put into a wider view as well. The problem is that as soon as we move from the particular, it is very easy to forget that individuals are affected by what is happening. The rest of this chapter tries to balance those two points.

The first argument must be that not placing jobs offshore will seriously damage your company's competitiveness and may lead to far more lost jobs. Saying so will not provoke a good response, however true it is. To say that if you don't do it someone else will isn't perceived as much of an argument in any highly charged situation. Suggesting that it is inevitable will also be poorly received and you will be open to accusations that you are putting your company's wealth before that of the community.

Nevertheless, these arguments about inevitability and competitive position are true. Even if your country somehow manages to block its own companies from moving work offshore, companies in other countries will inevitably be more competitive. You have to find a way of making these arguments in such a way that the emotional responses do not have force.

You need to put the actions you are taking in India positively, and you also need to be able to show what actions you are taking in your domestic market to meet the same demands. While that may sound cynical, it stems from a profound belief in corporate social responsibility and the imperatives it imposes.

You might like to mention that while America was apparently losing 10 million jobs offshore, an extra 12 million jobs were being created in the US. The people getting those new jobs may well not have been the ones who lost out, and there are many other factors to take into account, particularly that the economy was booming during that time and that the new jobs may not be as well paid or as productive as those lost. Yet there is something here that will strike home. Additionally, although it is hard to judge, the underlying belief is that the 12 new million jobs were more highly skilled and more highly paid than the 10 million that were lost.

We have started to help create a more buoyant and thriving economy in India – and that will contribute to the global economy and drive further job creation both in India and elsewhere. Trade on its own is an economic multiplier. International trade is a great stimulant for all economic activity. Stifling it never actually helped over the long term, while it may have protected some individuals initially. The short term is vital – because that is our immediate future – yet we are at a moment when taking a positive approach may well result in unexpected and dramatic improvements. Taking a negative approach will almost certainly rule them out.

This argument must be treated with great care, as quantifying it will be sensitive and challenging. When manufacturing jobs were lost to the East, it was said that the new western economies would be services based. Now that the services are going East as well, there is a vacuum, or at least the appearance of one.

There is, however, a replacement for those services jobs. We are moving, perhaps faster than people imagined, into an ideas economy. Manufacturing and services are the fulfillment of ideas. The essential driver for our economic activity in the future will be ideas. The shape of this economy is not clear and the West will certainly not have all the ideas, but it makes sense, and with a dynamic, developed economy in India we will have a huge new market.

It is worth reflecting again on the reciprocity that was raised in the previous chapter. Don't forget that if you are helped to enter the Indian market by your Indian supplier or partner, you will in fact be creating employment and some of that will be in your domestic market. The trading won't only be one way. Satyabrata Pal, Indian Deputy High Commissioner in London, has also drawn attention to the substantial inward investment that Indian business already makes in the West. It is the eighth largest inward investor in the UK, for example. India is already a major market for the UK and the US.

Individuals and communities will nevertheless initially suffer in the West, in the same way that individuals and communities in India will immediately benefit. It is worth considering a historical phenomenon that is always raised by both proponents and opponents of this global services revolution.

The Luddites

The Luddites were a movement in the UK during the Industrial Revolution at the end of the eighteenth century, named after the followers of General Lud, a mythical figure. The Luddites destroyed weaving machinery, which they saw as a threat to their livelihoods as skilled, artisan weavers.

Over the years Luddites have received a bad press and been cast as enemies of progress who didn't know what effect the mechanization of weaving would have. This is almost entirely unfair. They took action because they clearly understood what would happen to their jobs. To do so, they had to have a better sense of what mechanization and a factory system would mean than did most at that time.

What the Luddites didn't and probably couldn't appreciate was the general effect of the Industrial Revolution in the UK, which resulted in greater prosperity, far more employment, and a huge increase in international trade.

We can derive two points of significance from this. The first is that we, like the Luddites, should understand that there will be large-scale effects on individuals and local communities both West and East. If we can, we should comprehend the imperatives of corporate social responsibility in that light.

Secondly, we should, unlike the Luddites, see the positive effects of this change in the global economy, and create an appropriate approach to the opportunities. While the global services revolution will make the next few years both tough and exciting, it will also require us to develop a different sort of corporate governance, with the board providing not merely leadership, compliance, and vision, but cohesion as well. With many disparate departments potentially on different continents in different time zones, with different cultural perspectives, the new corporation will have to have both a stronger identity and a stronger *sense* of identity. Holding together a new, unified company that is fracturing into many different units is a new concept and an amazingly complex issue, which may well lead to better corporations.

In addition, as western populations age, people who are economically active are declining as a percentage of the total. We still need services to be provided. It may be that the West can go on importing people to do service jobs, as both Europe and the US have done since 1945, or it may be that now we have to export those jobs and let people stay in their own countries and provide services for the West offshore.

Before we had no alternative, but with the capabilities the interconnected world provides, not taking young, educated, dynamic people away from developing countries is a much more justifiable way of creating a global economy.

References

Chapter 1

1 *India 2020*, p. 21, http://planningcommission.nic.in/plans/planrel/pl_vsn2020.pdf.
2 *India Publishing Market Profile*, London, The Publishers Association and British Council, 2003.
3 www.ge.com.

Chapter 2

1 Denise Colgan and Elias Mazzawi, Cap Gemini Ernst & Young, "Transformational Outsourcing," *National Outsourcing Association News.*
2 Anant Koppar, "Critical success factors and what can go wrong," presentation to National Outsourcing Association Conference, London, July 2003.
3 www.wipro.com.
4 www.export.gov/safeharbor/.

Chapter 3

1 Arun Shourie, "We have a headstart, let's not put up our feet," *The Indian Express*, January 3, 2004.
2 www.aelink.free.fr/cmm/tr25_ovr.html.

Chapter 10

1 Fayezul H. Choudhury, Vice-President and Controller, World Bank, "Migrating the back office offshore – A World Bank perspective," presentation to London Emerging Markets Research Group, June 19, 2003.

Chapter 11

1 Angus Finnegan, Osborne Clarke, "Offshore contact centres: The legal pitfalls," presentation to National Outsourcing Association Conference, London, July 2003.
2 Sir Howard Davies, Financial Services Authority, speech at BBA Conference on Banking Supervision, June 2000.

3   Simon Ashby, Prudential Standards Division, Financial Services Authority, "The FSA approach to the supervision of outsourcing," presentation to National Outsourcing Association, March 26, 2003.

Chapter 14
1   MJ Aravind, Co-founder and Director, Daksh eServices, "De-risking the transition process," presentation to Emerging Markets Research Group, London, June 19, 2003.

Chapter 15
1   Institut de la Statistique du Québec.

Bibliography

Books

Grihault, Nicki (2003) *Culture Smart! India: A Quick Guide to Customs and Etiquette*, London, Kuperard.

Keay, John (2001) *The Great Arc: The Dramatic Tale of how India Was Mapped and Everest Was Named*, London, HarperCollins.

Mole, John (2003) *Mind Your Manners: Managing Business Cultures in Europe*, 3rd edn, London, Nicholas Brealey Publishing.

Moxham, Roy (2001) *The Great Hedge of India: The Quest for One of the Lost Wonders of the World*, London, Constable and Robinson.

Trompenaars, Fons and Hampden-Turner, Charles (1997) *Riding the Waves of Culture: Understanding Cultural Diversity in Business*, 2nd edn, London, Nicholas Brealey Publishing.

Surveys and data

India Publishing Market Profile, London, The Publishers Association and British Council, 2003.

India Digest, Indian High Commission, UK.

Publications from Institut de la Statistique du Québec.

Business research

Vivek Agrawal and Dian Farrell (2003) "Who wins in offshoring?," *McKinsey Quarterly*, no. 4, www.mckinseyquarterly.com.

Academic research

Ravi Aron (2002) *The Case For, and Against, Shifting Back-office Operations Overseas*, Philadelphia, PA, Wharton Business School.

Presentations and conferences

Business Process Outsourcing, Emerging Markets Research Group, June 19, 2003, London, www.emrgind.com

MJ Aravind, Co-founder and Director, Daksh eServices, "Enabling exceptional customer relationships: De-risking the transition process."

Ravi Aron, Professor, Wharton Business School, "The supply chain of information and the extended organizational form."

Frank Beechinor, OneClickHR plc, "Integrated onshore–offshore transaction processing – Transition management," "Setting up an offshore operation in India – An SME perspective."

Fayezul H. Choudhury, Vice President & Controller, The World Bank, "Migrating the back office offshore: A World Bank perspective."

Danelle Dinsdale, DLA, "Constructing the BPO deal."

John Leggate, Chief Information Officer, BP, "Offshore outsourcing: An introduction."

Christian Marchetti, Partner, Accenture, "Rhodia makes its move."

John Packham, Operations Director Offshore, Zurich Financial Services, "Offshore outsourcing: Turning strategy into reality."

Mark Underwood, Business Sector Director, Hays plc, "Hays offshore outsourcing."

National Outsourcing Association (NOA), 1st Annual Offshore Outsourcing Conference, July 23, 2003

Kevin Barrow, Tarlo Lyons Outsourcing Group, "Case Study: Creation of a financial services contact centre."

Angus Finnegan, Osborne Clarke, "Offshore contact centers: The legal pitfalls."

Mike Grime, Standard Chartered Bank, "Centralising in India."

Anant R. Koppar, Kshema, "Critical success factors and what can go wrong."

Adrian Quayle, Gartner, "Outsourcing 2003: Trends."

Dan Sandhu, Vertex India, "Strategies for process offshoring."

Saurabh Srivastavaartyn, NASSCOM, "Outsourcing to India: Prospects and strategic directions."

Sanjay Viswanathan, Quintant Europe, "How corporations can take advantage of India through the strategic location of service model."

Useful websites

Websites change frequently and their value varies over time, but the following are generally useful.

Government

Index of Ministry websites: http://goidirectory.nic.in/education.html.

Education Ministry: www.education.nic.in.

Central Advisory Board for Education: http://cabsec.nic.in/abr/abr15.htm.

Central Board for Secondary Education: www.cbseindia.org; www.cbse.nic.in.

Council for the Indian School Certificates Examinations: http://cisce.org.

Education Statistics, Ministry of Education:
www.education.nic.in/htmlweb/edusta1.htm.

National Council of Educational Research and Training (NCERT):
www.ncert.nic.in.

Finance Ministry: www.finmin.nic.in.

India Vision 2020, Report of the Committee:
http://planningcommission.nic.in/plans/planrel/pl_vsn2020.pdf.

Embassies and High Commissions, Ministry of External Affairs: for a complete list of Embassies and High Commission websites, go to http://meaindia.nic.in/. The full list can also be found at www.indianembassy.org.

Safe Harbor: www.export.gov/safeharbor/.

Indian business

National Association of Software and Services Companies (NASSCOM):
www.nasscom.org/
www.nasscom.org/nasscomnewsline.asp.

Stocks and shares

www.indiainfoline.com/stocks and shares.

Indian development statistics and facts

www.indiadevelopment.org/.
http://indiaimage.nic.in/.
www.indiaonestop.com/economy-macro-view.htm.
www.un.org/esa/analysis/devplan/cdp00p22.pdf.
www.nic.in/stat/.
Reserve Bank of India: www.rbi.in.
Indiainfoline, a small private information provider: www.indiainfoline.com.
World Bank: www.worldbank.org.
Asian Development Bank: www.adb.org.
www.mckinseyquarterly.com.
US–India Business Council: www.usibc.com/.

Regulatory authorities

US, Securities and Exchange Commission: www.sec.gov.
UK, Financial Services Authority: www.fsa.gov.uk.

Quality

CMM
http://aelinik.free.fr/cmm/tr25_o2.html#D230.
http://whatis.techtarget.com/definition/0,,sid9_gci763122,00.html.
Six Sigma
www.6-sigma.com/.

Newspapers

www.hinduonline.com.
www.hindustantimes.com.
www.timesofindia.com.
www.thestatesman.net.
www.expressindia.com.
www.asianageonline.com.

Magazines
www.india-today.com.
www.outlookindia.com.
www.flonnet.com.
www.economictimes.com.
www.financialexpress.com.
www.business-standard.com.
www.epw.org.

Academic research
Knowledge@Wharton: http://knowledge.wharton.upenn.edu.
www.dialogin.com.
www.cranfield.ac.uk.